W9-CTY-779

895

Selected Brontë Poems

Selected Brontë Poems

EDWARD CHITHAM and TOM WINNIFRITH

Basil Blackwell

© Edward Chitham and Tom Winnifrith 1985

First published 1985

Basil Blackwell Ltd
108 Cowley Road, Oxford OX4 1JF, UK

Basil Blackwell Inc.
432 Park Avenue South, Suite 1505,
New York, NY 10016, USA

All rights reserved. Except for the quotation of short passages for the
purposes of criticism and review, no part of this publication may be
reproduced, stored in a retrieval system, or transmitted in any form or by
any means, electronic, mechanical, photocopying, recording or otherwise,
without the prior permission of the publisher.

Except in the United States of America, this book is sold subject to the
condition that it shall not, by way of trade or otherwise, be lent, re-sold,
hired out, or otherwise circulated without the publisher's prior consent in
any form of binding or cover other than that in which it is published and
without a similar condition including this condition being imposed on the
subsequent purchaser.

British Library Cataloguing in Publication Data

Selected Brontë poems.
1. English poetry — 19th century
I. Chitham, Edward   II. Winnifrith, Tom
821'.8'08   PR1223
ISBN 0–631–14564–8
ISBN 0–631–14565–6   Pbk

Library of Congress Cataloging in Publication Data

Selected Brontë poems.
Contains more poems by Emily Brontë than by any other poet.
Bibliography: p.
Includes index.
1. Brontë family. 2. English poetry — 19th century.
I. Chitham, Edward.   II. Winnifrith, Tom.
III. Brontë, Emily, 1818–1848. Poems. Selections. 1985.
PR4166.C48 1985   821'.8'08   85–11155
ISBN 0–631–14564–8
ISBN 0–631–14565–6   Pbk

Typeset by Oxford Publishing Services, Oxford
Printed in Great Britain by Billing and Sons Ltd, Worcester

CONTENTS

ACKNOWLEDGEMENTS

We have already in previous editions acknowledged the help of various libraries in allowing access to and permission to quote from their collections of Brontë manuscripts, but take this opportunity to thank the Brontë Society at Haworth, the principal repository of Brontë material, for their prompt and courteous help. Mrs Margaret Smith and Mr Derek Roper have aided us in the reading of the poems, and we would like to thank them for their generosity in allowing us to use their readings which we have acknowledged in the notes. We would also like to thank for various kinds of assistance Dr Juliet Barker, Mrs Val Gladman and Mr David Martin.

The poems of Anne Brontë are based on the texts in Edward Chitham's edition, by permission of the Macmillan Press Ltd. Thanks are due to Oxford University Press for permission to adapt texts that will appear in the Clarendon edition of Emily Brontë's poems.

INTRODUCTION

In the course of the past five years the two editors have been engaged in editing the poetry of the four Brontë children. We have felt that the poems of the Brontës have not received the attention they have deserved, both as aids to understanding the Brontës' lives and works, and as poems in their own right. Nevertheless we are aware that the complete editions we have produced, or are endeavouring to produce, are rather forbidding for the general reader, because of the dense critical apparatus necessary to establish a correct text and because of the large number of poems of indifferent quality which disfigure the poetry of all four Brontës, and especially that of Charlotte.

We therefore felt it desirable to publish a selection of Brontë poems with notes designed to give the necessary literary and biographical background. Our selection has principally been introduced to bring out the best in each poet. For obvious reasons there are more poems by Emily in this selection; Charlotte, Branwell and Anne do, however, have considerable sections devoted to their poems, some of the best of which are much longer than those of Emily. The real or imagined love affairs of Charlotte, Branwell and Anne have not been allowed to dominate our selection, since poetry is an unreliable source for biographical conjecture. Nevertheless since there is interest in the Brontës' lives as well as in their works we have included poems, like the Valentine for Mr Weightman 'A Roland for your Oliver', which have biographical appeal, if not literary merit.

In textual matters we have endeavoured to print a text of which we think the authors would have approved. This may seem to involve several subjective judgements. At least we are not printing the Shakespeare Head version, edited by T. J. Wise and J. A. Symington, a highly inaccurate edition as a result of Wise's dishonest bungling. In general, we have endeavoured to produce the text of the latest manuscript, although punctuation, spelling and capitalization have been silently corrected. The Brontës were not greatly interested in punctuation and their manuscripts exhibit many anomalies or omissions. Where poems were printed in their lifetime, we have taken into account the published text. In the case of Charlotte and Branwell, this presents few problems; however, it is necessary to spend a little time explaining the position with regard to Emily and Anne.

It used to be thought that Charlotte's management of the production of the 1846 poem edition involved some editorial interpolation by her in the texts of her sisters' poems. In an article for *The Library*, Vol. VI, No. 2 (June 1984), Mr Derek Roper of Sheffield University has shown that there is no clear evidence for this belief, and that in the case of Emily there are a few indications that she may have collaborated positively in the work. In choosing his texts for this edition, Dr Chitham has therefore given more weight to the 1846 verbal variants than once would have been the case. To a lesser extent this applies also to the 1846 edition of Anne's poems, some of the variants of which have been adopted. So far as Charlotte is concerned, no one has ever doubted that the texts represent her final thoughts on those poems.

In this edition, Dr Winnifrith is responsible for text and notes on Charlotte and Branwell, and Dr Chitham on Emily and Anne. Likewise, the notes on Angria are Dr Winnifrith's and those on Gondal, Dr Chitham's. We have each read the other's work and taken note of slight variations in emphasis, but neither has acted as censor to the other. We have very rarely mentioned textual matters in detail in our notes. Readers interested to explore these in more detail are referred to our editions of Charlotte, Branwell and Anne, and to the forthcoming Clarendon edition of Emily.

BIOGRAPHICAL NOTE

The earliest poem in this selection was written by Charlotte Brontë in 1830 before her fourteenth birthday, when Anne was only ten, and the latest, again by Charlotte, was written on the occasion of Anne's death in 1849. Thus the period of nearly twenty years, during which these poems were written, encompass most but not all of the tragedies and triumphs of the Brontës' lives. Charlotte and Emily were too young to write poetry at Cowan Bridge when in 1825 their elder sisters Maria and Elizabeth died, and after the deaths of Emily and Anne in 1848 and 1849 Charlotte wrote no poetry, or none that has survived, in the five years of life that were left to her. These years saw the publication of *Shirley*, the writing of *Villette*, and the short-lived marriage to Mr Nicholls, but Charlotte after the succes of *Jane Eyre* had probably recognized that her talents for fiction were greater than her poetic gift, although she still showed an interest in poetry, when she issued a new selection of her sisters' work in 1851.

The Brontës' 'plays', inspired by the gift of some soldiers to Branwell, began in 1826, although the first manuscripts cannot be dated before 1829, and we have nothing of Emily and Anne until 1836. From 1829 until 1835, when Charlotte went to Roe Head as a teacher, she and Branwell poured forth an impressive amount of both verse and prose. Charlotte's studies at Roe Head as a pupil between 1831 and 1832 brought only a temporary lull. It is not certain when Anne and Emily broke away from Charlotte and Branwell. Gondal is well established by the time of the diary paper in November 1834, and possibly Charlotte's absence at school may have brought about the break.

The quantity and quality of the Brontës' early verse is certainly impressive, but it is not surprising. We live in an age when the writing and reading of poetry is confined to eccentric intellectuals, and very unfashionable among the young who have of course plenty of other sources of amusement and emotional expression. One such source is the acting of plays, strongly encouraged now, but thought very shocking in

Victorian times. In *Mansfield Park* (1814) Sir Thomas Bertram is deeply shocked at finding his grown-up children engaged in theatricals, and no doubt Mr Brontë, more evangelical than Jane Austen's stern parent, would have been even more shocked.

But he would not have been shocked by the writing of poetry, as he himself had been a poet. Admittedly, apart from religious fervour, Mr Brontë's poetry has nothing to commend it, and it would disfigure this collection if we included any selections from it. But Mr Brontë must take his place with the other poets that the young Brontës read as a source of their inspiration. There was rich supply of poetry in the library of Ponden House, to which the Brontës had accesss. The newspapers and periodicals they read contained verse as well as prose. Although we do not know the exact details of the curriculum followed by the Brontë children, whether at home, or more rarely at school, it is likely that the reading of poetry formed a large part. Charlotte translated Voltaire's *Henriade* as early as 1830, and though Branwell's translation of Horace was not completed until 1840 there is evidence of him trying his hand at Horace translations, and writing on other classical themes, much earlier than this.

Much of the Brontës' poetry is concerned with the stories of Angria and Gondal. Here, as is explained in two separate notes, we must distinguish between our knowledge of Angria, where we do have Charlotte's and Branwell's prose stories, and our appreciation of Gondal where only the poetry, like the tip of an iceberg, survives. The prose juvenilia of Charlotte and Branwell, not yet edited in a satisfactory fashion, is so baffling, and in places so boring, that the loss of the prose narratives of Gondal is not all that to be regretted, but at least we know most of what is happening in Angria. Some poems with an Angrian context can stand on their own, although originally composed as part of a prose narrative. Both Branwell in 1837 and the three sisters in 1846 adapted poems with an Angrian or Gondal context, so that they could be comprehensible to the general public.

Charlotte was at Roe Head as a teacher between 1835 and 1838. These were important and not very happy years for all four Brontës and for their poetic development. Emily and Anne both joined Charlotte as pupils at Roe Head, but Emily only remained three months in 1835, while Anne suffered both illness and religious depression in her two-year stay from October 1835 to the autumn of 1837. Branwell made an unsuccessful attempt to be an artist in London, probably in the autumn of 1835. Emily tried to become a teacher at Miss Patchett's school at

Law Hill near Halifax from September 1838 to March 1839, and found the work very demanding.

During these years Charlotte began to distance herself from Branwell, and though she wrote copiously and dreamed excessively of her Angrian world, she found the gap between her imagination and drab reality increasingly disturbing. Letters to Southey and Hartley Coleridge about a career in literature did not receive encouraging replies. Strong sexual feelings increased her anxiety. Branwell sent poems to *Blackwood's Magazine* and to Wordsworth, but these poems, printed in this selection, were not even acknowledged. During 1837 Branwell made fair copies of some of his Angrian poems. In 1838 he began a long and tedious poem, *Sir Henry Tunstall*, which he revised three times during the next four years. He was in Bradford for a year in 1838 and 1839, trying to earn a living as a portrait painter.

In 1839 Branwell and Emily returned home, and it was the turn of Anne and Charlotte to try their hand as governesses, Anne taking up a post with the Inghams of Blake Hall from April to December, while Charlotte was with the Sidgwicks of Stonegappe from May to July. The separation of the Brontës from each other, and in particular the splitting up of the pairs of Charlotte and Branwell, Emily and Anne, resulted in a turning away from Gondal and Angria to more personal poetry. It is of course difficult to separate personal poetry from the worlds of Gondal and Angria, and this is especially true of Emily, even though she did definitely divide her poems between a Gondal and non-Gondal notebook. Charlotte after writing a great deal of poetry at Roe Head appears to have written much less after her return home. Branwell, although still signing himself Northangerland on occasions, appears to have turned to more public themes, while Anne wrote several poems about her loneliness and religious doubts.

It is possible that some of her love poetry may have been inspired by her love for the Revd William Weightman, curate at Haworth from 1839 to 1842. There are dangers in giving an autobiographical interpretation to poems with so many fictional heroines around. Emily Brontë wrote about wild loves, but no wild lover has ever been found for her apart from the mythical Louis Parensell, a misreading of the title of a poem entitled *Love's Farewell*. On the other hand it is perhaps significant that Anne who was a governess with the Robinsons at Thorp Green from 1840 to 1845 is much more personal in her poetry than Emily, and that she did not include poems which could refer to Mr Weightman in her published selection. Emily remained at home apart from her visit to Brussels in 1842, taking on most of the domestic responsibilities when her aunt died in that year. This did not prevent her from writing Gondal and non-Gondal poems of extraordinary philosophical depth, perhaps worrying the more orthodox Anne.

We are on firmer ground when we come to Branwell's and Charlotte's love affairs. After an unsuccessful period as a railway clerk at Sowerby Bridge and Luddenden Foot from 1840 to 1842, during which he wrote some impressive if melancholy poetry, Branwell joined Anne at Thorp Green with the Robinsons at the beginning of 1843. In the previous summer he had had some poems published in the *Leeds Intelligencer* and *Halifax Guardian*, but wrote little at Thorp Green, where he seemed to be making a good impression. However on 17 June 1845 he was dismissed for behaviour bad beyond expression. He said this was the result of a love affair between him and Mrs Robinson, but there may have been a more sordid explanation. His remaining poems are depressing, though not without technical skill, and he cannot have become a hopeless drunkard as early as some accounts suggest.

Charlotte's love affair was an unreciprocated one with her teacher in Brussels, Monsieur Heger. She probably was not aware of her feelings until she returned without Emily to Belgium in 1843, and did not really feel her loss until she came back to Haworth at the beginning of 1844. At about this time she revised many of her earlier poems, giving them a vaguely continental flavour, and also wrote some new poems, printed in this section, where references to Monsieur Heger are very thinly veiled. The remaining part of the Brontë story is well known. One day in the autumn 1845, Charlotte discovered some poems by Emily. Emily was annoyed at the discovery, but was eventually persuaded that they should be published. With Charlotte taking the lead in looking for potential publishers the sisters eventually dispatched a selection to Aylott and Jones on 7 February 1846. The selection is very different from this one. The Brontës were not interested in their early work, they received no help from Branwell, they had to eliminate Gondal and Angria, and there is a certain amount of evidence to show that they pruned their work to suit Victorian taste.

The poems received some polite reviews, but sold few copies. Undaunted, the sisters set about publishing fiction; their career as poets was almost over. Emily wrote 'No coward soul is mine' in January 1846, and two undistinguished Gondal poems thereafter. Anne wrote some good poems in the last years of her life, including a very searching one in which she faces her own death in 1849. Branwell wrote some incoherent poems and a piece of irreverent doggerel about the Haworth doctor, while Charlotte finished her life as a poet with two moving poems on the deaths of Emily and Anne.

It is dangerous to use fiction as an aid to biography, and even more dangerous to use poetry. This is especially true of the Brontës who filled their drab lives with stories and poems about exciting fictional characters. The poem beginning 'Unloved I love, unwept I weep' was written long before Charlotte met Monsieur Heger, although she borrowed the line for another poem written nearer 1843. Nevertheless, because the Brontës wrote great novels their lives must be interesting, and because so much of their lives were occupied with poetry their poems must be interesting too. In addition, some of the poems which we have selected have not been sufficiently appreciated as works of art in their own right.

THE POETIC BACKGROUND
AND ACHIEVEMENT
OF THE BRONTËS

Since all three Brontë sisters figure in most literary reference books for their novels, it may seem hardly necessary to claim a place for their poetry as well. Should we not admit that the only reason for reading their verse is to shed light on the prose? To do so would be to commit a major injustice in the case of Emily, a minor injustice in the cases of Anne and Charlotte, and to neglect Branwell altogether, since he completed no large-scale novel as an adult. Emily is an important nineteenth-century poet, and each of the other three contribute work which cannot be dismissed, despite its faults or inadequacies.

It needs to be remembered that it was as poets that all four saw themselves at first. It was occasional verse that Branwell contributed to the *Halifax Guardian* and *Leeds Intelligencer*, and a volume of poems that the three 'Bells' used to test the market in 1846. Though it sold badly, the volume was not dismissed by critics. The stories have been bestsellers, but the poems, especially those of Emily, have retained their devotees even when sales were few. This is not surprising, for composition in verse came as naturally to the family as composition in prose.

Three early sources of poetic exemplars may be mentioned. First, Patrick Brontë was writing and reciting verse before the children were born. Second, their childhood was surrounded by the hymns of Wesley, Watts and others. Third, as they grew up they sang songs round the piano in the parlour, so that Moore and the rest entered their bones. Once the children could read well, they soon tackled the works of their Romantic predecessors, as well as the eighteenth-century poetry they had supplanted. To children with such a father, reading poetry seemed natural; soon it came to seem equally natural to write it.

Patrick Brontë had been born into an Irish peasant family where singing and reciting were second nature. It seems likely that he followed his father in composing what we might call folk-ballads. He taught himself to read Milton and the Ulster favourite, Burns. One may guess that at Cambridge he could hardly fail to encounter the work of Wordsworth and Coleridge, both of whom became favourites at Haworth. A great deal has been written of the family's enthusiasm for Cowper, a special mentor of Anne's. Byron, whose life Tom Moore wrote, is thought to have had a great influence on all the young Brontës, and we know they read a great deal of Scott's work, both prose and verse. It is harder to find firm evidence that Shelley was a hero of Emily's, but there are many pointers to such a conclusion. Campbell and Hood also seem to have figured in their reading. They read *Blackwood's* and *Fraser's* at times, the former regularly during their youth. Here they would encounter many minor poets of the day. A case has been made out for Tennyson as an influence. Despite this apparently varied, if uncritical, diet, the poems produced by the family have a slightly unfashionable and archaic ring at times. They appear to have had no interest in deliberate innovation, nor in keeping up with contemporary movements.

Early reviewers of the poems of the 'Bell' family, both in 1846 and on their reissue in 1848, found the work promising. The *Critic* called it 'genuine', 'a ray of sunshine', and refuted the notion that these new poets were producing 'servile copies'. They contained 'original thoughts, expressed in the true language of poetry'. The reviewer selected poems by all three sisters for quotation and praise. The *Athenaeum* considered that the 'instinct of song' ran in the family, though Anne's poems were not as good as those of Charlotte and Emily. W. A. Butler, in the *Dublin University Magazine*, found 'Cowperian amiability and sweetness' in the work, which he called 'unaffected and sincere'. When the poems were reprinted, they were said to have 'strength of thought and vigour of diction'. Charlotte is praised for her 'easy naturalness' and all are in a manner 'very far from commonplace'. But this writer did condemn the 'literary experiment' for which he said the Bells had a taste.

Of the four young Brontës, Branwell seems to have had the greatest interest in writing martial, epic poems. Many of these have an Angrian background, which is somewhat easier to elucidate than Gondal. Others seem to reflect Byron or Campbell, and a number contain references to Classical Greece. A Romantic and lyric strain is discerned in such poems as 'Memory', which has been wrongly ascribed to Emily. A group of poems concerning characters called 'Caroline' and 'Harriet' are sometimes thought to relate directly to the oldest of the Brontë children, Maria, who died when she was about twelve. It is generally agreed that her personality was such that she influenced both the lives and literary output of all the Brontës. Though he sometimes took his early poems and revised them, Branwell's verse may be divided into two largely discontinuous periods. His work prior to his engagement as a tutor at Thorp Green is more conventional, on the whole, and less imbued with first-hand feeling, than the poems produced during 1845–7. Some of the latter group echo or anticipate Anne's themes of the wearing power of time and the threat of death.

While these later poems of Branwell convey at times genuine pathos and artistic tension, Charlotte was clearly destined to become a storyteller. Unless a quantity of her latest verse has been lost—and this is very unlikely—she wrote only two poems after the publication of *Jane Eyre*. As with Branwell, much of her poetry was related to the Angrian story. There are many long poems of an epic nature, the quality of which is uneven. Charlotte seems to have found no difficulty in expressing herself in verse, and the inclusion of two poems in *Jane Eyre* shows that she regarded Sir Walter Scott's habit of doing so worthy of imitation. We may well find portions of the epic verse attractive, and concur with the reviewers of the 1846 collection in discovering sincerity and sweetness in the shorter lyrics. However, it can hardly be denied that Charlotte was right to pay more attention to novels than verse in her later years.

Anne's early death at the age of twenty-nine robbed the world of a developing social novelist with a satirical bent. Like Charlotte, she was a better novelist than poet. Nevertheless, her verse is still worth reading, and among critics Derek Stanford considers her one of the best Victorian women poets. A vein of deliberate understatement is found throughout Anne's poetry. She is perpetually rejecting opportunities for verbal fireworks. A steady development is evident, from the joyful but conventionally phrased 'Alexander and Zenobia' to the stark confrontation with death and faith evident in 'A dreadful darkness'. As P. J. M. Scott writes, by the end Anne has become 'capable of things quietly extraordinary'.

When we reach Emily Brontë, we are dealing with a poet whose talent and—sporadically—whose achievement in poetry is of a different order from those of her brother and sisters. It is not only that she has an exceptionally well-tuned ear (the same ear that allowed her to become a piano player worthy of tuition by one of the best tutors in Belgium), but that her themes are altogether less constricted than those of the others. Like Anne, she is much concerned with the problems of reconciling human emotional response to life with the annihilation or separation of loved ones in death. Unlike Anne, she is not finally satisfied with conventional Christian answers, whether theologically orthodox or not. Like Branwell, she is acutely interested in the subject of rebellion and strife, but hers is a cosmic rebellion without sure reconciliation. Emily's philosophical thought led her to no firm conclusions, and we must be willing to accept poems that strongly assert propositions contrary to those of other poems in the canon. There is also the problem of banal stanzas mixed in with work of high quality. On the whole, under Charlotte's guidance, Emily seems to have selected the best for the 1846 edition. This left some good poems to be published later, but a good deal of the remaining verse was indifferent. At her worst, Emily could rant in a way that was foreign to Anne. The selection she chose in 1846, or allowed Charlotte to choose, is free of such ranting.

The ambivalence in Emily Brontë's thought often leads to carefully balanced stanzas in an eighteenth-century mould. There is little doubt that the examples of Thomson, Cowper and the hymn writers were congenial to Emily's mind, or she would have abandoned them. The interplay and balance of opposites is evident as much in the poems as in *Wuthering Heights*, and some of the themes are the same. It is doubtful whether she should be called a nature poet; her 'nature' is more a matter of climate, season and weather than the delineation of natural species in all their variety. The difference between her and John Clare in this respect is illustrative. So often Emily takes us into the mood produced by a natural scene in a few words, while a poet like Clare delights in loving observation of the flora and fauna for their own sakes.

But although Emily takes precedence over the rest of the family there is justice in collecting their work together. So much of the family's work is collaborative. The roots of their literary composition grew in the soil of mutual inspiration and criticism. They copied out each other's poems and read them aloud to each other. Charlotte produced the 1846 volume as the work of a family team, and though it has been asserted that Branwell knew nothing of the publication, his presence was as much a condition of the production of the mature novels and poems as it had been when he led the nursery in acting scenes from plays they had made up together or writing jointly the Angrian story. To the end, the work of the Brontës retained its family likeness.

THE WORLD OF ANGRIA

Many of Charlotte and Branwell Brontë's poems have an Angrian origin, although revision for publication has sometimes obscured this. Much else about Angria is also obscure, as it took some time for the significance of Charlotte and Branwell's juvenile tales to be appreciated, and they still have not been properly edited. Dr Christine Alexander is editing Charlotte's juvenilia, and has cleared up many difficulties about the poetry of both Charlotte and Branwell in her preliminary volume, *The Early Writings of Charlotte Brontë* (Oxford, 1983). Previous Brontë scholars have given an incomplete picture of Angria and have tended to exaggerate the merits of the juvenilia and the resemblances between them and the adult novels.

In 1826 Mr Brontë bought some toy soldiers for Branwell. The four children named them and started creating stories about them. Charlotte called her favourite soldier The Duke of Wellington, the victor of Waterloo and a leading Tory politician. There is a manuscript of a story by Charlotte written in 1829 describing the setting up in Africa of a colony. Her story was entitled *The Twelve Adventurers*. By 1830 both Charlotte and Branwell were writing full and imaginative descriptions of this colony, whose capital was originally called Glass Town, but this was changed to Verreopolis and then Verdopolis. Contemporary political events and accounts of fashionable life were adapted to a rather improbable African setting.

The Duke of Wellington soon faded into the background, and was replaced as a chief character by his two sons, the Marquis of Douro and Lord Charles Wellesley. Charlotte wrote stories about the love affair between Douro and the daughter of his father's physician, Marian Hume; these stories had some basis in fact. Charlotte went to school in January 1831, and this acted as something of a check on the narrative. At some stage Emily and Anne must have broken away to form their own narrative, but in the absence of any of their juvenile prose this break is difficult to date.

Charlotte left Roe Head in May 1832. Branwell had written some stories during the time Charlotte was at school, although the dates of these stories suggest that he was generally inspired by her visits home in the holidays. He did introduce a new character, Rogue, who under the successive titles of Alexander Percy, Lord Ellrington and Duke of Northangerland, becomes his chief hero. Many of Branwell's narratives are tedious descriptions of war, with Rogue leading treacherous rebellions. Charlotte was more interested in painting the many affaires of Douro, although she did explore some of Percy's early loves.

In October 1833 Branwell introduced a new character Mary Percy, the daughter of Lord Ellrington, as he had become. Marian Hume is killed off early in 1834, and the way is clear for the two chief characters of Branwell and Charlotte to be united by the marriage of Mary and Douro. It is difficult to keep track of Douro's many love affairs, or to know what degree of marital infidelity is involved, since it was easy for either Brontë to kill off inconvenient spouses. The character of Douro becomes progressively more arrogant, and Mary Percy is treated no more kindly than Marian Hume or indeed Mina Laury, a girl of low birth, one of Douro's many mistresses.

Meanwhile there had been developments on the political front. In 1834 Douro, now called Zamorna, with Ellrington, now called Northangerland, as his Prime Minister sets up a new kingdom called Angria. This kingdom was formed after a hard-fought war. Branwell supplied details of its geography. Some old characters were taken from Verdopolis, some new ones were created. The main emphasis of the more interesting stories is on the growing rivalry between Zamorna and Northangerland with Mary Percy caught in the middle. Political developments in England supplied a model for the difficulties between King and Prime Minister, but the romantic touch of Mary Percy was the Brontës' own invention.

Charlotte left for Roe Head on 29 July 1835. While there, for the next three years, she wrote many poems with a vaguely Angrian background. These poems reflect the tension she felt between her own humdrum situation as a teacher and her wildly romantic imagination. Repressed sexual feelings played some part in causing her distress. Zamorna's marital infidelities increased during this period. Meanwhile, back at Haworth, Angria under Branwell's control was suffering civil war. The Government of Verdopolis was eager to destroy Angria and sought alliances from the Africans and the French. Zamorna returns and Northangerland joins Angria's enemies. At the battle of Edwardston Zamorna is defeated, and later captured, but is then sent into exile. Meanwhile Mary Percy mourns and then dies.

In October 1836 Charlotte wonders if Branwell has really killed Mary. He had, and Northangerland is full of gloom, but Charlotte need not have worried. Zamorna returns and leads a loyalist rebellion. He wins victories at Ardsley and then finally on 30 June 1837 at Evesham. Meanwhile Mary has been revived by Charlotte. From 1837 Charlotte and Branwell grew apart. Branwell wrote stories under the pseudonym Henry Hastings, while Charlotte in her stories cast doubt on this character as a drunken reprobate. Mary Percy's return to life does not mean that Zamorna returns to marital fidelity, as Zamorna continues to stray, most notably with Mina Laury, his long-suffering governess, who must owe something to Charlotte's own experiences. Both Branwell and Charlotte, as if the Battle of Evesham had ended the Angrian narrative, return to earlier scenes in the lives of their heroes. They also show an increasing interest in realism, and Yorkshire rather than Angria becomes the scene of their stories.

In the winter of 1839 Charlotte finished her last Angrian story *Caroline Vernon* and a manuscript beginning 'I have now written a great many books', which appears to bid farewell to Angria. She began a narrative, usually called *Ashworth*, in which Alexander Percy is settled in Yorkshire. Monsieur Heger is likely to have continued the education in realism. Branwell who had extracted in 1837 some of his Angrian poems from earlier manuscripts, possibly with a view to publication, does not seem to have been much interested in Angria after 1839. His last prose story *And The Weary are at Rest* is reworking of earlier Angrian material in a Yorkshire setting. He occasionally used the pseudonym Northangerland for his published poetry and, like Charlotte, continued to brood over Angrian themes in his later poems.

It will be seen, however, that Angria was a factor in the writing of Branwell and Charlotte Brontë for only about ten years. If we are to be strict, Angria as opposed to Glass Town was only invented in 1834, and thus it is only for half this period that it was in the minds of Charlotte and Branwell. It is a tribute to the vitality of the poems and stories between 1834 and 1839 that Angria has become the name under which we classify the juvenile writings of the two eldest Brontës, and has become a name with which Brontë scholars both belabour and befuddle each other. Many of the claims for the Angrian stories are extravagant. The plots and characters have something in common with Charlotte's mature novels with lonely women pining for imperious men, but there are important differences. The extravagant and unrealistic African setting of Angria is a vehicle for other improbabilities of design and language.

So far as the poems of Charlotte and Branwell are concerned, a knowledge of Angrian history is vaguely helpful, although, as both Charlotte and Branwell revised for publication poems with an Angrian setting and even poems that originally formed part of an Angrian prose story, we cannot feel all that underprivileged if like the original readers of the published poems we know nothing at all of Angria. Some poems of course have no connection with Angria. It is probably more helpful to know something of the circumstances under which Charlotte and Branwell wrote their poetry. There is only one history of the Brontës, whereas the history of Angria, as has been shown, is a series of interconnecting but sometimes contradictory stories. At times we almost wish that, as with Emily and Anne, no prose juvenilia from Charlotte and Branwell had survived. This would have made it easier for the poems to be judged in their own right.

THE GONDAL WORLD OF EMILY AND ANNE

'The Gondals are discovering the interior of Gaaldine.' That announcement, in the diary paper of 24 November 1834, is chronologically the first we ever hear of the secret islands of Emily and Anne Brontë. After this, the Gondals appear from time to time in the poems and diary papers of the two girls for twelve years, and Emily's last poem, written between 1846 and 1848, is set in an unnamed land which may still be Gondal. There have been a number of attempts to systematize the fragments of the Gondal 'saga' revealed in these poems and diary papers, and the new reader of Brontë poems is entitled to ask for some key to the 'story' of Gondal.

Disappointing as it may seem, there are some clear indications that no such key may be found. As we have seen, the Gondals were in existence as early as 1834, perhaps earlier. But by 1845 Anne was writing: 'We have not yet finished our "Gondal chronicles" that we began three years and a half ago.' Counting back three and half years from July 1845, we find the Christmas holidays, 1841–2, as Anne's starting date. Previously they were mere incidents, provisional and unrelated, without a chronological framework. What is more, these chronicles were not finished by 1845. After that it is most unlikely that they were ever finished.

The Gondals had emerged from 'plays', once the poetry of all the Brontë children. It is likely that the two younger girls, who at that time were, in the words of Ellen Nussey (Charlotte's best friend), 'like twins', first acted isolated incidents, then wrote about what they had acted. This writing was in prose and verse. Even at this stage there may have been some continuity. In the 1837 diary paper Emily mentions a 'life' of 'Augustus Almeda', who may be male, but may be her self-identification, to whom we shall return shortly. During this period, poems were sometimes started without any clear idea who were to be the heroines of the events described. It seems possible that by the end of 1841 the girls felt that the muddle of character and plot needed clarifying and setting into one single story.

That story was destined never to be completed. Even in 1845, Anne says in her diary paper that the Gondals are 'not in firstrate playing condition'. She seems to have felt that the childish game had had its day, and at twenty-five she might well think so. Once, according to Ellen, the girls 'were to be seen with their arms lacing each other'. This close friendship faded. An attempt was made in 1846 to revive the Gondals, but it foundered. Both Emily and Anne had moved beyond it.

Some Gondal poetry by both sisters is included in this anthology. In general, Gondal verse is not Emily's best, but there are a few very strong poems with Gondal ascriptions in the manuscripts. Looked at from a biographical and psychological point of view rather than a poetic one, Gondal was important for Emily for many years and not destructive to Anne's talent. This facet of their imaginative life cannot be excluded from our selection. Bright lyrics like 'Geraldine, the moon is shining' and 'O wander not so far away' have therefore been included. The reader may be justified in asking 'Who was Geraldine?' Such questions take us into the realm of psychology rather than poetic criticism.

About twenty of Emily's poems are ascribed to, or refer in the text to, a Gondal character whose name was apparently A. G. Almeda. One poem with the initials A.G.A. refers to 'Augusta'. The G. seems to stand for Geraldine, a name with Irish antecedents. The initials together may stand for 'Augusta Geraldine Almeda', who seems to have been a ruthless queen of Gondal. She has great energy and emotion. Some see in her the original of Catherine in *Wuthering Heights*. For Emily, at times, she seems to have fulfilled the role of lawless *alter ego*, in whose character she could dwell and act without harming her own real-life personality. When we understand how circumscribed was the life of a clergyman's daughter in the 1840s, we may understand why this persona was necessary to a girl with such emotional drive as Emily seems to have had. Nevertheless, the persona was probably of more psychological than poetic value.

Examination of these Gondal poems by both sisters suggests that they might sometimes be started without a clear idea how they would end. For example, 'Why do I hate that lone green dell?' was written on 9 May 1838. It is ascribed to A.G.A. But the first part of the poem is such that it may perhaps have been begun with a particular Yorkshire dell in mind. The whitening bones may simply have been those of a dead moorland sheep, for the imaginations of Emily and Anne used the day-to-day events of their lives as material to be transformed into Gondal plays, or into poetry, or both. It is most unlikely that the poem refers to a dell that has already been identified as the scene of a Gondal crime. The girls' imagination seems to have worked the other way round: they found a sinister dell on the moors, imagined a Gondal crime there, and then wrote a poem; or else they wrote part of the poem first, then thought of a suitable Gondal event and characters.

Later the same month, Emily wrote a poem about a child and her mother, sailing on a stormy sea: 'This shall be thy lullaby'. In the earlier manuscript the poem is ascribed to 'Blanche'. The child is addressed as 'thou bright-haired child'. In 1839 the ascription disappears, and the child is called 'my dark-haired child'. Blanche's name disappears from Gondal poetry and never returns. There are in existence two lists of Gondal characters, written by Anne. Not one of the thirty-five or more names appears in Emily's poetry, though surnames do coincide.

Altogether, Gondal names seem to be as curious a mixture as the fragments of story line. Some are everyday names such as Albert, Edward, Arthur, Eliza, Helen. Others are more exotic, and have a Celtic or Continental flavour: Desmond, Flora, Una, Zirilla, Roderic. Others again, including place-names, seem to have evolved out of the girls' own names. For example, the following Gondal names contain the syllable 'El' or 'Al', which sounds like a childish version of part of 'Emily': Almedore, Alfred, Eldred, Elderno, Elnor, Elmor, Elbë, Gerald, Geraldine, and of course Gondal itself. The same tendency to ring the changes on an existing name is evidenced by the names of the two islands: Gondal and Gaaldine are almost anagrams. Besides Geraldine we also find that Anne invents a 'Geralda', and Douglas rides up 'Gobelrin's' glen. It is hard to believe that these names can have been produced in a random fashion. They look like subconscious choices of Emily, showing her propensity for choosing artistic material from inside herself as well as for closely related 'pairs': twins, opposites, civil wars, mirror images, portrait likenesses.

Of the Gondal 'story line' itself it is hard to say anything for certain. We hear of proud and treacherous kings, revolts, battles between kinsmen, orphans, deaths amid carnage and outcasts ranging over snowy mountains. There are long sea journeys, and at least one character seems to be exiled to England. With such fragmentary patterns we should be content. If ever the Gondal chronicles were completed (and after 1845 there seems so little time in which the Brontë's could have completed them while not writing their novels and greater poems), they were certainly lost or destroyed. If Gondal was the practice-ground for the production of *Wuthering Heights* it had its value. So far as the elucidation of the individual poems is concerned, their air of mystery might not be solved even if we could miraculously rediscover the

Gondal background. All the best poems seem to stand better without Gondal references, and many of the very best are not Gondal poems at all.

CHRONOLOGICAL LIST
OF POEMS

CHARLOTTE BRONTË'S POEMS

1   *Pleasure (A Short Poem or else not say I)* 'True pleasure breathes not city air' 8 February 1830
2   *The Vision (A Short Poem)* 'The gentle showery Spring had passed away' 13 April 1830
3   *Matin* 'Long hath earth lain beneath the dark profound' 12 November 1830
4   *St John in the Island of Patmos* 'The holy exile lies all desolate' 30 August 1832
5   'The cloud of recent death is past away' 27 November 1832
6   'O Hyle! thy waves are like Babylon's streams' February 1833 (?)
7   'Justine, upon thy silent tomb the dews of evening weep' February 1833 (?)
8   *The Red Cross Knight* 'To the desert sands of Palestine' 2 October 1833
9   *Lament* 'Lament for the Martyr who dies for his faith' 28 November 1834
10 *Memory* 'When the dead in their cold graves are lying' 13 February, 2 August and 20 October 1835
11 'We wove a web in childhood' 19 December 1835
12 *Reason* 'Unloved I love, unwept I weep' Around 1836
13 'Again I find myself alone, and ever' Around 1837
14 'When thou sleepest, lulled in night' Around 1837
15 *Stanzas* 'If thou be in a lonely place' 14 May 1837. Copied in 1845. Revised for publication 1846.
16 'Sit still—a breath, a word may shake' Around 1837
17 'Obscure and little seen my way' Around 1837
18 'Is this my tomb, this humble stone' 4 June 1837
19 'Why should we ever mourn as those' Around 1837
20 *Presentiment* 'Sister, you've sat there all the day' 1837. Copied around 1843. Revised for publication 1846.

BRANWELL BRONTË'S POEMS

EMILY BRONTË'S POEMS

SELECTED POEMS
OF
CHARLOTTE BRONTË

PLEASURE

(A Short Poem or else not say I)

TRUE pleasure breathes not city air,
  Nor in Art's temples dwells,
In palaces and towers where
  The voice of Grandeur dwells.

No! Seek it where high Nature holds
  Her court 'mid stately groves,
Where she her majesty unfolds,
  And in fresh beauty moves;

Where thousand birds of sweetest song,
  The wildly rushing storm
And hundred streams which glide along,
  Her mighty concert form!

Go where the woods in beauty sleep
  Bathed in pale Luna's light,
Or where among their branches sweep
  The hollow sounds of night.

Go where the warbling nightingale
  In gushes rich doth sing,
Till all the lonely, quiet vale
  With melody doth ring.

Go, sit upon a mountain steep,
  And view the prospect round;
The hills and vales, the valley's sweep,
  The far horizon's bound.

25   Then view the wide sky overhead,
         The still, deep vault of blue,
      The sun which golden light doth shed,
         The clouds of pearly hue.

      And as you gaze on this vast scene
30   Your thoughts will journey far,
      Though hundred years should roll between
         On Time's swift-passing car.

      To ages when the earth was young,
         When patriarchs, grey and old,
35   The praises of their god oft sung,
         And oft his mercies told.

      You see them with their beards of snow,
         Their robes of ample form,
      Their lives whose peaceful, gentle flow,
40   Felt seldom passion's storm.

      Then a calm, solemn pleasure steals
         Into your inmost mind;
      A quiet aura your spirit feels,
         A softened stillness kind.

THE VISION

(A Short Poem)

THE gentle showery Spring had passed away,
   And no more breathed the fragrant air of June;
Summer had clad in glorious array
   Each hill and plain; and now the harvest-moon
5   Shone on the waving corn,—brown Autumn's
      golden boon!

In that glad time, as twilight softly crept
   Over the earth, I wandered to a place
Where stillness reigned as if the whole world slept,—
   For there of noise remained no wearying trace:
10   But deepest silence sat on all nature's face.

It was a wild glen; near it frowned huge rocks
    Which hung their dark beams o'er its stony bed;
And, in their caverned sides, faint echo mocks
    When rolls some fragment down, with rumbling
      dread
15   And horrid noise, launched from the mountain's
      head.

The valley now was still; a midnight calm
    Fell on it as I sat beneath a tree
Whose leaflets glistened with the dew's mid balm
    Wept by the evening star so freshly free,
20   And filling all the air with soft humidity.

'Mong the huge trees which canopied that glen
    I saw the sky with many a bright star hung,
And through the midst alone sailed glorious gem
    The moon, who still her trembling lustre flung
25   Unchanged, as when the spheres together tuneful
      sung.

At intervals her light fell through the trees
    And with mild glory silvered all the vale,
While through those branches whispered not a breeze:
    No hollow blast did sad and mournful wail,
30   But solemn silence walked beneath the moonbeams pale.

Yet black the gaunt rocks rose before my eyes,
    And their black caverns filled the heart with dread;
They stood in grand relief from out the skies
    Whose clear vaults archèd o'er each shaggy head,
35   And from whose quivering stars a radiant light was shed.

I gazed upon this scene till slumber fell
    Upon my eyelids; then methought I saw
On my entrancèd sight a vision swell
    Whose glory passed the bounds of Nature's law,
40   And filled the spirit with a mingled joy and awe!

A land was spread before me where the trees
    Formed woods of emerald clearness, and high bowers
Through which there whispered many a murmuring breeze
    Perfumed with incense of a hundred flowers,
45   Watered by clouds of light which fell in fragrant showers.

I heard sweet voices, not like human sound,
　　But tuneful of articulate harmony;
I saw no shape, but oft there floated round
　　A zephyr soft, and breathing from the sky,
50　　As if some unseen form in light wings flitted by!

At length the air 'gan brighten; faint there shone
　　A rainbow path through all the expanse of blue,
And music of a soft melodious tone,
　　Subdued by distance, through heaven's wide arch flew,
55　　Falling upon the ear, calm as the twilight dew.

Louder it rose: sweet harp and timbrel clear
　　Rang tunefully to many a sweeter voice;
These mingling fell upon the listening ear
　　While all the echoes answered to the noise,
60　　And Nature seemed united to rejoice!

Then a bright chariot glided through the air
　　Attended by a glorious company
Of beings radiant surpassing fair;
　　Around them rolled of light a mighty sea;
65　　And now the music played with loudest melody.

And while this scene slow passed before my eyes,
　　Dazzled with splendour, suddenly I woke,
And, lo! the light dawn tinged the eastern skies,
　　Showing the rugged front of many a rock,
70　　And faintly gilding each wide-branching oak.

MATIN

LONG hath earth lain beneath the dark profound
　　Of silent-footed, planet-crested night:
Now from the chains of slumber soft, unbound,
　　She springs from sleep to hail the glorious birth of light.

5　A solemn hush lay on her hills and woods,—
　　Now, as the day approaches, fast dispelling;
For at the touch of the bright orient-floods
　　Thousands of voices rise, in mingled murmurs swelling.

First the sun's glories tip the lofty hills,
    Then roll impetuous down the dusky vale;
Sings sweet in light the pebbled crystal rill,
    And joy expands the buds or flowers that woo the gale.

Oh! I might sing of pastures, meads, and trees
    Whose verdant hue is tinged with solar beams;
And I might sing of morn's fresh, bracing breeze
    That, with awaking breath, ripples the glassy streams;

And of the merry lark who soars on high,
    Aye rising in his course towards the sun;
Of his descending from the vaulted sky
    To the expectant nest, when that sweet song is done.

These I could sing if thou wert near me now,—
    Thou whom I love, my soul's most fair delight;
If the fair orbs that beam beneath thy brow
    Shed on my darkling page their ray divinely bright.

But now great waters of the mighty deep,
    Howling like famished wolves, roll us between;
Oh! sad and bitter drops I mournful weep
    To think of those vast leagues of tossing billows green.

Come from the fairy valley where thou dwellest,—
    Shady and green is Britain's favoured isle;
Come, for all gloom and sadness thou dispellest,
    And chase away my grief with one sweet sunny smile.

Methinks I see thee sitting calm and lonely
    Beneath the umbrageous elm upon the lawn;
Naught near thee but the woodland warblers only
    Singing their matin-song; and perhaps some gentle
      fawn.

Or pearly dews thy footsteps may be brushing,
    Tripping as cheerful as the lambkin gay
Beside the cataract that thunderous rushing
    Covers its shaken banks with white-churned bells and
      spray.

Hark! Africa unto her desert sand now calls thee,
    Where the bright sun pours his most fervid beams;
Alas! the chain of love for aye enthralls me:
    My prisoned heart still pants even in shifting dreams.

45 I hear thy voice, I see thy figure nightly;
    Thou comest to me in midnight slumber deep!
And through the dark thy blue eyes, glimmering brightly,
    Beaming upon me in unquiet haunted sleep.

Oh! how I loved to hear thy low sweet singing
50   When evening threw her quiet shades around;—
The moon, her mild light through the casement flinging
    Seemed from the sky to list the half-angelic sound.

Thou to the scene a calmer beauty lending,
    With eyes steeped in the lingering light of song;
55 And o'er the harp, thy form so graceful, bending,
    What melting notes then stole the dusky air along.

Oh! when within thy still, retired bower
    Shall I once more hear that dear entrancing strain?
Would I could bring back the oft-desired hour
60   My sad bereavèd heart might beat with joy again!

May still I hope for thy long-wished returning:
    Comes swiftly o'er the dark and raging sea!
Come, for my soul with hope deferred is burning;
    Then will I sing a song worthy of morn and thee!

ST JOHN IN THE ISLAND OF PATMOS

THE holy exile lies all desolate
    In that lone island of the Grecian sea.
And does he murmur at his earthly fate,
    The doom of thraldom and captivity?

5   No. Lulled by rushing of the unquiet breeze
    And the dull solemn thunder of the deep,
Under the hanging boughs of loftiest trees
    Behold the Apostle sunk in silent sleep.

And, is that chamber dreamless, as the lone
    Unbroken, frozen stillness of the grave?
Or is his soul on some far journey gone
    To lands beyond the wildly howling wave?

Where Zion's daughter views with tear-dimmed eye
    Her proud all-beauteous temple's lofty form,
Piercing with radiant front the blue bright sky
    And mourns with veiled brow the coming storm?

Haply his spirit lingers where the palm
    Upspringing from the flowery verdant sod
Throws a dark solemn shade, a breezeless calm,
    Over the house where he first spoke to God.

Or to his freed soul is it once more given
    To wander in the dark, wild, wilderness,
The herald of the Lord of Earth and Heaven
    Who came, in mercy came, to heal and bless?

No. From his eyes a veil is rent away,
    The will of God is gloriously revealed;
And in the full light of eternal day
    Jehovah's fixed decrees are all unsealed.

The armed hosts of God, in panoply,
    Of splendour most insufferably bright,
Rush forth triumphant from the parting sky
    Whose wide arch yawns before those floods of light.

He hears the voice of Archangels tell
    The doom, the fiery, fearful doom of Earth,
And as the trumpets' tones still louder swell
    On the dark world red plagues are poured forth.

At once ten thousand mighty thunders sound,
    With one wild howl the sea yields up her dead.
A flaming whirlwind sweeps the trembling ground,
    The skies are passed away in fear and dread.

All earth departs; at God's supreme behest
  Sinners are bound in the black depths of hell.
The souls of righteous men forever rest
  Where Angel harps in sounds harmonious swell.

45 And now the new Jerusalem descends
  Beaming with rainbow radiance from on high;
In awe and fear the holy prophet bends
  As that bright wonder rushes on his eye.

He hears the last voice, ere Heaven's gates are sealed,
50   Proclaim that all God's works are consummate;
That unto him the Almighty hath revealed
  The unfathomed mysteries of Time and Fate.

He wakes from his wonderous trance and hears
  Faint distant warblings from the distant sky;
55 Floating like tuneful music of the spheres
  Sweet as the voice of Angel harmony
Sounding Jehovah's praise to all eternity.

THE cloud of recent death is past away,
  But yet a shadow lingers o'er his tomb
To tell that the pale standard of decay
  Is reared triumphant o'er life's sullied bloom.

5 But now the eye bedimmed by tears may gaze
  On the fair lines his gifted pencil drew,
The tongue unfaltering speak its meed of praise
  When we behold those scenes to Nature true—

True to the common Nature that we see
10   In England's sunny fields, her hills and vales,
On the wild bosom of her storm-dark sea
  Still heaving to the wind that o'er it wails.

How many winged inhabitants of air,
  How many plume-clad floaters of the deep,
15 The mighty artist drew in forms as fair
  As those that now the skies and waters sweep;

From the great eagle, with his lightning eye,
  His tyrant glance, his talons dyed in blood,
To the sweet breather-forth of melody,
20   The gentle merry minstrel of the wood.

Each in his attitude of native grace
  Looks on the gazer life-like, free and bold,
And if the rocks be his abiding place
  Far off appears the winged marauder's hold.

25 But if the little builder rears his nest
  In the still shadow of green tranquil trees,
And singing sweetly 'mid the silence blest
  Sits a meet emblem of untroubled peace,

'A change comes o'er the spirit of our dream,'—
30 Woods wave around in crested majesty;
We almost feel the joyous sunshine's beam
  And hear the breath of the sweet south go by.

Our childhood's days return again in thought,
  We wander in a land of love and light,
35 And mingled memories, joy—and sorrow—fraught
  Gush on our hearts with overwhelming might.

Sweet flowers seem gleaming 'mid the tangled grass
  Sparkling with spray-drops from the rushing rill,
And as these fleeting visions fade and pass
40 Perchance some pensive tears our eyes may fill.

These soon are wiped away, again we turn
  With fresh delight to the enchanted page
Where pictured thoughts that breathe and speak and
      burn
  Still please alike our youth and riper age.

45 There rises some lone rock all wet with surge
  And dashing billows glimmering in the light
Of a wan moon, whose silent rays emerge
  From clouds that veil their lustre, cold and bright.

And there 'mongst reeds upon a river's side
50   A wild bird sits, and brooding o'er her nest
Still guards the priceless gems, her joy and pride,
        Now ripening 'neath her hope-enlivened breast.

We turn the page: before the expectant eye
        A traveller stands alone on some desert heath;
55   The glorious sun is passing from the sky
        While fall his farewell rays on all beneath;

O'er the far hills a purple veil seems flung,
        Dim herald of the coming shades of night;
E'en now Diana's lamp aloft is hung,
60   Drinking full radiance from the fount of light.

Oh, when the solemn wind of midnight sighs,
        Where will the lonely traveller lay his head?
Beneath the tester of the star-bright skies
        On the wild moor he'll find a dreary bed.

65   Now we behold a marble Naiad placed
        Beside a fountain on her sculptured throne,
Her bending form with simplest beauty graced,
        Her white robes gathered in a snowy zone.

She from a polished vase pours forth a stream
70   Of sparkling water to the waves below
Which roll in light and music, while the gleam
        Of sunshine flings through shade a golden glow.

A hundred fairer scenes these leaves reveal;
        But there are tongues that injure while they praise:
75   I cannot speak the rapture that I feel
        When on the work of such a mind I gaze.

Then farewell, Bewick, genius' favoured son,
        Death's sleep is on thee, all thy woes are past;
From earth departed, life and labour done,
80   Eternal peace and rest are thine at last.

O HYLE! thy waves are like Babylon's streams
   When the daughters of Zion hung o'er them in woe;
When the sad exiles wept in their desolate dreams,
   And sighed for the sound of their calm Kedron's flow.

5   The palms are all withered that shadowed thy shore,
    The breezes that kiss thee through sepulchres sweep:
For the plume of the Ethiop, the lance of the Moor
   All under the sods of the battle-field sleep.

O Hyle! that moonlight shines colder on thee
10   Than afar off it shines on the sad lake of graves
And drear as the voice of its wild waters be
   'Tis joy to the sound of thy desolate waves.

O Hyle! thy children are scattered afar;
   All gone is their glory, all faded their fame;
15 Crushed is their banner-staff, vanished their star,
   Unburied their ashes, forgotten their name.

JUSTINE, upon thy silent tomb the dews of evening
    weep,
Descending twilight's wings of doom around and o'er
    thee sweep,
The flowers are closed on thy grave, Justine, the
    fern-leaves bend and fade
And the fitful night-wind dies and swells as it ushers in the
    shade.

5   A lonely light in heaven smiles,—one pale star in the west;
The night-clouds rise in giant piles far along Gambia's
    breast.
I am come, and come alone, Justine, to spend one hour
    with thee,
But the turf with its flowers and fern-leaves green doth
    hide thee jealously.

'O long and still hath been thy sleep beneath that grassy
    grave:
10 Years have rolled on their billows deep, and time its
    whelming wave.'
Yet, still I do remember my young nurse ere she died,
When the gloom of dark December had quenched the
    summer's pride.

Lone lay she in the latticed room which crowns that
    turret grey;
And I used to think its death-bed gloom prophetic of
    decay
15 In the placid sunny summer eves when the light of sunset
    fell
Through the chequering play of those ivy leaves with
    smiles of sad farewell.

How did I love to climb the stair which to her chamber
    led,
That I might drop a childish tear on Justine's dying bed;
I felt she was not long for earth,—her pale cheek told
    me so;
20 She who had loved me from my birth I knew was soon
    to go.

How wearily her eye would turn to the lattice and the
    sky,
Within, a wild wish seemed to burn that yet she might not
    die,
As golden clouds went sailing on, and the sound of winds
    and trees
Came, as unto a mariner comes the deep moan of the
    seas.

25 Then her daughter, and her foster-son, she'd to her
    bosom press,
And say, with such a bitter moan, 'May God my children
    bless!'
And then I called her 'Mother', and weepingly I said
I would be Mina's brother when she was cold and dead.

That vow has since been broken,—as when lightning
    shivers trees,
30 Those words, in anguish spoken, have been scattered to
    the breeze.
'Justine, if God has given a glance of earth to thee,
Thou hast even wept in Heaven my withering crimes to
    see.'

But let me not remember those hours of darkness past,
Nor blow the dying ember to light with such a blast.
35 I do not know repentance, I cannot bend my pride
Nor deprecate my conscience even at thy cold grave side.

Life's fitful fever over, thou sleepest well, Justine
Pale flowers thine ashes cover and grass mounds ever
    green,
The fox-glove here is drooping its silent peal of bells,
40 And the shadowy yew-tree stooping of rest eternal tells.

O, might I find a dwelling but half so calm as thine,
When my life-storm stills its yelling, when my comet-fires
    decline!
But the wild, the raging, billow is a fitter home for me:
The coral for the willow; for the turf the tossing sea.

THE RED CROSS KNIGHT

TO the desert sands of Palestine,
    To the kingdoms of the East,
For love of the Cross and Holy Shrine,
    For hope of heavenly rest,
5 In the old dark times of faintest light
Aye wandered forth each Red Cross Knight.

Warmed by the Palmer's strange wild tale,
    Warmed by the Minstrel's song,
They took plumed helm and coat of mail
10   And sabre keenly strong;
They left, O high and gallant band!
For unknown shores their own sweet land.

The Cross was still their guiding-star,
  Their weapon and their shield;
In vain the lance and scymitar
  Opposing squadrons wield!
For still victorious from the fight
Came back each noble Red Cross Knight.

In vain shrill pipe and timbrels' swell
  Rose from the turbaned host,
For still the bloody Infidel
  The wreath of conquest lost;
And still that garland's hallowed light
Crowned gloriously the Red Cross Knight.

The Lion King of Christendom
  Was gathered where his fathers rest;
And ne'er again did battle-hum
  Sound from the calling East;
And on Britannia's Island-shore
The Red Cross Knight was seen no more.

Six hundred circles of our earth
  Moved around the God of Light,
When, lo! a great and glorious birth
  Broke forth on Afric's night.—
Now flow, my strain, more swiftly flow:
Drink inspiration's spirit-glow.

For Gifford is thy wondrous theme:
  The bravest and best of men;
Whose life has been one martial dream,
  The war against the Saracen;
Reviver of the holy sign
Which whelmed with slaughter Palestine.

Hail, great Crusader! lift the Cross!
  Kingdoms call to thy banners' shade!
And, heedless of all earthly loss,
  Through blood, through fire, through carnage
wade;
Led by that high and heavenly gem,
The living star of Bethlehem.

Wade to the city of renown,
    And rescue Zion from her foe;
Take to thyself a radiant crown,
    And pour on him eternal woe;
Then shall earth's mightiest bless thy name
And yield to thee the palm of Fame.

LAMENT

LAMENT for the Martyr who dies for his faith,
  Who prays for his foes with his failing breath,
Who sees, as he looks to the kindling sky,
God and His Captain, the Saviour, nigh;
    Who sees the mighty recompense,
    When soul is conquering flesh and sense;
    Sees heaven and all its angels bright,
    At the very end of his mortal fight,
    At the black close of that agony
    Which sets the impatient spirit free;
    Then, as in Christ he sinks to sleep,
    Weep for the Dying Martyr, weep.

And the soldier, laid on the battle-plain
    Alone at the close of night, alone,
The passing off of some war-like strain
    Blent with his latest moan;
His thoughts all for his father-land,
His feeble heart, his unnerved hand
Still quiveringly upraised to wield
Once more his bright sword on the field,
While wakes his fainting energy
To gain her yet one victory;
As he lies bleeding, cold and low,
As life's red tide is ebbing slow,
Lament for fallen bravery.

For the son of wisdom, the holy sage,
Full of knowledge, and hoar with age,
Him who had walked through the times of night,
As if on his path a secret light
Lustrous and pure and silent fell;

To all, save himself, invisible,
A secret ray from Heaven's own shrine
Poured on that spirit half divine,
And making a single Isle of light
In the wide blank ocean of Pagan night;
Lament for him as you see him laid
Waiting for Death on the Dungeon bed,
The sickly lamp beside him burning,
   Its dim ray falling on sorrow and gloom;
Around him his sad disciples mourning,
   As they watch for the hour of awful doom;
And he, by coming death unshaken,
   As if that slumber would soon be o'er,
As if all freshened he should waken
   And see the light of morn once more.

Ay, on the sage's, the soldier's bier
I could drop many a pitying tear,
And as the martyr sinks to sleep
I could in love, in sorrow weep.
But, Percy, for that rose of thine,
Maria Stuart, bright, divine,
Divine and bright the mortal form,
The eternal soul a venomed worm,
For her I'd never heave a sigh.
Unmoaned I'd let the fair fiend die,
Seductive in her treachery,
Most dazzling in her crimes.
The flower of France should fade away
And Scotland's heather Hell decay
Ere her death mass left its chimes.
And I could smile vindictively
To know the earth I walked was free
From her who kissed her lord to death,
And poisoned him with kindness's breath,
One moment fondly o'er him bending,
The next her gentle spirit lending
To plots that well might wake a shiver
In bosoms crime has deathed forever.
Accursed woman o'er thy tomb
My scorn flings down its sternest gloom.

35

40

45

50

55

60

65

70

MEMORY

WHEN the dead in their cold graves are lying
   Asleep, to wake never again;
When past are their smiles and their sighing,
   Oh! why should their memories remain?

5   Though sunshine and spring may have lightened
     The wild flowers that blow on their graves;
Though summer their tombstones have brightened,
    And autumn have pall'd them with leaves;

Though winter have wildly bewailed them
10   With her dirge-wind as sad as a knell;
Though the shroud of her snow-wreath have veiled
    them,
    Still how deep in our bosoms they dwell!

The shadow and sun-sparkle vanish,
    The cloud and the light flee away;
15   But man from his heart may not banish
    The thoughts that are torment to stay.

The reflection departs from the river
    When the tree that hung o'er is cut down,
But on Memory's calm current for ever
20   The shade without substance is thrown.

When quenched is the glow of the ember,
    When the life-fire ceases to burn,
Oh! why should the spirit remember?
    Oh! why should the parted return?

25   Because that the fire is *still* shining,
    Because that the lamp is still bright;
While the body in dust is reclining
    The soul lives in glory and light.

WE wove a web in childhood,
　　A web of sunny air;
We dug a spring in infancy
　　Of water pure and fair;

5 　　We sowed in youth a mustard seed,
　　We cut an almond rod;
We are now grown up to riper age—
　　Are they withered in the sod?

Are they blighted, failed and faded,
10 　　Are they mouldered back to clay?
For life is darkly shaded;
　　And its joys fleet fast away.

Faded! the web is still of air,
　　But how its folds are spread,
15 And from its tints of crimson clear
　　How deep a glow is shed.
The light of an Italian sky
Where clouds of sunset lingering lie
　　Is not more ruby-red.

20 But the spring was under a mossy stone,
　　Its jet may gush no more.
Hark! sceptic, bid thy doubts be gone,
　　Is that a feeble roar
Rushing around thee? Lo! the tide
25 Of waves where armèd fleets may ride
Sinking and swelling, frowns and smiles,
An ocean with a thousand isles
　　And scarce a glimpse of shore.

The mustard-seed in distant land
30 　　Bends down a mighty tree,
The dry unbudding almond-wand
　　Has touched eternity.
There came a second miracle
Such as on Aaron's sceptre fell,
35 And sapless grew like life from heath,
Bud, bloom and fruit in mingling wreath
All twined the shrivelled off-shoot round
As flowers lie on the lone grave-mound.

Dream that stole o'er us in the time
40 When life was in its vernal clime,
Dream that still faster o'er us steals
  As the mild star of spring declining
The advent of that day reveals,
  That glows in Sirius' fiery shining:

45 Oh! as thou swellest, and as the scenes
  Cover this cold world's darkest features,
Stronger each change my spirit weans
  To bow before thy god-like creatures.

When I sat 'neath a strange roof-tree
50 With nought I knew or loved round me,
Oh how my heart shrank back to thee,
Then I felt how fast thy ties had bound me.

That hour, that bleak hour when the day
  Closed in the cold autumn's gloaming,
55 When the clouds hung so bleak and drear and grey
  And a bitter wind through their folds was roaming.
There shone no fire on the cheerless hearth,
  In the chamber there gleamed no taper's twinkle.
Within, neither sight nor sound of mirth,
60 Without, but the blast, and the sleet's chill sprinkle.

Then sadly I longed for my own dear home
  For a sight of the old familiar faces,
I drew near the casement and sat in its gloom
  And looked forth on the tempest's desolate traces.

65 Ever anon that wolfish breeze
  The dead leaves and sere from their boughs was
    shaking,
And I gazed on the hills through the leafless trees
  And felt as if my heart was breaking.

Where was I ere an hour had passed:
70 Still listening to that dreary blast,
Still in that mirthless lifeless room,
Cramped, chilled, and deadened by its gloom?

No! thanks to that bright darling dream,
Its power had shot one kindling gleam,
75   Its voice had sent one wakening cry,
And bade me lay my sorrows by,
And called me earnestly to come,
And borne me to my moorland home.
I heard no more the senseless sound
80   Of task and chat that hummed around,
I saw no more that grisly night
Closing the day's sepulchral light.

The vision's spell had deepened o'er me:
Its lands, its scenes were spread before me,
85   In one short hour a hundred homes
Had roofed me with their lordly domes,
And I had sat by fires whose light
Flashed wide o'er halls of regal height,
And I had seen them come and go
90   Whose forms gave radiance to the glow,
And I had heard the matted floor
Of ante-room and corridor
Shake to some half-remembered tread
Whose haughty firmness woke even dread,
95   As through the curtained portal strode
Some spurred and fur-wrapped Demi-God,
Whose ride through that tempestuous night
   Had added somewhat of a frown
To brows that shadowed eyes of light
100   Fit to flash fire from Scythian crown,
Till sweet salute from lady gay
Chased that unconscious scowl away;
And then the savage fur-cap doffed,
   The Georgian mantle laid aside,
105   The satrap stretched on cushion soft,
   His loved and chosen by his side,
That hand, that in its horseman's glove
   Looked fit for nought but bridle rein,
Caresses now its lady-love
110   With fingers white that show no stain
They got in hot and jarring strife,
When hate or honour warred with life,—
Nought redder than the roseate ring
That glitters fit for Eastern King.

115 In one proud household where the sound
     Of life and stir rang highest round,
     Hall within hall burned starry bright
     And light gave birth to richer light,
     Grandly its social tone seemed strung,
120 Wildly its keen excitement rung,
     And hundreds 'mid its splendours free,
     Moved with unfettered liberty,
     Not gathered to a lordly feast,
     But each a self-invited guest:
125 It was the kingly custom there
     That each at will the house should share.

     I saw the master not alone,
     He crossed me in a vast saloon,
     Just seen then sudden vanishing
130 As laughingly he joined the ring
     That closed around a dazzling fire,
     All listening to a lady's lyre.
     He was in light and licensed mood,
     Fierce gaiety had warmed his blood,
135 Kindled his dark and brilliant eye
     And toned his lips' full melody.

     I saw him take a little child
        That stretched its arms and called his name.
     It was his own, and half he smiled
140   As the small eager creature came
     Nestling upon his stately breast,
        And its fair curls and forehead laying
     To what but formed a fevered nest—
        Its father's cheek where curls were straying
145 Thicker and darker on a bloom
     Whose hectic brightness boded doom.

     He kissed it and a deeper blush
     Rose to the already crimson flush,
     And a wild sadness flung its grace
150 Over his grand and Roman face.
     The little, heedless, lovely thing
     Lulled on the bosom of a King,

Its fingers 'mid his thick locks twining,
Pleased with their rich and wreathed shining,
155 Dreamed not what thoughts his soul were haunting
Nor why his heart so high was panting.

I went out in a summer night,
   My path lay o'er a lonesome waste,
Slumbering and still in clear moon-light,
160   A noble road was o'er it traced.
Far as the eye of man could see
   No shade upon its surface stirred,
All slept in mute tranquillity,
   Unbroke by step or wind or word.

165 That waste had been a battle-plain,
   Head-stones were reared in the waving fern.
There they had buried the gallant slain
   That dust to its own dust might return,
And one black marble monument
170   Rose where the heather was rank and deep,
Its base was hid with the bracken and bent,
   Its sides were bare to the night-wind's sweep.

A Victory carved in polished stone,
   Her trumpet to her cold lips held,
175 And strange it seemed as she stood alone
That not a single note was blown,
   That not a whisper swelled.

It was Eamalia's ancient field,
   I knew the desert well,
180 For traced around a sculptured shield
These words the summer moon revealed:
   'Here brave Macarthy fell!
The men of Keswick leading on.
Their first, their best, their noblest one,
185   He did his duty well.'

REASON

UNLOVED I love, unwept I weep,
    Grief I restrain, hope I repress;
Vain is this anguish, fixed and deep,
    Vainer desires or dreams of bliss.

5 My life is cold, love's fire being dead;
        That fire self-kindled, self-consumed;
    What living warmth erewhile it shed,
        Now to how drear extinction doomed!

    Devoid of charm how could I dream
10   My unasked love would e'er return?
    What fate, what influence lit the flame
        I still feel inly, deeply burn?

    Alas! there are those who should not love;
        I to this dreary band belong;
15 This knowing let me henceforth prove
        Too wise to list delusion's song.

    No, Syren! Beauty is not mine;
        Affection's joy I ne'er shall know;
    Lonely will be my life's decline,
20   Even as my youth is lonely now.

    Come Reason—Science—Learning—Thought—
        To you my poor heart I dedicate;
    I have a faithful subject brought;
        Faithful because most desolate.

25 Fear not a wandering, feeble mind:
        Stern Sovereign, it is all your own
    To crush, to cheer, to loose, to bind;
        Unclaimed, unshared, it seeks your throne.

    Soft may the breeze of summer blow,
30   Sweetly its sun in valleys shine;
    All earth around with love may glow,—
        No warmth shall reach this heart of mine.

Vain boast and false! Even now the fire
　Though smothered, slacked, repelled, is burning
At my life's source; and stronger, higher,
　Waxes the spirit's trampled yearning.

It wakes but to be crushed again:
　Faint I will not, nor yield to sorrow;
Conflict and force will quell the brain;
　Doubt not I shall be strong to-morrow.

Have I not fled that I may conquer?
　Crost the dark sea in firmest faith
That I at last might plant my anchor
　Where love cannot prevail to death?

AGAIN I find myself alone, and ever
　The same voice like an oracle begins
Its vague and mystic strain, forgetting never
　Reproaches for a hundred hidden sins,
And setting mournful penances in sight,
Terrors and tears for many a watchful night.

Fast change the scenes upon me all the same,
　In hue and drift the regions of a land
Peopled with phantoms, and how dark their aim
　As each dim guest lifts up its shadowy hand
And parts its veil to shew one withering look,
That mortal eye may scarce unblighted brook.

I try to find a pleasant path to guide
　To fairer scenes—but still they end in gloom;
The wilderness will open dark and wide
　As the sole vista to a vale of bloom,
Of rose and elm and verdure—as these fade
Their sere leaves fall on yonder sandy shade.

My dreams, the Gods of my religion, linger
　In foreign lands, each sundered from his own,
And there has passed a cold destroying finger
　O'er every image, and each sacred tone
Sounds low and at a distance, sometimes dying
Like an uncertain sob, or smothered sighing.

25   Sea-locked, a cliff surrounded, or afar
         Asleep upon a fountain's marble brim—
      Asleep in heart, though yonder early star,
         The first that lit its taper soft and dim
      By the great shrine of heaven, has fixed his eye
30   Unsmiling though unsealed on that blue sky.

      Left by the sun, as he is left by hope:
         Bowed in dark, placid cloudlessness above,
      As silent as the Island's palmy slope,
         All beach untrodden, all unpeopled grove,
35   A spot to catch each moonbeam as it smiled
      Towards that thankless deep so wide and wild.

      Thankless he too looks up, no grateful bliss
         Stirs him to feel the twilight-breeze diffuse
      Its balm that bears in every spicy kiss
40   The mingled breath of southern flowers and dews,
      Cool and delicious as the fountain's spray
      Showered on the shining pavement where he lay.

      WHEN thou sleepest, lulled in night,
         Art thou lost in vacancy?
      Does no silent inward light,
         Softly breaking, fall on thee?
5   Does no dream on quiet wing
         Float a moment 'mid that ray,
      Touch some answering mental string,
         Wake a note and pass away?

      When thou watchest, as the hours
10   Mute and blind are speeding on,
      O'er that rayless path, where lowers
         Muffled midnight, black and lone;
      Comes there nothing hovering near,
         Thought or half reality,
15   Whispering marvels in thine ear,
         Every word a mystery?

Chanting low an ancient lay,
　　Every plaintive note a spell,
Clearing memory's clouds away,
20　　Showing scenes thy heart loves well?
Songs forgot, in childhood sung,
　　Airs in youth beloved and known,
Whispered by that airy tongue,
　　Once again are made thine own.

Be it dream in haunted sleep,
25　　Be it thought in vigil lone,
Drink'st thou not a rapture deep
　　From the feeling, 'tis thine own?
All thine own; thou need'st not tell
30　　What bright form thy slumber blest;—
All thine own; remember well
　　Night and shade were round thy rest.

Nothing looked upon thy bed,
　　Save the lonely watch-light's gleam;
35　Not a whisper, not a tread
　　Scared thy spirit's glorious dream;
Sometimes, when the midnight gale
　　Breathed a moan and then was still,
Seemed the spell of thought to fail,
40　　Checked by one ecstatic thrill;

Felt as all external things,
　　Robed in moonlight, smote thine eye;
Then thy spirit's waiting wings
　　Quivered, trembled, spread to fly;
45　Then the aspirer wildly swelling
　　Looked, where 'mid transcendency
Star to star was mutely telling
　　Heaven's resolve and fate's decree.

Oh! it longed for holier fire
　　Than this spark in earthly shrine;
50　Oh! it soared, and higher, higher,
　　Sought to reach a home divine.
Hopeless quest! soon weak and weary

Flagged the pinion, drooped the plume,
55 And again in sadness dreary
Came the baffled wanderer home.

And again it turned for soothing
To the half finished, broken dream;
While, the ruffled current smoothing,
60 Thought rolled on her startled stream.
I have felt this cherished feeling,
Sweet and known to none but me;
Still I felt it nightly healing
Each dark day's despondency.

STANZAS

IF thou be in a lonely place,
If one hour's calm be thine,
As Evening bends her placid face
O'er this sweet day's decline;
5 If all the earth and all the heaven
Now look serene to thee,
As o'er them shuts the summer even,
One moment—think of me!

Pause, in the lane, returning home;
10 'Tis dusk, it will be still:
Pause near the elm, a sacred gloom
Its breezeless boughs will fill.
Look at that soft and golden light,
High in the unclouded sky;
15 Watch the last bird's belated flight,
As it flits silent by.

Hark! for a sound upon the wind,
A step, a voice, a sigh;
If all be still, then yield thy mind,
20 Unchecked, to memory.
If thy love were like mine, how blest
That twilight hour would seem,
When, back from the regretted Past,
Returned our early dream!

25 If thy love were like mine, how wild
  Thy longings, even to pain,
For sunset soft, and moonlight mild,
  To bring that hour again!
But oft, when in thine arms I lay,
30 I've seen thy dark eyes shine,
And deeply felt their changeful ray
  Spoke other love than mine.

My love is almost anguish now,
  It beats so strong and true;
35 'Twere rapture, could I deem that thou
  Such anguish ever knew.
I have been but thy transient flower,
  Thou wert my god divine;
Till, checked by death's congealing power,
40 This heart must throb for thine.

And well my dying hour were blest,
  If life's expiring breath
Should pass, as thy lips gently prest
  My forehead cold in death;
45 And sound my sleep would be, and sweet,
  Beneath the churchyard tree,
If sometimes in thy heart should beat
  One pulse, still true to me.

SIT still—a breath, a word may shake
 The calm that like a tranquil lake
Falls settling slowly o'er my woes.
Perfect, unhoped-for sweet repose,
5 O leave me not—forever be
Thus more that Heaven than God for me.

An hour ago how lone I lay
Watching the taper's pallid ray,
As struggling through the night it shed
10 A light upon that statue's brow
To the cold rigid, marble head
Giving a strange half life-like glow

That startled sleep—and oftimes brought
Terror of night and dread of thought.
I scarce that dread may now recall,
For thou art here, mine own, my all.

Let me now in the silence tell
What I have felt when far away
The ocean's wide and weltering swell
Parted us further day by day,
And scarce as thou went wandering on
Could I in thought those lands portray
Where wrapt perchance in slumber lone
My lord 'mid foes and dangers lay—
Confused the dream of stormy waves
And battle-fields and gory graves
And woods untrodden—ways unknown
Still, round my midnight couch was thrown.

If the soft evening star arose
To seal some cloudless day's repose
And would bring peace with tranquil ray
Where pain had tortured many a day,
Would touch the heart that yearned for thee
With a kind balm like sympathy,
How following on that glimpse of rest
Redoubling anguish wracked this breast,
Anguish because no [—] eye
Could see the light of that sweet sky.
And as to my wide halls I turned,
How dim the torch and hearthlight burned.

Beneath their gilded domes there fell
The gloom of lonely hermit's cell,
And music if awakened died
As if wild gales repining sighed
Through vaulted crypt, through columned
    aisle
Threading some old religious pile.

Is it so now? O, nearer still
Claps me and kiss the tear away
That starts—as that remembrance chill
Crosses with clouds my radiant day.
Close not thy dark eyes, for divine
To me their full and haughty shine.
Do I repent that long-past hour
Of moonlight-love and mystery
When the wide forest's arching bower
Heard me vow lasting faith to thee?
Suffering and loneliness and wrong
Are nothing to a heart like mine.
They only firmer knit the strong
True ties that twine its strings with thine.
I might reproach and chide thee now
For days when coldness dimmed thy brow,
But only burning love will speak
In tears, for words are far too weak.

OBSCURE and little seen my way
Through life has ever been,
But winding from my earliest day
  Through many a wondrous scene.
None ever asked what feelings moved
  My heart, or flushed my cheek,
And if I hoped, or feared or loved
  No voice was heard to speak.

I watched, I thought, I studied long,
The crowds I moved unmarked among,
I nought to them and they to me
But shapes of strange variety.
The Great with all the elusive shine
Of power and wealth and lofty line
I long have marked and well I know.

IS this my tomb, this humble stone
Above this narrow mound?
Is this my resting place, so lone,

So green, so quiet round?
5 Not even a stately tree to shade
The sunbeam from my bed,
Not even a flower in tribute laid
As sacred to the dead.

I look along those evening hills,
10   As mute as earth may be,
I hear not even the voice of rills—
Not even a cloud I see.
How long is it since human tread
Was heard on that dim track
15 Which, through the shadowy valleys led,
Winds far, and farther back?

And was I not a lady once,
My home a princely hall?
And did not hundreds make response
20   Whene'er I deigned to call?
Methinks, as in a doubtful dream,
That dwelling proud I see
Where I caught first the early beam
Of being's day's spring free.

25 Methinks the flash is round me still
Of mirrors broad and bright;
Methinks I see the torches fill
My chambers with their light,
And o'er my limbs the draperies flow
30   All gloss and silken shine,
On my cold brow the jewels glow
As bright as festal wine.

Who then disrobed that worshipped form?
Who wound this winding sheet?
35 Who turned the blood that ran so warm
To Winter's frozen sleet?
O can it be that many a sun
Has set, as that sets now,
Since last its fervid lustre shone
40   Upon my living brow?

Have all the wild dark clouds of night
  Each eve for years drawn on
While I interred so far from light
  Have slumbered thus alone?
45 Has this green mound been wet with rain—
  Such rain as storms distil
When the wind's high and warning strain
  Swells loud on sunless hill?

And I have slept where roughest hind
50   Had shuddered to pass by,
And no dread did my spirit find
  In all that snow-racked sky,
Though shook the iron-rails around
  As, swept by deepened breeze,
55 They gave a strange and hollow sound
  That living veins might freeze.

O was that music like my own?—
  Such as I used to play
When soft, clear and holy shone
60   The summer moon's first ray,
And saw me lingering still to feel
  The influence of that sky?
O words may not the peace reveal
  That filled its concave high,

65 As rose and bower how far beneath
  Hung down o'ercharged with dew,
And sighed their sweet and fragrant breath
  To every gale that blew
The hour for music, but in vain,
70   Each ancient stanza rose
To lips that could not with their strain
  Break Earth's and Heaven's repose.

Yet first a note and then a line
  The fettered tongue would say,
75 And then the whole rich song divine
  Found free a gushing way.
Past, past, forgotten, I am here,
  They dug my chamber deep,
I know no hope, I feel no fear,
80   I sleep—how calm I sleep!

WHY should we ever mourn as those
 Whose 'star of hope' has ceased to smile?
How dark soe'er succeeding woes,
 Be still and wait and trust the while.

5   A time will come when future years
 Their veil of softening haze shall fling
Over that mournful vale of tears
 Which saw thy weary wandering.

Wild, rough, and desolate the way
10   To every pilgrim here below;
All rough the path, all dim and grey
 The lonely wastes through which we go.

But think of Beulah's bowers, the home
 That waits thee when this path is trod,
15   Lying all free from clouds and gloom,
 Celestial in the smile of God.

One stream to cross, one sable flood,
 Silent, unsounded, deep and dim:
It blights the flesh, it chills the blood;
20   But, deathless spirit! trust in Him;

For on the shore of Heaven, that lies
 So sweet, so fair, so bathed in light,
Angels are waiting; lift thine eyes,
 Behold them where they walk in white!

25   A little while, an hour of pain,
 One struggle more, one gasp for breath,
And it is over; ne'er again
 Shall sin or sorrow, hell or death,

Prevail o'er him; he passed away
30   A shade, a flower, a cloud from earth;
On glory look, forget decay,
 And know in Heaven an angel's birth.

PRESENTIMENT

'SISTER, you've sat there all the day,
    Come to the hearth awhile;
The wind so wildly sweeps away,
    The clouds so darkly pile.
That open book has lain, unread,
    For hours upon your knee;
You've never smiled nor turned your head;
    What can you, sister, see?'

'Come hither, Jane, look down the field;
    How dense a mist creeps on!
The path, the hedge, are both concealed,
    Even the white gate is gone;
No landscape through the fog I trace,
    No hill with pastures green;
All featureless is Nature's face,
    All masked in clouds her mien.

'Scarce is the rustle of a leaf
    Heard in our garden now;
The year grows old, its days wax brief,
    The tresses leave its brow.
The rain drives fast before the wind,
    The sky is blank and grey;
O Jane, what sadness fills the mind
    On such a dreary day!'

'You think too much, my sister dear;
    You sit too long alone;
What though November days be drear?
    Full soon will they be gone.

I've swept the hearth, and placed your chair,
    Come, Emma, sit by me;
Our own fireside is never drear,
Though late and wintry wane the year,
    Though rough the night may be.'

'The peaceful glow of our fireside
    Imparts no peace to me:
My thoughts would rather wander wide
    Than rest, dear Jane, with thee.
I'm on a distant journey bound,
    And if, about my heart,
Too closely kindred ties were wound
    'Twould break when forced to part.

'"Soon will November days be o'er"—
    Well have you spoken, Jane:
My own forebodings tell me more—
    For me, I know my presage sure,
    They'll ne'er return again.
Ere long, nor sun nor storm to me
    Will bring or joy or gloom;
They reach not that Eternity
    Which soon will be my home.'

Eight months are gone, the summer sun
    Sets in a glorious sky;
A quiet field, all green and lone,
    Receives its rosy dye.
Jane sits upon a shaded stile,
    Alone she sits there now;
Her head rests on her hand the while
    And thought o'ercasts her brow.

She's thinking of one winter's day,
    A few short months ago,
When Emma's bier was borne away
    O'er wastes of frozen snow.
She's thinking how that drifted snow
    Dissolved in spring's first gleam,
And how her sister's memory now
    Fades, even as fades a dream.

The snow will whiten earth again,
    But Emma comes no more;
She left, 'mid winter's sleet and rain,

70   This world for Heaven's far shore.
On Beulah's hills she wanders now,
    On Eden's tranquil plain;
To her shall Jane hereafter go,
    She ne'er shall come to Jane!

WHAT does she dream of, lingering all alone
    On the vast terrace, o'er the stream impending?
Through all the still, dim night no life-like tone
    With the soft rush of wind and wave is blending.
5 Her fairy step upon the marble falls
With startling echo through those silent halls.

Chill is the night, though glorious, and she folds
    Her robe upon her breast to meet that blast
Coming down from the barren Northern wolds.
10   There, how she shuddered as the breeze blew past
And died on yonder track of foam, with shiver
Of giant reed and flag fringing the river.

Full, brilliant shines the moon—lifted on high
    O'er noble land and nobler river flowing,
15 Through parting hills that swell upon that sky
    Still with the hue of dying daylight glowing,
Swell with their plumy woods and dewy glades,
Opening to moonlight in the deepest shades.

Turn, lady, to thy halls, for singing shrill
20   Again the gust descends—again the river
Frets into foam—I see thy dark eyes fill
    With large and bitter tears—thy sweet lips quiver.

      'OH, let me be alone,' he said,
        And he was left alone.
None wished to stay—a sense of dread
    Came with that hollow tone.
5 Upon his couch he rose to see
    If through the chamber wide
There shone an eye to watch how he
    Could yield to pain his pride.

No, all was void—before his bed
  A lofty arch disclosed
How gloomily the sky was spread
  With clouds where sad storms reposed,
Unwilling still to break, but full
  Of awful days to be,
When that high concave dense and dull
  Should burst convulsively.

The light that touched the sufferer's brow
  Was brassy, faint and wan,
Yet showed it well what sense of woe
  Worked in that dying man.
He looked forth on the dreary sky
  And back he sank again,
But not to sleep or faint, his eye
  Showed strength still strove with pain.

He spoke, for burning fever wrought
  So wildly in his brain
He knew not whether voice or thought
  Took up the frenzied strain.
He spoke aloud, his vision wild
  Seemed something to portray,
And as the phantom waned, he smiled
  And beckoned it to stay.

'Be mine for evermore, I go
  Where none shall watch us rove.
O heal this anguish, soothe this woe
  And then my true heart prove.
Shall I not by the cane-brake find
  Some home, some rest for thee,
Where haply on thy breast reclined
  My future heaven shall be?

'These are my father's halls, but here
  I feel I may not stay.
I grieve not so these arms may bear
  Mine Idol too away;
And thou wilt go, that heavenly smile
  Forgives and grants me more
Than hours and months and years of toil
  And fondness can restore.

'O is it Fever brings that form
   So near my dying bed,
And waves that hand so soft and warm
   Above my throbbing head?
Is it delirium shews her now
   With pitying aspect nigh,
With dark curls o'er her snow-white brow,
   With love in that deep eye?

'Hollow and vapour-like it seems,
   I see but cannot feel,
Like glorious thoughts, like golden dreams
   Which youth and hope reveal.
But I must wake, I know she said
   She never loved but one,
And all my adoration paid
   In fire she seemed to shun.

'Again if raised from this death-bed
   I'll peril life to try
If she for whom I fought and bled
   Will let me hopeless die;
And if an angel's voice divine
   From God should bid me tell
In what bright heaven of glorious shine
   My spirit longed to dwell,

'I'd say let it be shadowy night,
   On earth let stars look down,
And let her lips in their dim light
   Confess her heart my own.
Be it in black and frozen wild,
   Be it in lonely wood,
So she but loved and cheered and smiled
   I'll buy such bliss with blood.'

The white lips of the dying man
   Turned whiter still, and he
With up-turned eyes and aspect wan
   Seemed stricken with agony.
He felt himself alone, he knew
   All the cold lonely room around.

THE TOWN BESIEGED

WITH moaning sound a stream
     Sweeps past the Town's dark walls;
Within her streets a bugle's voice
Her troops to slumber calls.

5   The sentinels are set,
     The wearied soldiers sleep;
     But some shall know tomorrow night
     A slumber far more deep.

     A chill and hoary dew
10   On tower and bastion shines.
     What dew shall fall when war arrays
     Her fiery battle lines?

     Trump and triumphant drum
     Her conflict soon shall spread;
15   Who then will turn aside and say
     'We mourn the noble dead'?

     Strong hands, heroic hearts
     Shall homeward throng again;
     Redeemed from battle's gory grasp
20   Where will they leave the slain?

     Beneath a foreign sod
     Beside an alien wave;
     Watched by the martyr's holy God
     Shall sleep the martyred brave.

A ROLAND for your Oliver
     We think you've justly earned;
You sent us such a valentine,
     Your gift is now returned.

5   We cannot write or talk like you;
     We're plain folks every one;
You've played a clever jest on us,
     We thank you for the fun.

Believe us when we frankly say
   (Our words, though blunt, are true),
At home, abroad, by night or day,
   We all wish well to you.

And never may a cloud come o'er
   The sunshine of your mind;
Kind friends, warm hearts, and happy hours
   Through life, we trust, you'll find.

Where'er you go, however far
   In future years you stray,
There shall not want our earnest prayer
   To speed you on your way.

A stranger and a pilgrim here
   We know you sojourn now;
But brighter hopes, with brighter wreaths,
   Are doomed to bind your brow.

Not always in these lonely hills
   Your humble lot shall lie;
The oracle of fate foretells
   A worthier destiny.

And though her words are veiled in gloom,
   Though clouded her decree,
Yet doubt not that a juster doom
   She keeps in store for thee.

Then cast hope's anchor near the shore,
   'Twill hold your vessel fast,
And fear not for the tide's deep roar,
   And dread not for the blast.

For though this station now seems near,
   'Mid land-locked creeks to be,
The helmsman soon his ship will steer
   Out to the wide blue sea.

Well officered and staunchly manned,
  Well built to meet the blast;
With favouring winds the bark must land
  On glorious shores at last.

FRANCES

S HE will not sleep, for fear of dreams,
  But, rising, quits her restless bed,
And walks where some beclouded beams
  Of moonlight through the hall are shed.

5 Obedient to the goad of grief,
  Her steps, now fast, now lingering slow,
In varying motion seek relief
  From the Eumenides of woe.

Wringing her hands, at intervals—
10 But long as mute as phantom dim—
She glides along the dusky walls,
  Under the black oak rafters grim.

The close air of the grated tower
  Stifles a heart that scarce can beat,
15 And, though so late and lone the hour,
  Forth pass her wandering, faltering feet;

And on the pavement spread before
  The long front of the mansion grey,
Her steps imprint the night-frost hoar,
20 Which pale on grass and granite lay.

Not long she stayed where misty moon
  And shimmering stars could on her look,
But through the garden archway soon
  Her strange and gloomy path she took.

25 Some firs, coëval with the tower,
  Their straight black boughs stretched o'er her head;
Unseen, beneath this sable bower,
  Rustled her dress and rapid tread.

There was an alcove in that shade,
30   Screening a rustic seat and stand;
Weary, she sat her down, and laid
    Her hot brow on her burning hand.

To solitude and to the night
    Some words she now, in murmurs, said;
35   And trickling through her fingers white,
    Some tears of misery she shed.

'God help me in my grievous need,
    God help me in my inward pain;
Which cannot ask for pity's meed,
40   Which has no licence to complain;

'Which must be borne; yet who can bear,
    Hours long, days long, a constant weight—
The yoke of absolute despair,
    A suffering wholly desolate?

45 'Who can for ever crush the heart,
    Restrain its throbbing, curb its life?
Dissemble truth with ceaseless art,
    With outward calm mask inward strife?'

She waited—as for some reply;
50   The still and cloudy night gave none;
Ere long, with deep-drawn, trembling sigh,
    Her heavy plaint again begun.

'Unloved—I love; unwept—I weep;
    Grief I restrain—hope I repress:
55 Vain is this anguish—fixed and deep;
    Vainer, desires and dreams of bliss:

'My love awakes no love again,
    My tears collect, and fall unfelt;
My sorrow touches none with pain,
60   My humble hopes to nothing melt.

'For me the universe is dumb,
    Stone-deaf, and blank, and wholly blind;
Life I must bound, existence sum
    In the strait limits of one mind;

65 'That mind my own. Oh! narrow cell;
    Dark—imageless—a living tomb!
There must I sleep, there wake and dwell
    Content,—with palsy, pain, and gloom.'

Again she paused; a moan of pain,
70   A stifled sob, alone was heard;
Long silence followed—then again
    Her voice the stagnant midnight stirred:

'Must it be so? Is this my fate?
    Can I nor struggle, nor contend?
75 And am I doomed for years to wait,
    Watching death's lingering axe descend?

'And when it falls, and when I die,
    What follows? Vacant nothingness?
The blank of lost identity?
80   Erasure both of pain and bliss?

'I've heard of Heaven—I would believe;
    For if this earth indeed be all,
Who longest lives may deepest grieve;
    Most blest, whom sorrows soonest call.

85 'Oh! leaving disappointment here,
    Will man find hope on yonder coast?
Hope, which, on earth, shines never clear,
    And oft in clouds is wholly lost.

'Will he hope's source of light behold,
90   Fruition's spring, where doubts expire,
And drink, in waves of living gold,
    Contentment, full, for long desire?

'Will he find bliss, which here he dreamed?
    Rest, which was weariness on earth?
95 Knowledge, which, if o'er life it beamed,
    Served but to prove it void of worth?

'Will he find love without lust's leaven,
    Love fearless, tearless, perfect, pure,
To all with equal bounty given;
100   In all, unfeigned, unfailing, sure?

'Will he, from penal sufferings free,
    Released from shroud and wormy clod,
All calm and glorious, rise and see
    Creation's Sire—Existence' God?

105 'Then, glancing back on Time's brief woes,
    Will he behold them, fading, fly;
Swept from Eternity's repose,
    Like sullying cloud from pure blue sky?

'If so, endure, my weary frame;
110   And when thy anguish strikes too deep,
And when all troubled burns life's flame,
    Think of the quiet, final sleep;

'Think of the glorious waking-hour,
    Which will not dawn on grief and tears,
115 But on a ransomed spirit's power,
    Certain and free from mortal fears.

'Seek now thy couch, and lie till morn,
    Then from thy chamber, calm, descend,
With mind nor tossed, nor anguish-torn,
120   But tranquil, fixed, to wait the end.

'And when thy opening eyes shall see
    Mementos on the chamber wall,
Of one who has forgotten thee,
    Shed not the tear of acrid gall.

125 'The tear which, welling from the heart,
        Burns where its drop corrosive falls,
    And makes each nerve in torture start,
        At feelings it too well recalls:

    'When the sweet hope of being loved
130   Threw Eden-sunshine on Life's way;
    When every sense and feeling proved
        Expectancy of brightest day:

    'When the hand trembled to receive
        A thrilling clasp, which seemed so near,
135 And the heart ventured to believe
        Another heart esteemed it dear:

    'When words, half love, all tenderness,
        Were hourly heard, as hourly spoken,
    When the long sunny days of bliss
140   Only by moonlight nights were broken:

    'Till, drop by drop, the cup of joy,
        Filled full, with purple light was glowing,
    And Faith, which watched it sparkling high,
        Still never dreamt the overflowing.

145 'It fell not with a sudden crashing,
        It poured not out like open sluice;
    No, sparkling still, and redly flashing,
        Drained, drop by drop, the generous juice.

    'I saw it sink, and strove to taste it—
150   My eager lips approached the brim;
    The movement only seened to waste it—
        It sank to dregs, all harsh and dim.

    'These I have drunk, and they for ever
        Have poisoned life and love for me;
155 A draught from Sodom's lake could never
        More fiery, salt, and bitter be.

'Oh! Love was all a thin illusion;
    Joy but the desert's flying stream;
And glancing back on long delusion
160   My memory grasps a hollow dream.

'Yet whence that wondrous change of feeling,
    I never knew, and cannot learn;
Nor why my lover's eye, congealing,
    Grew cold and clouded, proud and stern.

165 'Nor wherefore, friendship's forms forgetting,
    He careless left and cool withdrew,
Nor spoke of grief nor fond regretting,
    Nor even one glance of comfort threw.

'And neither word nor token sending,
170   Of kindness, since the parting day,
His course, for distant regions bending,
    Went, self-contained and calm, away.

'O bitter, blighting, keen sensation,
    Which will not weaken, cannot die,
175 Hasten thy work of desolation,
    And let my tortured spirit fly!

'Vain as the passing gale, my crying;
    Though lightning-struck, I must live on;
I know at heart there is no dying
180   Of love, and ruined hope, alone.

'Still strong and young, and warm with vigour,
    Though scathed, I long shall greenly grow;
And many a storm of wildest rigour
    Shall yet break o'er my shivered bough.

185 'Rebellious now to blank inertion,
    My unused strength demands a task;
Travel, and toil, and full exertion
    Are the last, only boon I ask.

'Whence, then, this vain and barren dreaming
   Of death, and dubious life to come?
I see a nearer beacon gleaming
   Over dejection's sea of gloom.

'The very wildness of my sorrow
   Tells me I yet have innate force;
My track of life has been too narrow,
   Effort shall trace a broader course.

'The world is not in yonder tower,
   Earth is not prisoned in that room,
'Mid whose dark panels, hour by hour,
   I've sat, the slave and prey of gloom.

'One feeling—turned to utter anguish,
   Is not my being's only aim;
When, lorn and loveless, life will languish,
   But courage can revive the flame.

'He, when he left me, went a-roving
   To sunny climes beyond the sea;
And I, the weight of woe removing,
   Am free and fetterless as he.

'New scenes, new language, skies less clouded,
   May once more wake the wish to live;
Strange foreign towns, astir and crowded,
   New pictures to the mind may give.

'New forms and faces, passing ever,
   May hide the one I still retain,
Defined and fixed, and fading never,
   Stamped deep on vision, heart, and brain.

'And we might meet—time may have changed him;
   Chance may reveal the mystery,
The secret influence which estranged him;
   Love may restore him yet to me.

190

195

200

205

210

215

220

'False thought—false hope—in scorn be banished!
   I am not loved—nor loved have been!
Recall not, then, the dreams scarce vanished;
   Traitors! mislead me not again!

225   'To words like yours I bid defiance,
   'Tis such my mental wreck have made;
Of God alone, and self-reliance,
   I ask for solace—hope for aid.

      'Morn comes—and ere meridian glory
230   O'er these, my natal woods, shall smile,
Both lonely wood and mansion hoary
   I'll leave behind, full many a mile.'

GILBERT

I THE GARDEN

ABOVE the city hung the moon,
   Right o'er a plot of ground
Where flowers and orchard-trees were fenced
   With lofty walls around:
5   'Twas Gilbert's garden—there to-night
   A while he walked alone;
And, tired with sedentary toil,
   Mused where the moonlight shone.

This garden, in a city heart,
   Lay still as houseless wild,
10   Though many-windowed mansion fronts
   Were round it closely piled;
But thick their walls, and those within
   Lived lives by noise unstirred;
15   Like wafting of an angel's wing,
   Time's flight by them was heard.

Some soft piano-notes alone
   Were sweet as faintly given,
Where ladies, doubtless, cheered the hearth

20 With song that winter-even.
The city's many-mingled sounds
    Rose like the hum of ocean;
They rather lulled the heart than roused
    Its pulse to faster motion.

25 Gilbert has paced the single walk
    An hour, yet is not weary;
And, though it be a winter night,
    He feels nor cold nor dreary.
The prime of life is in his veins,
30   And sends his blood fast flowing,
And Fancy's fervour warms the thoughts
    Now in his bosom glowing.

Those thoughts recur to early love,
    Or what he love would name,
35 Though haply Gilbert's secret deeds
    Might other title claim.
Such theme not oft his mind absorbs,
    He to the world clings fast,
And too much for the present lives,
40   To linger o'er the past.

But now the evening's deep repose
    Has glided to his soul;
That moonlight falls on Memory,
    And shows her fading scroll.
45 One name appears in every line
    The gentle rays shine o'er,
And still he smiles and still repeats
    That one name—Elinor.

There is no sorrow in his smile,
50   No kindness in his tone;
The triumph of a selfish heart
    Speaks coldly there alone.
He says: 'She loved me more than life;
    And truly it was sweet
55 To see so fair a woman kneel
    In bondage at my feet.

'There was a sort of quiet bliss
  To be so deeply loved,
To gaze on trembling eagerness
  And sit myself unmoved;
60 And when it pleased my pride to grant
  At last some rare caress,
To feel the fever of that hand
  My fingers deigned to press.

65 ''Twas sweet to see her strive to hide
  What every glance revealed;
Endowed, the while, with despot-might
  Her destiny to wield.
I knew myself no perfect man,
70   Nor, as she deemed, divine;
I knew that I was glorious—but
  By her reflected shine;

'Her youth, her native energy,
  Her powers new-born and fresh—
75 'Twas these with Godhead sanctified
  My sensual frame of flesh.
Yet, like a god did I descend
  At last to meet her love;
And, like a god, I then withdrew
80   To my own heaven above.

'And never more could she invoke
  My presence to her sphere;
No prayer, no plaint, no cry of hers
  Could win my awful ear.
85 I knew her blinded constancy
  Would ne'er my deeds betray,
And, calm in conscience, whole in heart,
  I went my tranquil way.

'Yet, sometimes, I still feel a wish,
  The fond and flattering pain
90 Of passion's anguish to create
  In her young breast again.
Bright was the lustre of her eyes

When they caught fire from mine;
95   If I had power—this very hour,
            Again I'd light their shine.

'But where she is, or how she lives,
        I have no clue to know;
I've heard she long my absence pined,
100   And left her home in woe.
But busied, then, in gathering gold,
        As I am busied now,
I could not turn from such pursuit,
        To keep a broken vow.

105   'Nor could I give to fatal risk
            The fame I ever prized;
Even now, I fear, that precious fame
        Is too much compromised.'
An inward trouble dims his eye,
110   Some riddle he would solve;
Some method to unloose a knot,
        His anxious thoughts revolve.

He, pensive, leans against a tree,
        A leafy evergreen—
115   The boughs the moonlight intercept,
        And hide him like a screen;
He starts—the tree shakes with his tremor,
        Yet nothing near him passed;
He hurries up the garden alley
120   In strangely sudden haste.

With shaking hand he lifts the latchet,
        Steps o'er the threshold stone;
The heavy door slips from his fingers—
        It shuts, and he is gone.
125   What touched, transfixed, appalled his soul?—
            A nervous thought, no more;
'Twill sink like stone in placid pool,
        And calm close smoothly o'er.

2 THE PARLOUR

Warm is the parlour atmosphere,
  Serene the lamp's soft light;
The vivid embers, red and clear,
  Proclaim a frosty night.
Books, varied, on the table lie,
  Three children o'er them bend,
And all, with curious, eager eye,
  The turning leaf attend.

Picture and tale alternately
  Their simple hearts delight,
And interest deep, and tempered glee,
  Illume their aspects bright.
The parents, from their fireside place,
  Behold that pleasant scene,
And joy is on the mother's face,
  Pride in the father's mien.

As Gilbert sees his blooming wife,
  Beholds his children fair,
No thought has he of transient strife,
  Or past though piercing fear.
The voice of happy infancy
  Lisps sweetly in his ear,
His wife, with pleased and peaceful eye,
  Sits, kindly smiling, near.

The fire glows on her silken dress,
  And shows its ample grace,
And warmly tints each hazel tress,
  Curled soft around her face.
The beauty that in youth he wooed
  Is beauty still, unfaded;
The brow of ever placid mood
  No churlish grief has shaded.

Prosperity, in Gilbert's home,
  Abides, the guests of years;
There Want or Discord never come,
  And seldom Toil or Tears.

130

135

140

145

150

155

160

165 The carpets bear the peaceful print
  Of Comfort's velvet tread,
And golden gleams, from plenty sent,
  In every nook are shed.

  The very silken spaniel seems
170   Of quiet ease to tell,
As near its mistress' feet it dreams,
  Sunk in a cushion's swell;
And smiles seem native to the eyes
  Of those sweet children three;
175 They have but looked on tranquil skies,
  And know not Misery.

Alas! that Misery should come
  In such an hour as this;
Why could she not so calm a home
180   A little longer miss?
But she is now within the door,
  Her steps advancing glide;
Her sullen shade has crossed the floor,
  She stands at Gilbert's side.

185 She lays her hand upon his heart,
  It bounds with agony;
His fireside chair shakes with the start
  That shook the garden tree.
His wife towards the children looks,
190   She does not mark his mien;
The children, bending o'er their books,
  His terror have not seen.

In his own home, by his own hearth,
  He sits in solitude,
195 And circled round with light and mirth,
  Cold horror chills his blood.
His mind would hold with desperate clutch
  The scene that round him lies;
No—changed, as by some wizard's touch,
200   The present prospect flies.

A tumult vague—a viewless strife
  His futile struggles crush;
'Twixt him and his, an unknown life
  And unknown feeling rush.
205 He sees—but scarce can language paint
  The tissue Fancy weaves;
For words oft give but echo faint
  Of thoughts the mind conceives.

Noise, tumult strange, and darkness dim
  Efface both light and quiet;
210 No shape is in those shadows grim,
  No voice in that wild riot.
Sustained and strong, a wondrous blast
  Above and round him blows;
215 A greenish gloom, dense overcast,
  Each moment denser grows.

He nothing knows—nor clearly sees,
  Resistance checks his breath,
The high, impetuous, ceaseless breeze
220   Blows on him, cold as death.
And still the undulating gloom
  Mocks sight with formless motion:
Was such sensation Jonah's doom,
  'Gulfed in the depths of ocean?

225 Streaking the air, the nameless vision,
  Fast-driven, deep-sounding, flows;
Oh! whence its source, and what its mission?
  How will its terrors close?
Long-sweeping, rushing, vast and void,
230   The Universe it swallows;
And still the dark, devouring tide
  A Typhoon tempest follows.

More slow it rolls; its furious race
  Sinks to a solemn gliding;
235 The stunning roar, the wind's wild chase,
  To stillness are subsiding;

And, slowly borne along, a form
　The shapeless chaos varies;
Poised in the eddy of the storm,
240　　Before the eye it tarries:

A woman drowned—sunk in the deep,
　On a long wave reclining;
The circling waters' crystal sweep,
　Like glass, her shape enshrining.
245　Her pale dead face, to Gilbert turned,
　Seems as in sleep reposing;
A feeble light, now first discerned,
　The features well disclosing.

No effort from the haunted air
250　　The ghastly scene could banish;
That hovering wave, arrested there,
　Rolled—throbbed—but did not vanish.
If Gilbert upward turned his gaze,
　He saw the ocean-shadow;
255　If he looked down, the endless seas
　Lay green as summer meadow.

And straight before, the pale corpse lay,
　Upborne by air or billow,
So near, he could have touched the spray
260　　That churned around its pillow.
The hollow anguish of the face
　Had moved a fiend to sorrow;
Not death's fixed calm could rase the trace
　Of suffering's deep-worn furrow.

265　All moved; a strong returning blast,
　The mass of waters raising,
Bore wave and passive carcase past,
　While Gilbert yet was gazing.
Deep in her isle-conceiving womb,
270　　It seemed the ocean thundered,
And soon, by realms of rushing gloom,
　Were seer and phantom sundered.

Then swept some timbers from a wreck,
   On following surges riding;
275   Then seaweed, in the turbid rack
   Uptorn, went slowly gliding.
The horrid shade, by slow degrees,
   A beam of light defeated,
And then the roar of raving seas,
280   Fast, far, and faint, retreated.

And all was gone—gone like a mist,
   Corse, billows, tempest, wreck;
Three children close to Gilbert pressed,
   And clung around his neck.
285   'Good-night! good-night!' the prattlers said,
   And kissed their father's cheek;
'Twas now the hour their quiet bed
   And placid rest to seek.

The mother with her offspring goes
   To hear their evening prayer;
290   She nought of Gilbert's vision knows,
   And nought of his despair.
Yet, pitying God, abridge the time
   Of anguish, now his fate!
295   Though, haply, great has been his crime,
   Thy mercy, too, is great.

Gilbert, at length, uplifts his head,
   Bent for some moments low,
And there is neither grief nor dread
300   Upon his subtle brow.
For well can he his feelings task,
   And well his looks command;
His features well his heart can mask,
   With smiles and smoothness bland.

305   Gilbert has reasoned with his mind—
   He says 'twas all a dream;
He strives his inward sight to blind
   Against truth's inward beam.
He pitied not that shadowy thing,

310
  When it was flesh and blood;
 Nor now can pity's balmy spring
  Refresh his arid mood.

 'And if that dream has spoken truth,'
  Thus musingly he says;
315
 'If Elinor be dead, in sooth,
  Such chance the shock repays:
 A net was woven round my feet,
  I scarce could further go,
 Ere shame had forced a fast retreat,
320
  Dishonour brought me low.

 'Conceal her then, deep, silent Sea,
  Give her a secret grave!
 She sleeps in peace, and I am free,
  No longer Terror's slave:
325
 And homage still, from all the world,
  Shall greet my spotless name,
 Since surges break and waves are curled
  Above its threatened shame.'

3 THE WELCOME HOME

 Above the city hangs the moon,
330
  Some clouds are boding rain;
 Gilbert, erewhile on journey gone,
  To-night comes home again.
 Ten years have passed above his head,
  Each year has brought him gain;
335
 His prosperous life has smoothly sped,
  Without or tear or stain.

 'Tis somewhat late—the city clocks
  Twelve deep vibrations toll,
 As Gilbert at the portal knocks,
340
  Which is his journey's goal.
 The street is still and desolate,
  The moon hid by a cloud;
 Gilbert, impatient, will not wait,—
  His second knock peals loud.

345 The clocks are hushed; there's not a light
         In any window nigh,
     And not a single planet bright
         Looks from the clouded sky;
     The air is raw, the rain descends,
350   A bitter north-wind blows;
     His cloak the traveller scarce defends—
         Will not the door unclose?

     He knocks the third time, and the last;
         His summons now they hear:
355 Within, a footstep, hurrying fast,
         Is heard approaching near.
     The bolt is drawn, the clanking chain
         Falls to the floor of stone;
     And Gilbert to his heart will strain
360   His wife and children soon.

     The hand that lifts the latchet, holds
         A candle to his sight,
     And Gilbert, on the step, beholds
         A woman clad in white.
365 Lo! water from her dripping dress
         Runs on the streaming floor;
     From every dark and clinging tress
         The drops incessant pour.

     There's none but her to welcome him;
370   She holds the candle high,
     And, motionless in form and limb,
         Stands cold and silent nigh;
     There's sand and seaweed on her robe,
         Her hollow eyes are blind;
375 No pulse in such a frame can throb,
         No life is there defined.

     Gilbert turned ashy-white, but still
         His lips vouchsafed no cry;
     He spurred his strength and master-will
380   To pass the figure by,—
     But, moving slow, it faced him straight,

It would not flinch nor quail:
Then first did Gilbert's strength abate,
His stony firmness fail.

385   He sank upon his knees and prayed;
The shape stood rigid there;
He called aloud for human aid,
No human aid was near.
An accent strange did thus repeat
390   Heaven's stern but just decree:
'The measure thou to her didst mete,
To thee shall measured be!'

Gilbert sprang from his bended knees,
By the pale spectre pushed,
395   And, wild as one whom demons seize,
Up the hall-staircase rushed;
Entered his chamber—near the bed
Sheathed steel and firearms hung—
Impelled by maniac purpose dread
400   He chose those stores among.

Across his throat a keen-edged knife
With vigorous hand he drew;
The wound was wide—his outraged life
Rushed rash and redly through.
405   And thus died, by a shameful death,
A wise and wordly man,
Who never drew but selfish breath
Since first his life began.

HE saw my heart's woe, discerned my soul's anguish,
How in fever, in thirst, in atrophy it pined;
Knew he could heal, yet looked and let it languish,—
To its moans spirit-deaf, to its pangs spirit-blind.

5   But once a year he heard a whisper low and dreary
Appealing for aid, entreating some reply;
Only when sick, soul-worn, and torture-weary,
Breathed I that prayer, heaved I that sigh.

He was mute as is the grave, he stood stirless as a tower;
    At last I looked up, and saw I prayed to stone:
I asked help of that which to help had no power,
    I sought love where love was utterly unknown.

Idolater I kneeled to an idol cut in rock!
    I might have slashed my flesh and drawn my heart's best
        blood:
The Granite God had felt no tenderness, no shock;
    My Baal had not seen nor heard nor understood.

In dark remorse I rose; I rose in darker shame;
    Self-condemned I withdrew to an exile from my kind;
A solitude I sought where mortal never came,
    Hoping in its wilds forgetfulness to find.

Now, Heaven, heal the wound which I still deeply feel;
    Thy glorious hosts look not in scorn on our poor race;
Thy King eternal doth no iron judgment deal
    On suffering worms who seek forgiveness, comfort, grace.

He gave our hearts to love: He will not love despise,
    E'en if the gift be lost, as mine was long ago;
He will forgive the fault, will bid the offender rise,
    Wash out with dews of bliss the fiery brand of woe;

And give a sheltered place beneath the unsullied throne,
    Whence the soul redeemed may mark Time's fleeting
        course round earth;
And know its trials over and its sufferings gone,
    And feel the peril past of Death's immortal birth.

AT first I did attention give,
  Observance—deep esteem;
His frown I failed not to forgive,
His smile—a boon to deem.

Attention rose to interest soon,
Respect to homage changed;
The smile became a valued boon,
The frown like grief estranged.

The interest ceased not with his voice,
The homage tracked him near.
Obedience was my heart's free choice—
Whate'er his mood severe.

His praise infrequent—favour rare,
Unruly deceivers grew.
And too much power a haunting fear
Around his anger threw.

His coming was my hope each day,
His parting was my pain.
The chance that did his steps delay
Was ice in every vein.

I gave entire affection now,
I gave devotion sure,
And strong took root and fast did grow
One mighty feeling more.

The truest love that ever heart
Felt at its kindled core
Through my veins with quickened
    start
A tide of life did pour.

A halo played about the brows
Of life as seen by me,
And troubling bliss within me rose,
And anxious ecstacy.

I dreamed it would be nameless bliss
As I loved loved to be,
And to this object did I press
As blind as eagerly.

But wide as pathless was the space
That lay our lives between,
And dangerous as the foaming race
Of ocean's surges green,

And haunted as a robber path
Through wilderness or wood,
For might and right, woe and wrath
Between our spirits stood.

45   I dangers dared, I hindrance scorned
I omens did defy;
Whatever menaced, harassed, warned
I passed impetuous by.

On sped my rainbow fast as light,
50   I flew as in a dream,
For glorious rose upon my sight
That child of shower and gleam,

And bright on clouds of suffering dim
Shone that soft solemn joy.
55   I care not then how dense and grim
Disasters gather nigh.

I care not in this moment sweet,
Though all I have rushed o'er
Should come on pinion strong and fleet
60   Proclaiming vengeance sore.

Hate struck me in his presence down,
Love barred approach to me,
My rival's joy with jealous frown
Declared hostility.

65   Wrath leagued with calumny transfused
Strong poison in his veins
And I stood at his feet accused
Of false [—] stains

Cold as a statue's grew his eye,
70   Hard as a rock his brow,
Cold hard to me—but tenderly
He kissed my rival now.

She seemed my rainbow to have seized,
Around her form it closed,
And soft its iris splendour blazed
Where love and she reposed.

My darling, thou wilt never know
The grinding agony of woe
 That we have borne for thee.
Thus may we consolation tear
E'en from the depth of our despair
 And wasting misery.

The nightly anguish thou art spared
When all the crushing truth is bared
 To the awakening mind,
When the galled heart is pierced with grief,
Till wildly it implores relief,
 But small relief can find.

Nor know'st thou what it is to lie
Looking forth with streaming eye
 On life's wilderness.
'Weary, weary, dark and drear,
How shall I the journey bear,
 The burden and distress?'

O since thou art spared such pain
We will not wish thee here again;
 He that lives must mourn.
God help us through our misery
And give us rest and joy with thee
 When we reach our bourne!

There's little joy in life for me,
And little terror in the grave;
I've lived the parting hour to see
 Of one I would have died to save.

5   Calmly to watch the failing breath,
            Wishing each sigh might be the last;
        Longing to see the cloud of death
            O'er those belovèd features cast.

        The cloud, the stillness that must part
10   The darling of my life from me;
        And then to thank God from my heart,
            To thank Him well and fervently;

        Although I knew that we had lost
            The hope and glory of our life;
15   And now, benighted, tempest-tossed,
            Must bear alone the weary strife.

SELECTED POEMS
OF
BRANWELL BRONTË

THE CXXXVIITH PSALM

BY the still streams of Babylon
We sat in sorrowing sadness down,
All weeping when we thought upon
  Our Zion's holy dome;

There hung our harps, unheeded now,
From the dark willow's bending bough,
Where mourning o'er the waves below
  They cast their evening gloom.

There round us stood that Iron band
  Who tore us from our home;
And in their far off stranger land
  Compelled our feet to roam.

They turned them to our native west
  And laughed with victor tongue;
Now sing—they said in stern behest—
  Your Zion's holiest song!—

How can we name Jehovah's name
So far away from Jordan's stream?

Jerusalem! Jerusalem!
  May hand and heart decay
If I forget thy diadem
  And sceptre passed away!
If 'mid my brightest smiles of joy
  I do not think of thee,

25 Or cease one hour my thoughts to employ
    On Salem's slavery,
Let this false tongue forget to speak,
And this torn heart with anguish break!

Remember, God, how Edom's sons
30   In Zion's darkest day
Rejoiced above her prostrate wall
    Like Lions o'er their prey;
How ruthlessly they shouted then
    As dark they gathered round,
35 'Down with it! Yea, Down with it
    Even to the very ground!'

Daughter of Babel, worn with woe
    And struck with misery,
As thou hast served God's people—so
40   Shall thy destruction be!
And in thine own dark hour of death,
    When foemen gather round,
Happy be they who on thy stones
Of ruin take thy little ones
45   And dash them to the ground!

MORNING

MORN comes and with it all the stir of morn,
New light new life upon its sunbeams borne.
The Magic dreams of Midnight fade away,
And Iron Labour rouses with the day.
5 He who has seen before his sleeping eye
The times and smiles of childhood wandering by,
The memory of years, gone long ago
And sunk and vanished now in clouds of woe,
He who, still young, in dreams of days to come
10 Has lost all memory of his native home,
Whose untracked future opening far before
Shews him a smiling heaven and happy shore,
While things that are frown dark and drearily
And sunshine only beams on things to be:

15 To such as these night is not all a night,
For one in eve beholds his morning bright,
The other basking in his earliest morn
Feels noontide summer o'er his feelings dawn.
But that worn wretch who tosses night away,
20 And counts each moment to returning day,
Whose only hope is dull and dreamless sleep,
Whose only choice to wake and watch and weep,
Whose present pains of body and of mind
Shut out all glimpse of happiness behind,
25 Whose present darkness hides the faintest light
Which yet might struggle through a milder night,
And He like *one* whom present cares engage
Without the glare of youth or gloom of age,
Who must not sleep upon his idle oar
30 Lest life's wild Tempests dash him to the shore,
Whom high Ambition calls aloud to awake,
Glory his goal, and death or life his stake,
And long and rugged his rough race to run
Ere he can stop to enjoy his Laurels won,
35 To these the night is weariness and pain
And blest the hour when day shall rise again!
'Mid visions of the Future or the past
Others may wish the shades of night to last,
Round these alone the *present* ever lies,
40 And these will first awake when morning calls Arise!

LINES

WE leave our bodies in the Tomb,
Like dust to moulder and decay,
But, while they waste in coffined gloom,
Our parted spirits, where are they?
5 In endless night or endless day?
Buried as our bodies are
Beyond all earthly hope or fear?
Like them no more to reappear,
But festering fast away?
10 For future's but the shadow thrown
From present and, the substance gone,
Its shadow cannot stay!

MISERY

PART I

HOW fast that courser fleeted by,
  With arched neck backward tossed on high,
And snorting nostrils opened wide,
And foam-flecked chest and gory side.
  I saw his Rider's darkened form
As on they hurried through the storm.
Forward he pressed, his plume behind
Flew whistling in the wintry wind,
But his clenched teeth and angry eye
Seemed wind and tempest to defy,
And eagerly he bent his sight
To pierce the darkness of the night,
And oft he gazed and gazed again
Through the rough blast and driving rain.
  Look up and view the midnight heaven
Where mass o'er mass continual driven
The wild black storm clouds fleet and change;
Like formless phantoms vast and strange
That bend their gloomy brows from high
And pass in midnight darkness by;
And still they pass and still they come
Without a flash to break the gloom.
  I cannot see the foam and spray
Which mark that raging torrent's way,
But I can hear the ceaseless roar
Where swollen and chafed its waters pour.
There, where yon blackened oaks on high
Blend wildly with the midnight sky,
Tossing their bare and groaning boughs
Like some dread fight of Giant foes;—
There, where that glimpse of Moonlight shines,
  From the wild wrack of heaven sent down,
And spreads its silver trembling lines
  Amid the darkness, then is gone;—
There stays the Horseman—wide before,

Deep and dark the waters roar,
But down the lone vale far away
Glances one solitary ray.
The sound of winds and waters rise,
40 And sweeps the sleet-shower o'er the skies,
While dreariest darkness all around
Makes still more drear each sight or sound.
But heeds not such that Cavalier:
Reining his trembling Charger there,
45 He halts upon the river's brink,
Where all its wild waves surge and sink,
Shades with his hand his anxious eye
And through the night looks eagerly.
　　Why smiled he when that far off light
50 Again broke twinkling on his sight?
Why frowned he when it sunk again
'Mid the darksome veil of rain?
Till brightly flashing forth once more,
It streams and twinkles far before.

55 'Oh through the tempests of this life
　　However loud they sound,
However wild their storms and strife
　　May burst and thunder round,
Though reft and riven each aid and prop,
60 There may be Heaven!—There may be Hope!
I thought just now that Life or Death
　　Could never trouble me,
For that I should draw my future breath
　　In silent apathy,
65 That o'er the pathway of my fate
　　Though steady beat the storm,
As I walked alone and desolate
　　I'd to that path conform.
Affection should not chain me,
70 　　Or Sorrow hold me down,
But Despair itself sustain me,
　　Whom itself had overthrown.
I thought that fame and glory
　　Were names for shame and woe,
75 That Life's deceitful story

I had finished long ago,
That all its novelty was gone,
    And that thus to read again
The same dull page in the same sad tone
    Was not even change of pain.
Defeat had crushed me into dust,
    But only laid my head
Where head and heart and spirit must
    Be soon for ever laid.
My fearless followers all were slain,
    My power and glory gone,
My followers met that fate of men
    And Power—! I am *NOW* alone!
Not so!—I *thought* it—till that light
    Glanced glittering down the glen,
And on my spirit's dreary night
    Flashed brightness back again.
Yes! I had thought I had stood alone,
That I need sigh or weep for none,
Had quenched my love in apathy,
Since none would sigh or weep for me.
Yes! But that single silver beam
    Which flashes on my eye
Hath waked me from my dreary dream
    And made the darkness fly;
Then pardon that the storms of woe
    Have whelmed me in a drifting sea,
With death and dangers struggling so
    That I—a while—forgot even Thee.
This moment as I gain the shore,
    And clouds begin to disappear,
Even steadier, brighter than before
    Thou shinest, my own—my Guardian Star!'

'Oh could I speak the long lost feeling,
The inward joy its Power revealing,
The glimpse of something yet to come
Which yet may give a happy Home.
Oh could I speak my thoughts of thee
Whom soon again my eyes shall see.
The dove that bore the Olive leaf

Could never bring such glad relief
To wanderers o'er the shoreless main
As in my weariness and pain
That single light has given to me.
120   My gallant horse, speed swiftly thou,
Soon shall a hand caress thee now,
Grateful that thou has borne me on
Through deadliest deeds and dangers gone,
A touch thou mayest be proud to own
125   Though thou so oft hast felt my own!
Oh that fair hand and faithful heart
From mine what power can ever part?
What Power?—Ha! well indeed I know
The very fire which burns me now,
130   The very energy of soul
     Which to thine arms impels me on,
When once I've gained that wished for goal
     Will—like a comet from the sun,
Hurl me with power that scorns control
135   Far from thy beams of Happiness,
     Into the expanse of wild distress
Where passion's lightnings burst and battles'
     thunders roll!'

     Impetuous then that Horseman sprung
Down the steep bank—His armour rung
140   'Mid the wild water's roar,
And dashing through the old oak trees,
His Courser's hoofs upon the breeze
Their reckless rattle swiftly cease
     In the dark night before!

145   Who that hath felt the feeling wild
     Which struck upon the excited mind
When, perhaps, long since—while yet a child,
     In awful mystery undefined,
Old tales and legends often told,
150   While winter nights fell long and drear,
Have made his heart's blood curdle cold
     Their dreary fates to hear,
Of Ancient Halls where Destiny

Has brooded with its raven wing;
155　Of castles stern whose riotry
　　　Hid not the gloomy crimes within;
　Of Death beds, where the sick man lying
　　　'Mid anxious list'ners standing by,
　Ere he had told the secret, dying,
160　　　Had left a sealèd mystery;
　Of Heirs who to some fearful doom
　　　Succeeded with their ancient Hall;
　Of Marriage Feasts where ghosts would come
　　　The new-made Bride to call;—
　He that hath still in memory
165　　　Kept fast those dreams of childhood's hours,
　Who these far visions yet may see
　　　Of Castle halls and feudal Towers,—
　To him I show this stormy Night
　　　That seems to darken on my sight!

170　Far above their forest trees
　　　These dreary turrets rise,
　And round their walls the midnight breeze
　　　Comes shrieking from the skies.
　Scarce can I note the central tower
175　　　Amid the impetuous storm,
　Till shimmering through the pelting shower
　　　The moonbeams mark its form.
　Far downward to the raving stream
　　　The woody banks decline,
180　Where waters flashing in the beam
　　　Through deepest darkness shine.
　Those giant oaks their boughs are tossing
　　　As wild winds wilder moan,
　Trunks and leaves confusedly crossing
185　　　With a ceaseless groan.
　And over all the castle walls
　　　Rise blacker than the night,
　No sign of man amid their Halls
　　　Save that lone turret light.
　The upward path is wild and steep,
190　　　Yet hear that horseman come,
　Not toiling up, with cautious creep,

But hotly hasting home.
The steed is to the stables led,
195   But where's the Rider gone?
Up that high turret staircase sped
      With gladdened haste alone.
The Ante Room looks hushed and still
      With lattice curtained close,
200   The tempests sweeping round the hill
      Disturb not its repose.
All's soft and calm, a holy balm
      Seems sleeping in the air,
But what on earth has power to charm
205   A spirit chafed with care?
The warrior hastes to seek that power,
      He knows the only one
Whose love can soothe his lonely hour
      Or hush his rising groan;
210   And where that soft and solemn light
      Shines through the opened door,
He hastens in with armèd tread
      Across the chequered floor;
And entering—Though a sacred stream
215   Of radiance round him fell,
It could not with its silent beam
      His eager spirit quell.

'Maria!'—But the silence round
      Would give him no reply,
220   And straightway did that single sound
      Without an echo die.

'Where hath my Gentle Lady gone?
      I do not find her here.'
Lo, on that stately couch alone
225   Reclines thy Lady fair.
But—cold and pale is her marble brow,
      Dishevelled her sunny hair.
Oh! is it in peaceful slumber now
      That she lieth so silent there?
230   'Heaven bless thy dreams!' Lord Albert cried,
      But his heart beat impatiently,

And as he hasted to her side
    He scarce had power to see.
All wildly the scenes of his former life
235   Flashed back upon his eyes,
And at once a shade of despair and strife
    Before him seemed to arise!
But as the sailor to his ship
    Clings with more frenzied power
240 As louder thundering o'er the deep
    Fresh billows whelm him o'er,
So madly on his only prop
    This war-worn man reclined,
He could not, would not deem his hope
245   Delivered to the wind!

Yet then why is this start of bewildered fright?
    And whence can arise this fear?
Is it not now in the depth of night?
    And sleeps not thy Lady there?
250 And art not thou on the Castle height
    From war's alarms afar?
See—is that sleep?—
               —With opened eyes
Chilly white and cold she lies!
255 Sunk her cheeks and blanched her lip
    That trembles as with suffering—
She sleeps not till the eternal sleep
    Its dreamless rest shall bring!
Heaven had occupied her mind
260 To onward hasting Death resigned,
But 'mid those strange uncertainties
    Which crowd their ghastly phantoms round,
When all our Reason's guiding ties
    Are from the parting soul unbound,
265 She thought when first she heard that tread
    That Death himself was hasting near,
The conjured vision of his form
    Obeyed her ready fancies' fear,
And to her dim eyes seemed to appear,
270   Till—that one word—and all was clear!
Then—sinking Reason rose again,

Then—joined the links of memory's chain,
Then—spite of all her dying pain,
  She felt—she knew her Lord was there!
275 Oh! when across that dreary sea
The light broke forth so suddenly,
What soul can feel, what tongue express
The burst of raptured happiness
  That from her spirit chased its care,
280   For—She was dying! But—He was there!

Ah! swiftly, surely art thou gliding
  Over Death's unfathomed sea,
Dark and deep the waves dividing
  Thee from earth and earth from thee!
285 Life, thy own, thy happy land
Parted far on either hand,
  As the mighty waters widen
  Onward to Eternity!
Shores of life, farewell for ever,
290   Where thy happiness has lain,
Lost for ever! Death must sever
  All thy hopes and joys and pain!
Yet, how blest the sound must be
  Which comes upon thy dying ear
295 From off the dim departing shore,
  Although its landmarks disappear,
Still sounding o'er the eternal roar
  The voice of Him thou hold'st so dear!
  'Tis as when the Mariner,
300 Just parted from his native home,
  After a night of dread and fear
Whose storms have riven the waves to foam,
When night's dark hours have swept away
All save the sounding of the sea,
305 Morn breaks where all looks new and strange,—
But Hark!—a sweet a sudden change,
For on his ear strikes soft from far
  In Sabbath chime his native bells;
He starts, and bursts the joyful tear
310 For things unutterably dear
  That farewell music tells!

Yet stay—why do I wander so
To wile me from that scene of woe?
   There stood the armèd man,
315 The very wildness of Despair
In his red eyeballs' stricken glare,
   His cheek so ghostly wan!
And on her couch his Lady lying
Still and slow and surely dying,
320 Yet, with an enraptured smile
   And glistening of her glassy eye,
As her weak arms she would the while
   Have stretched to clasp him standing by;
But they would not her will obey,
325 And motionless beside her lay.
Then her white lips moved to speak,
   But nothing could she say!
This was Death's triumphant hour,
Grasped by his tremendous power
330   She must pass away!

'Speak Maria!—speak, my love!
   Let me hear thy voice.
Nought on earth or Heaven above
   Could make me so rejoice!
335 Speak, O speak, and say to me
I am not come too late to thee!
Oh tell me that my arm can save
Thy sinking spirit from the grave
Maria! O my only love
340   Tell me thou wilt not die,
And naught below and naught above
   Shall feel so blest as I!
O would that I were far away
Alone upon a stormy sea!
345 Might I awake on yonder plain
Where I have left my soldiers slain,
So I *could* wake and rise and know
   That this was but a fearful dream,
That *thou* at least wert smiling now
350   As once in love and beauty's beam!
But here's the truth which now I know!
My God, My God, I cannot bear Thy blow!'

All was vain! she moved not, spoke not,
Speech or sound the silence broke not,
355 But he flung him o'er her lying
As he would catch her spirit flying.
All was vain!—That spirit flies
To God, Who gave it, in the skies!
That within his arms which lay
360 Was but a lifeless form of clay,
Nought of feeling in that face,
No return to his embrace,
Not a wish or power to save
Its own cold members from their grave.
365   Go, Lord Albert, go again,
Drown thought amid a world of storms.
    Go—For thy Despair is vain
And thy Hope lies food for worms!

MISERY

PART II

WIDE I hear the wild winds sighing
O'er the hills and far away,
Heaven in clouds before them flying
    Through the drear December day,
5   Dull and dark its evening ray,
As o'er the waste the ceaseless rain,
Drives past, is gone, and then again
Sweeps cold and drenching by, in showers of sleety
        spray.

And now the watery mountains rise
10 All dimly mingling with the skies,
At times some black brow darkening forth
Bleared by the tempest from the North,
And then, as fast the clouds sail on,
All its crags and heath knolls gone;
15 The changing veil of sleet drives o'er the waste alone.

Alone I list to hear the sigh
Of the wild blast passing by;
Hark, far away with mournful moan
It bends the heath on the old gray stone,
20 Then rising in the ash tree's bough
Scatters the withered leaves below;
Blackens the wall with pelting spray
And wails and wanders far away.
Oh when I hear that wintery sound,
25 The very voice of a mountain land,
A thousand feelings crowding round
 Start up and rise on every hand,
And wake to life as the wild winds wake,
 And pass with them away,
30 Sunbeams that o'er the spirit break
 Amid the dreariest day;
But hush!—And hark, that solemn wail,
 'Tis past—and yet—'tis on my ear,
Shrill, piercing through the misty veil
35 Like voice of the departing year!
Oh hush!—Again and yet again
Bursts forth that loud and longdrawn strain,
Soldiers! attend! it calls you back
From the pursuers' bloody track,
40 And wildly o'er your foeman's fall
Resounds your evening bugle call!

The battle is done with the setting sun,
The struggle is lost and the victory won,
'Tis over. No sighs, no anguished cries,
45 From the wild wreck of conflict rise.
The senseless corse on earth reclining
Nor feels defeat nor knows repining,
And they who survive in their agony
Now stiff and spent and speechless lie,
50 Their dim eyes wander toward the sky,
 Yet seek and see no comfort there,
For here upon this stormy heath
The laboured faintness of the breath,
The chill approach of Iron Death,
55 Demands a sterner care;

And well I know that life's last light
Just bordering on Eternal night,
When all these souls shall take their flight,
 Must crush those souls with fear.

60 Then there they lie and wildly o'er them
   Howls the wind with hollow tone,
While between its banks before them
   Hear the torrent chafe and groan
   Heavily with sullen tone,
65   Yet still careering swiftly on;
And torn with shot, a shattered tree
  Shakes its bare arms to the bitter gale,
O'er the blood-red eddies that rapidly
  Down the swollen streamlet curling sail;
70 And the blackened stones of a fallen wall
  Dashed down by the iron-hail of war
With their earthy bank above them thrown
  Obstructs the torrent's passage there,
Till angrily its waters roar
75 All white with froth and red with gore;
And—There!—a shattered carcase lies
Without the power to look or rise.
'Tis He!—the Conquered Chieftain—he
Whose look could once give victory,
80 But sightless now—
The shot has torn his eyes away,
And his slashed face is gashed with clay
Cast backward in the eddying Flood
That washes off his bursting blood,
85 The stones across his body thrown
That as he fell drove following down.
Oh scarce we know the human form
In this chief victim of the storm.
Yet—though thus crushed and torn he be,
90 Though hence he never more shall rise,
Though just as now still waves shall wash
From the crushed bones the wasting flesh,
  There shall he lie, as there he lies.
Yet still! oh still! look down and see
95 How vast may mortal misery be,

For in that bloody battered cell
Still Life and Soul and Memory dwell.
Never when he was fair and young
Did feeling thrill more fresh and strong,
100 Never the Hell-hounds of despair
Had wilder power to worry there.
  'O could I untormented die
    Without this gnawing agony
That wrings my heart so—!
                              Heavily and slow
105   The blood ebbs forth, but parts not so the soul:
Hither I came with pain, hence must I go
Still, still in pain!—Is such our changeless doom?
    God! shall such destiny unroll,—
110 Its agonies beyond the tomb?
All Dark without, All Fire within,
Can Hell have mightier hold on sin?
But yet, through all, my dying mind
From such a present turns behind
115 To—what has been—and then looks o'er
The dark, dark void of things before,
The land of souls beyond the sable shore!
    Oh how my eyes have stretched to see that land!
How even when sunk in life's bewildering roar
120   All my strained thoughts have striven to reach its
      strand,
    Have striven its mysteries to understand,
Though dark indeed the unreturning sea
That separates what lies beyond from me;
Though those vast waves which bear such thousands
      thither
125 Have never brought again one spirit hither,
    If spirits those who pass may truly be,
Those fearful passengers, whose sightless eyes
    And blanched lips and tongues which cannot
      move,
May either see the expanse which round them lies,
130   Or tell the scenes which open where they rove.
    Now might I send across yon sea that Dove
Which bore the Olive branch! Oh might it bear
From hence some token, toward me hovering here,

Even though it were the fruit of bitterness,
135 So I might cease this doubt and fearfulness
When I embark to sail—I know not where,
I scarce know whence—or how—but such distress,
Vain is the hope that it will end!—and then
How vain the wish to know where lies our pain!
140 Oh, it lies here—and if my mind
Survives, it will not lag behind,
And if indeed—I truly die,
Lost—in the abyss of vacancy,
Why *then* the sum of all will be
145 That I on earth have lived to see
Twice twenty winters beat on me,
Not one whole day of happiness
And year on year of mad distress!

'They say when on the bed of death
150   The wasted sick man lingering lies,
His breast scarce heaving with his breath,
    And cold his brow and quenched his eyes,
    See! how resignedly he dies.
Aye! what a look of peace and love
155 That glazed eye casts to heaven above:
Even those white lips will scarcely quiver
Though he must leave this world for ever,
And though his children round him stand
'Tis not for them that outstretched hand.
160 Angels shall press those clay cold fingers
In the unknown void round which he lingers.

    'Ha! does the *victim* reason so
Thus bound beneath that fatal blow?
No! There indeed he lies inert,
165 For death's cold frost congeals his heart,
Yet while that dim and dazing eye
Can wander o'er one stander by,
While those mute lips, that silent tongue
Can one short broken gasp prolong,
170 While in that whirled and burning brain
Reason's last spark can wax and wane,
So long across that parting soul

Unmixed—unmingled—torments roll;
He—look on death with smiling eye,
175   He—content and peaceful die,
He—no, like fire one burning strife
Convulses each riven string of life,
And could those lips be moved to say,
Could those stiff hands be clasped to pray,
180   That only voice and prayer would be,
"Oh save me from that fatal sea
Where hell and Death join agony!"

'I am dying, and what a rayless gloom
Seems dark'ning round my dreary tomb.
185   I know no light—I see no ray
To guide me on my heavenly way.
      There was a light—but it is gone.
There was a Hope—but all is o'er.
      And powerless, sightless, left alone,
190   I go where thou has gone before,
And yet I shall not see thee more.
Ha! said I that the dying man
Could only think of present pain,
Oh no! For scenes gone long ago
195   Make the main torrent of this woe.
I meant he thinks of pain alone;
It skills [?] not whether come or gone;
All dark alike to him and me
What has been or is to be.
200   And keen I feel much misery now,
For where, Maria, where art Thou
Lost, though I seem to see thee now?
Thy smiling eyes and shining brow,
And sunny cheek and golden hair,
205   In all thy beauty smiling there?
How often has thy bright blue eye
Driven sorrow shrinking from its shine,
And banished all my misery
Before one heavenly look of thine!
210   How often has that look divine
Roused up this heart from bitterness,
And bowed it in its worst distress

To kneel before thy shrine,
While I was thine and thou wert mine.
215 When troubles hastened thickening on,
When every hope of rest seemed gone,
When 'mid the blight of hating eyes
I stood bewildered, sick by woe,
What was the star which seemed to rise
220 To light me on and guide me through?
What was that form so heavenly fair,
Untouched by time, unmarked with care,
To whose fond heart I clung to save
My sinking spirit from its grave?
225 Maria! hadst thou never been,
    This hour I should not living be,
But while I strove with fate, between
    The strife thou camest to set me free,
And wildly did I cling to thee.
230 I could not, would not, dared not part,
Lest hell again should seize my heart.

'Can I forget how toward my eye
    Still ever gazed, for guidance, thine,
As if I were thy star on high,
235   Though well I knew 'twas thou wert mine.
That azure eye, that softened smile,
    That heavenly voice whose tones to me
The weariest wintriest hours could wile,
    And made me think that still might be
240   Some years of happiness with thee;
That thou, amid my life to come,
Shouldst be my hope, my heaven, my home,
But—we are sundered—thee, thy grave,
And me, this dreary wild will have.
245 What'er the world to come may be
I must never look on thee.
If there's no God, no Heaven, no Hell,
Thou within thy grave must dwell—
I, here black'ning in the storm—
250 Both a banquet for the worm.
If there *is* a heaven above,
    Thou I know art shining there

At the Almighty throne of love,
    Angel bright and angel fair:
255 From Heaven thou wanderest like the Dove
    To the wild world of waters here,
But never made o'er it to rove,
    Thou hast left its waves of sin and care,
    Back for thine Ark, while I staid where
260 The rottenest mass of carnage lay,
A Raven resting on its prey.
    O God, my fear lies there
Without a hope to meet me there,
But howling in despair.
265 But, Oh why will the parted return to our heart
    When the sods have grown green on their tomb?
Oh, why will the twilight refuse to depart
    When it only gives depth to the gloom?
Oh why, in the snow and storms of December,
270   When branches lie scattered and strewn,
Do we oftest and clearest and brightest remember
    The sunshine and summer of June?
Oh why, mid the hungry and cottageless waste
    Do we dream of the goblet filled high?
275 Why will our spirits when famishing taste
    Of such visionlike revelry?
Moralist, speak!—is't in life's deepest sorrow
    That these gleams of the past which hath vanished
        away,
Though misery and mourning await on the morrow,
280   May strengthen to bear through the shades of to-day?
Since we have had our sunshine, we must have our storm
If once with an angel, then now with a worm.
Christian, speak, sayest thou cares and annoy
Are probations on earth to a heavenly joy,
285 Or next will thou point to the desolate sea
And show me the mariner drifting away,
Behind him the shores of his vanishing home,
Around him the billows all crested with foam.
Yet he casts not a look upon ocean or shore,
290 But fixes his eyes on his haven before.
Sayest thou thus, now smile on his joys and his sorrow,
And press toward Heaven, his Haven of to-morrow?

Aye Man! on let him press till that heaven shall break
  In lightnings and thunders and tempests and gloom.
295 Then let the Spirit in safety speak!
    Where is the rest beyond the tomb?
    Where are the joys of his heavenly home?
Then let the moralist seek for his strength
  And smile on the past in its visionlike form.
300 Then let the Christian, anchored at length,
    See light in the darkness and sun through the storm.
Away with all this false disguise,
See midnight truth with noonday eyes,
The past has had a single joy,
305 But when that past is long gone by,
When cares have driven cares away,
When general darkness clouds the day,
That single star amid the sky
Will shed a brighter light on high,
310 And in the horizon only one
Is yet the ALL which can be shewn.
And still as gloomier frowns that night,
Brighter it flashes on the sight,
And still—oh still—as time flies by,
315 While other things in shades may die,
'Tis but one more present to my eye
My one sole star of memory!
Well o'er me shining let it be
That thus one glimmering I may see
320 Fixed far above to show my gloom,
And light my spirit to its Tomb!
Yet how I wander! grasping now
At the glorious dream of a world to come,
Then recalling back, I scarce know how
325 Upon that hideous, hopeless gloom,
The Nothingness within the tomb.
Thinking on Thee, and then again
Shrinking within my present pain.
All wide, all wandering—This is death,
330 And I would calmly meet him now,
As stern I'd feel my faltering breath
As I have seen my power laid low,
But for the thought—

Oh, what's to come!

335 God, if there be a God, look down,
  Compassionate my fall!
Oh clear away thy awful frown,
  And hearken to my call!
Nay—all is lost—I cannot bear
340 In mouldering dust to disappear,
And Heaven will not the gloom dispel,
Since if there is heaven, my home is Hell—
No Hope, no Hope, and Oh, farewell.
The form so long kept treasured here
345 Must thou then ever disappear?
Gone long, but kept in memory's shrine,
Now dying again as memory dies.
First passes from earth my star divine,
And now 'tis passing from the skies.
350 Then thou art gone and Heaven is gone,
And sights and sounds and all are gone.

'Oh what a shade is life—I am dying,
And how like A DREAM IS EXISTENCE FLYING.'

See through the shadows of the night,
355   Burst hotly, hasting onward there,
A wounded charger vast and white
  All wildly mad with pain and fear.
With hoofs of thunder on he flies
Shaking his white mane to the skies,
360 Till on his huge knees tumbling down,
Across the fallen chieftain thrown,
With a single plunge of dying force
His vast limbs hide Albert's corse.

S TILL and bright, in twilight shining,
  Glitters forth the evening star;
Closing rosebuds, round me twining,
  Shed their fragrance through the air;
5 Slow the river pales its glancing,
Soft its waters cease their dancing,
Calm and cool the shades advancing

Speak the hours of slumber near!
Why this solemn silence given
   To the close of fading day?
Feels the earth the hush of heaven?
   Can the expanse of nature pray?
And when daylight's toil is done,
Grateful for summer sunshine gone,
Can it before the Almighty's throne
   Its glad obeisance pay?
Such a hush of sacred sadness
   Wide around the weary wild,
O'er the whirl of human madness
   Spreads the slumbers of a child.
These surrounding sweeps of trees
Swaying to the evening breeze
With a voice like distant seas
   Making music mild.
Percy Hall above them lowering,
   Darker than the dark'ning sky,
With its halls and turrets towering
   Wakes the wind in passing by.
Round that scene of wondrous story
In their old ancestral glory
All its oaks so huge and hoary
   Wave their boughs on high.

Among these Turrets there is one
The soonest dark when day is done,
And when Autumn's winds are strongest
Moans the most and echoes longest.
So—on the steps that lie before
A solitary archèd door,
In that lone gable far away
   From sights and sounds of social joy,
Fronting the expanse so dim and grey
   There sits a lonely boy.
One hand is in his curling hair
   To part it from his brow,
And that young face so soft and fair
   Is lifted heavenward now.
On the cold stone he has laid him down

To watch that silver line
Beneath the power of twilight's frown
50   In the wide west decline.
For heaven still guides his azure eyes
      Toward its expanse so wild,
As veiled in darkness there he lies,
      A little Angel Child!

55 Oh who has known, or who can tell
      The Fountain of those feelings high
Which, while in this wild world we dwell,
      At times will lift us up on high,
      In a celestial sympathy
60 With yon blue vault, yon starry dome,
      As if the spirit deemed the sky
Was even on earth its only home,
And while the eye is dim with tears,
      The feelings wrapt in dreams sublime,
65 How dead seem earthly hopes and fears,
      How all forgot the course of time!
And yet the soul can never say
      What are the thoughts which make it glow.
We feel they are, but *what* are they?
70   'Tis this which we must never know
      While lingering in this world of woe.
Yet did man's soul descend from heaven
With feelings by its Maker given
All high, all glorious, all divine,
75   And from his hand perfected gone
With such a bright reflected shine
      As the full moon bears from the sun.
But then—the soul was clothed in clay,
So straight its beauty passed away,
80 And through a whirl of misery driven
Earth's shadow came 'tween it and heaven.
A darkened orb the moon became,
Lost all its lustre, quenched its flame!
Or entering on this morbid life,
85 The clouds of war, the storms of strife,
Continual passing, veil it round
With gloomy wreaths of shade profound.

So, only shining fitfully,
A single gleam of light we see,
90 As pass the clouds on either hand
To show the clear calm heaven beyond.
Yet at one moment soars our soul
   Into those wayward dreams divine,
Till back again the darkness roll
95   And hide the uncertain shine.
Yet shall a time come rapid on
When all these clouds that round us frown,
From Heaven's vast vault all past and gone,
Leave the full moon in glory there,
100 To shine for ever bright and fair.
When this dull clay is cast away
These THOUGHTS shall shine with cloudless ray
And we shall understand what now
But dimly is revealed below
In yon lone child's uplifted eyes.
105   Such dreams can scarce be dim,
So late upon those morbid skies
   The moon has risen to him;
So late his soul has passed from heaven
   That it can scarce forget
110 The visions bright whose haloed light
   Is round its musings yet.
Silent he sits on the darkened stone,
   With night around him falling,
As if to him that hollow moan
115   From the old tree tops were calling.
He listens to the eerie wind
   Around his Father's dwelling,
Till later following on his mind
   More glorious thoughts seem swelling.
120 For both his little hands were stretched
   In rapture to the sky,
When wilder from the wilderness
   Each blast came howling by
Toward clouds all southward resting wide
125   Above the Atlantic sea,
While o'er them far the darksome air
   Is haloed lustrously.

He fears some wondrous sight
  To him were opening soon,
130   Till, lo!—that sudden shining light,
  'The MOON, the glorious MOON!'

Oh, soft and sweet is the silver beam
  That floods the turret high,
While fairy woodlands round it seem
135   All glinting gloriously.
Each window glitters cold and clear
  Upon the southern tower,
And—though the shade is darker made
  Around his lonely bower—
140   Yet o'er his face a solemn light
  Comes smiling from the sky,
And shows to light the lustre bright
  Of his uplifted eye.
The dimless, heedless carelessness
145   Of happy Infancy,
Yet such a solemn tearfulness
  Commingling with his glee,
The parted lips, the shining hair
  Cast backward from his brow,
150   Without a single shade of care,
But bathed amid that moonlight air,
  Oh, who so blest as thou!
The moon in glory o'er the grove
  Majestic marches on,
155   With all the vault of heaven above
  To canopy her throne;
And from her own celestial rest,
Upon the dark wood's waving crest
  Serenely she looks down,
160   Yet beaming still, as if she smiled,
Most brightly on that beauteous child.
But what thought he as there he lay
  Beneath the archèd door,
Amid the ever trembling play
165   Of moonshine through the bower,
Gazing with blue eyes dimmed with tears
To that vast vault of shining spheres,

Till its mysterious power
Makes the bright drops unnoticed break
170   In dewy lustre o'er his cheek?

'Oh, how I could wish to fly
Far away through yonder sky,
O'er those trees upon the breeze
    To a paradise on high!
175   Why am I so bound below
That I must not, cannot go,
Lingering here for year on year
    So long before I die?
Now how glorious seems to be
180   Heaven's huge concave stretched o'er me.
But—Every star is hung so far
    Away from where I lie.
I love to see that Moon arise—
It suits so with the silent skies.
185   I love it well, but cannot tell
    Why it should make me cry.
Is't that it brings before me now
Those wondrous times gone long ago,
When Angels used from Heaven to come
190   And make this earth their happy home?
When Moses brought from Egypt's strand
God's favoured tribes through seas and sand
Victorious to the promised land!
When Salem rose, her Judah's pride,
195   Where David lived and Jesus died!
Is't that I know this very moon
Those vanished wonders gazed upon,
When Shepherds watched their flocks by night,
    All seated on the ground,
200   And angels of the Lord came down,
    And glory shone around?
Is't that I think upon the sea,
Just now it's beaming beauteously,
Where I so oft have longed to be,
205   But never yet have been?
Is't that it shines so far away
On Lands beyond that Ocean's spray,

'Mong lonely Scotland's hills of grey
   And ENGLAND's groves of green?
210 Or is't that through yon deep blue dome
It seems so solemnly to roam,
As if upon some unknown Sea,
   A vessel's stately form,
It o'er the waves was wandering free
215   Through calm and cloud and storm?
I cannot tell but it's in heaven,
   And though I view it here
Till I am mouldering dust to dust,
My parted spirit never must
220   Behold its brightness near.
I am crying to think that mighty throng
Of Glorious Stars to heaven belong,
That they can never, never see
A little earthly child like me;
225 Still rolling on, still beaming down,
And I unnoticed and unknown,
Though Jesus once in ages gone
   Called children to his knee.
So, where He reigns in glory bright
230 Above these starry skies of night,
Amid his paradise of light,
   Oh, why might I not be!
Oft, when awake on Christmas morn,
In sleepless twilight laid forlorn,
235 Strange thoughts have o'er my mind been borne
   How he has died for me;
And oft, within my chamber lying,
Have I awaked myself with crying
From dreams where I beheld him dying
240   Upon the accursed tree;
And often has my mother said,
While on her lap I laid my head,
She feared for time I was not made,
   But for Eternity!
245 So I can read my title clear
   To mansions in the skies,
And let me bid farewell to fear
   And wipe my weeping eyes.

I'll lay me down on this marble stone
   And set the world aside,
To see upon its ebon throne
   Yon moon in glory ride.
I'll strive to pierce that midnight vault
   Beyond its farthest star,
Nor let my spirit's wanderings halt
   'Neath Eden's crystal bar;
For sure that wind is calling me
   To a land beyond the grave,
And I must not shrink upon the brink
   Of Jordan's heavenly wave;
But I'll fall asleep in its waters deep,
   And wake on that blest shore
Where I shall neither want or weep
   Or sigh or sorrow more.
Oh, Angels come! Oh, Angels come!
And guide me to my Heavenly Home!'

Guide thee to heaven!—Oh, lovely child,
Little knowest thou the tempests wild
Now gathering for thy future years
Their blighting floods of bitter tears.
Little thou knowest how long and dread
Must be thy path ere thou art laid
Within thy dark and narrow bed,
Or how, then, thou wilt shrink to be
Launched out upon Eternity,
All those celestial visions flown,
All Hope of Heaven for ever gone!
   This passionate desire for Heaven
Is but the beam of brightness given
Around thy spirit at its birth,
And not yet quenched in clouds of earth,—
The inward yearnings of the soul
Toward its original and goal,
Before that goal is hid from sight
Amid the gloom of mortal night.
To that just entering into Time
This world is like a stranger clime,
Where—nothing kindred—nothing known—

Leaves thy young spirit all alone
290   To spend its hours in thinking on
The native home whence it has gone.
     But—Oh! at last a time will come
When Heaven is lost, and earth is home;
Where pleasures glimmering on thy sight
295   As soon as seen shall sink in night
Whilst thou pursuest them through the gloom,
Sinking like meteors to the tomb.
This light shall change to lightning then,
This love of Heaven to Hell of men.
300   So if thou seekest a glorious name
Thy path shall lead through blood and flame,
From crime to crime, imparting healing,
Blessed thyself and others blessing;
For that which from on high is thrown
305   Will always fall most rapid down,
And sink the deepest—So with thee,
Thy quick and passionate heart shall be
But farther plunged in misery.
Then those around thee oft may find
310   Earth and its joys to suit their mind,—
For dust to dust, the sons of earth
Will love the land that gave them birth,
Yet never thou, or if thou dost
Full quickly thou shalt find it Dust!

315   He sleeps!—in slumber calm and deep,
An infant's blest and balmy sleep,
Dreaming of heaven those closèd eyes,
And glorious visions of the skies,
And tremblingly their fringes lie
320   On the young cheek of infancy;
The softened curls of golden hair
Just moving in the moonlight air;
But his white brow so sweetly still,
So free from every shade of ill,
325   Shall it be so for ever?—No!
Who in this world would wish it so?
Yon is the image of a man
Destined to lead the foremost van
Of coming time, and in his hand

330 The future chooses to command.
'Tis he whose never dying name
Shall see a future world of flame.
PERCY! awake thee from thy sleep.
Awake! to bid thy country weep.

THE light of thy ancestral hall,
    Thy Caroline, no longer smiles:
She has changed her palace for a pall,
    Her garden walks for minster aisles:
5   Eternal sleep has stilled her breast
        Where peace and pleasure made their shrine;
    Her golden head has sunk to rest—
        Oh, would that rest made calmer mine!

To thee, while watching o'er the bed
10   Where, mute and motionless, she lay,
How slow the midnight moments sped!
        How void of sunlight woke the day!
Nor ope'd her eyes to morning's beam,
        Though all around thee woke to her;
15 Nor broke thy raven-pinioned dream
        Of coffin, shroud, and sepulchre.

Why beats thy breast when hers is still?
        Why linger'st thou when she is gone?
Hop'st thou to light on good or ill?
20   To find companionship alone?
Perhaps thou think'st the churchyard stone
        Can hide past smiles and bury sighs:
That Memory, with her soul, has flown;
        That thou can'st leave her where she lies.

25 No! joy *itself* is but a shade,
        So well may its remembrance die;
But cares, life's conquerors, never fade,
        So strong is their reality!
Thou may'st forget the day which gave
30   That child of beauty to thy side,
But not the moment when the grave
        Took back again thy borrowed bride.

OH! on this first bright Mayday morn,
    That seems to change our earth to Heaven,
May my own bitter thoughts be borne,
    With the wild winter it has driven!
Like this earth, may my mind be made
    To feel the freshness round me spreading,
    No other aid to rouse it needing
Than thy glad light, so long delayed.
    Sweet woodland sunshine!—none but thee
    Can wake the joys of memory,
Which seemed decaying, as all decayed.

O! may they bud, as thou dost now,
    With promise of a summer near!
Nay—let me feel my weary brow—
    Where are the ringlets wreathing there?
Why does the hand that shades it tremble?
    Why do these limbs, so languid, shun
    Their walk beneath the morning sun?
Ah, mortal Self! couldst thou dissemble
    Like Sister-Soul! But forms refuse
    The real and unreal to confuse.
But, with caprice of fancy, She
Joins things long past with things to be,
Till even I doubt if I have told
    My tale of woes and wonders o'er,
Or think Her magic can unfold
    A phantom path of joys before—
Or, laid beneath this Mayday blaze—
Ask, 'Live I o'er departed days?'
Am I the child by Gambia's side,
Beneath its woodlands waving wide?
Have I the footsteps bounding free,
The happy laugh of infancy?

FAR off, and half revealed, 'mid shade and light,
Black Comb half smiles, half frowns; his mighty
form
Scarce bending into peace, more formed to fight
A thousand years of struggles with a storm
Than bask one hour subdued by sunshine warm
To bright and breezeless rest; yet even his height
Towers not o'er this world's sympathies; he smiles—
While many a human heart to pleasure's wiles
Can bear to bend, and still forget to rise—
As though he, huge and heath-clad on our sight,
Again rejoices in his stormy skies.
Man loses vigour in unstable joys.
Thus tempests find Black Comb invincible,
While we are lost, who should know life so well!

OH Thou, whose beams were most withdrawn
When should have risen my morning sun,
Who, frowning most at earliest dawn,
Foretold the storms through which 'twould run;

Great God! when hour on hour has passed
In an unsmiling storm away,
No sound but bleak December's blast,
No sights but tempests, through my day,

At length, in twilight's dark decline,
Roll back the clouds that mark Thy frown,
Give but a single silver line—
One sunblink, as that day goes down.

My prayer is earnest, for my breast
No more can buffet with these storms;
I must have one short space of rest
Ere I go home to dust and worms;

I must a single gleam of light
Amid increasing darkness see,
Ere I, resigned to churchyard night,
Bid day farewell eternally!

My body is oppressed with pain,
   My mind is prostrate 'neath despair—
Nor mind nor body may again
   Do more than call Thy wrath to spare,

25 Both void of power to fight or flee,
   To bear or to avert Thy eye,
With sunken heart, with suppliant knee,
   Implore a peaceful hour to die.

When I look back on former life,
   I scarcely know what I have been,
30 So swift the change from strife to strife
   That passes o'er the 'wildering scene.

I only feel that every power—
   And Thou hadst given much to me—
35 Was spent upon the present hour,
   Was never turned, my God, to Thee;

That what I did to make me blest
   Sooner or later changed to pain;
That still I laughed at peace and rest,
40   So neither must behold again.

THE TRIUMPH OF MIND OVER BODY

MAN thinks too often that the ills of life,
Its ceaseless labour, and its causeless strife,
With all its train of want, disease, and care,
Must wage 'gainst spirit a successful war;
5 That when such dark waves round the body roll,
Feeble and faint will prove the struggling soul;
That it can never triumph or feel free,
While pain that body binds, or poverty.

   No words of mine have power to rouse the brain
10 Oppress'd with grief—the forehead bowed with pain;
For none will hear me if I tell how high
Man's soul can soar o'er body's misery:

But, where Orations, eloquent and loud,
Prove weak as air to move the listening crowd,
15   A single syllable—if timely spoken—
That mass inert has roused—its silence broken,
And driven it, shouting for revenge or fame,
Trampling on fear or death—led by a *single name!*

So now, to him whose worn-out soul decays
20   Neath nights of sleepless pain or toilsome days,
Who thinks his feeble frame must vainly long
To tread the footsteps of the bold and strong;
Who thinks that—born beneath a lowly star—
He cannot climb those heights he sees from far;
25   To him I name one name—it needs but one—
Nelson—a world's defence—a Kingdom's noblest son!

Ah! little child, torn early from thy home
Over a weary waste of waves to roam;
I see thy fair hair streaming in the wind
30   Wafted from green hills left so far behind;
Like one lamb lost upon a gloomy moor,
Like one flower tossed a hundred leagues from shore.
Thou hast given thy farewell to thine English home,
And tears of parting dim thy views of fame to come.

35   I seem to see thee, clinging to the mast,
Rocked roughly o'er the northern ocean's waste;
Stern accents only shouted from beneath,
Above, the keen wind's bitter biting breath,
While thy young eyes are straining to descry
40   The Ice blink gleaming in a Greenland sky,
All round the presages of strife and storm
Engirdling thy young heart and feeble form.

Each change thy frame endured seemed fit to be
The total round of common destiny;
45   For next—upon the Wild Mosquito shore
San Juan's guns their deadly thunders pour,
Though, deadlier far, that pestilential sky
Whose hot winds only whisper who shall die.
Yet, while—forgotten all their honours won—

50   Strong frames lay rotting neath a tropic sun,
        And mighty breasts heaved in death's agony,
        Death only left the storm-worn *Nelson* free.

        Death saw him laid on rocky Teneriffe,
        Where stern eyes sorrowed o'er their bleeding chief
55   Borne down by shot and beaten back by fate,
        Yet keeping front unblenched and soul elate.

        Death saw him, calm, off Copenhagen's shore,
        Amid a thousand guns' heaven-shaking roar,
        Triumphant riding o'er a fallen foe
60   With hand prepared to strike, but heart to spare the blow.

        Death touched, but left him, when a tide of blood
        Dyed the dark waves of Egypt's ancient flood,
        As mighty L'Orient fired the midnight sky
        And first bedimmed Napoleon's destiny;
65   When in that blaze flashed redly sea and shore,
        When far Aboukir shook beneath its roar,
        When fell on all one mighty pause of dread
        As if wide heaven were shattered overhead,
        Then—From the pallet where the hero lay—
70   His forehead laced with blood and pale as clay—
        He rose—revived by that tremendous call—
        Forgot the wound which lately caused his fall,
        And bade the affrighted battle hurry on,
     Nor thought of pain or rest till victory should be won!

75   I see him sit—his coffin by his chair—
        With pain-worn cheek and wind dishevelled hair,
        A little, shattered wreck, from many a day
        Of cares and storms and battles passed away;
        Prepared at any hour God bade, to die,
80   But not to stop or rest or strike or fly;
        While—like a burning reed—his spirit's flame
        Brightened, as it consumed his mortal frame.
        He knew his lightning course must soon be o'er,
        That death was tapping at his cabin door,
85   That he should meet the grim yet welcome guest
        Not on a palace bed of downy rest,

But where the stormy waters rolled below,
And, pealed above, the thunders of his foe;
That no calm sleep should smooth a slow decay
90 Till scarce the mourners knew life passed away,
But stifling agony and gushing gore
Should fill the moments of his parting hour;
He knew—but smiled—for, as that polar star
A thousand years—as then—had shone from far,
95 While all had changed beneath its changeless sky—
So, what *to* earth belonged *with* earth should die;
While he—all soul—would take a glorious flight,
Like yon—through time—a still and steady light;
Like yon, to England's sailors given to be
100 The guardian of her fleets—the Pole Star of the sea!

    A Vessel lies in England's proudest port
Where venerating thousands oft resort,
And, though ships round her anchor, bold and gay,
They seek her only, in her grim decay;
105 They tread her decks—all tenantless—with eyes
Of awe-struck musing—not of vague surprise;
They enter in a cabin, dark and low,
And o'er its time-stained floor with reverence bow:
Yet nought appears but rafters, worn and old,
110 No mirrored walls—no cornice bright with gold:
Yon packet steaming through its smoky haze
Seems fitter far to suit the wanderer's gaze;
But—'tis not present time they look at now,
They look at six and thirty years ago:
115 They see where fell the 'Thunderbolt of war'
On the storm swollen waves of TRAFALGAR;
They read a tale to wake their pain and pride
In that brass plate, engraved—'HERE NELSON DIED!'

    As 'wise Cornelius' from his mirror bade
120 A magic veil of formless clouds to fade,
Till gleamed before the awe-struck gazer's eye
Scenes still to come or passed for ever by;
So let me, standing in this darksome room,
Roll back a generation's gathered gloom,
125 To shew the morn and evening of a sun
The memory of whose light still cheers old England on.

Where ceaseless showers obscure the misty vale,
And winter winds through leafless osiers wail,
Beside a stream with swollen waves rushing wild,
130   Sits—calm amid the storm—yon fair haired child.
He *cannot* cross, so full the waters flow—
So bold his little heart, he *will not* go;
Patient of hindrances, but deeming still
Nothing impossible to steadfast will;
135   While from the old Rectory, his distant home,
'All hands' to seek their darling truant roam,
And *one*—his mother—with instinctive love,
Like that which guides aright the timid dove—
Finds her dear child—his cheeks all rain bedewed,
140   The unconscious victim of those tempests rude,
And, panting, asks him why he tarries there?
Does he not dread his fate—his danger fear?
That child replies—all smiling in the storm—
'Mother—what is this Fear?—I never saw its form!'
145   Ah! oft, since then, he heard the tempests sound,
Oft saw far mightier waters surging round,
Oft stood unshaken—death and danger near,
Yet saw no more than then the phantom Fear!

Now wave the wand again—Be England's shore
150   Sunk far behind the horizon's billowy roar;
And Lo! again this cabin dark and grim,
Beheld through smoke wreaths, indistinct and dim!
'Where is my child' methinks the mother cries:
No! far away that mother's tombstone lies!
155   Where is her child? He is not surely here,
Where reign, undoubted sovereigns, Death and Fear?

A prostrate form lies, neath a double shade
By stifling smoke and blackened timber made,
With head that backward rolls, whene'er it tries
160   From its hard, thunder shaken bed to rise.
Methought I saw a brightness on its breast,
As if in royal orders decked and dressed;
But its wan face, its grey locks crimson died,
Have surely nought to do with power or pride;
165   For death his mandate writes on its white brow—

'Thine earthly course is run—come with me now!'
Stern faces o'er this figure weeping bend
As they had lost a father and a friend,
While, all unanswered, burst yon conquering cheer,
170　Since He—their glorious chief is dying here.
They heed it not—but, with rekindled eye,
As He, even Death would conquer ere he die,
He asks—'What was't?—What deed had England done?
What ships had struck?—Was victory nobly won?
175　Did Collingwood—did Trowbridge face the foe?
Whose ship was first in fight—who dealt the sternest blow?'

　　I could not hear the answer—lost and drowned
In that tremendous crash of earthquake sound,
But, I could see the dying Hero smile,
180　As pain and sickness vanquished—bowed, awhile,
To *soul*, that soared—prophetic—o'er their sway,
And saw, beyond death's night Fame's glorious day;
That deemed no bed so easy as a tomb
Neath old Westminster's hero sheltering gloom,
185　That knew the laurel round his dying brow
Should bloom for ever as it flourished now,
That felt, this pain he paid, was cheaply given
Honour on earth and happiness in heaven:
That was a smile as sweet as ever shone
190　O'er his wan face in hours of childhood gone;
A smile which asked as plainly—'What is fear?'
As then unnoticed, though as then, so near.

　　Now faint and fainter rolled the cannon's sound
On his dull ear—each object, wavering round,
195　Mocked his dim eye—nor face, nor form seemed known;
He only felt that his great work was done,
That one brave heart was yearning at his side,
So, murmuring 'Kiss me, Hardy'—Nelson smiling died!

　　Oh! When *I* think upon that awful day
200　When all I know or love must fade away—
When, after weeks or months of agony,
Without one earthly hope to succour me,
I must lie back, and close my eyes upon

The farewell beams of the descending sun;
205 Must feel the warmth I never more may know
Mock my fast freezing frame of pain and woe,
Must feel a light is brightening up the sky
As shining clouds and summer airs pass by;
While I—a shrouded corpse, my bed must leave
210 To lie forgotten in my narrow grave,
The world all smiles above my covering clay;
I silent—senseless—festering fast away:
And, if my children, mid the churchyard stones,
Years hence, shall see a few brown mouldering bones;
215 Perhaps a skull, that seems, with hideous grin,
To mock at all this world takes pleasure in,
They'll only from the unsightly relics turn,
Or into ranker grass the fragments spurn;
Nor know that *these* are the remains of him
220 Whom they'll remember, like a faded dream,
As one who danced them on a father's knee
In long departed hours of happy infancy.

Then—then I ask—with humble—earnest prayer—
O Mighty Being! give me strength to dare
225 The certain fate, the dreadful hour to bear,
As thou didst NELSON! 'mid the battles roar
Lying, pale with mortal sickness—choked with gore,
Yet, thinking of thine England—saved, that hour,
From her great foeman's empire crushing power;
230 Of thy poor frame so gladly given, to free
Her thousand happy homes from slavery;
Of stainless name for her—of endless fame for thee.

Give me—Great God!—give all who own thy sway
Soul to command, and body to obey:
235 When dangers frown—a heart to beat more high;
When doubts confuse—a more observant eye;
When fortunes change—a power to bear their blight;
When Death arrives—to Life, a calm '*good night*.'
We are Thy likeness—Give us on to go
240 Through Life's long march of restlessness and woe,
Resolved thy Image shall be sanctified

By holy confidence—not human pride.
We have our task set—Let us do it well;
Nor barter ease on earth with pain in Hell.
245 We have our Talents, from thy treasury given—
Let us return thee good account in heaven.

    I know this world, this age is marching on;
Each year more wondrous than its parent gone;
And shall *I* lag behind it sad and slow?
250 With wish to rise but void of power to go?
Forbid it God! Who hast made me what I am;
Nor, framed to honour, let me sink in shame;
But, as yon Moon, which *seems* 'mid clouds to glide,
Whose dark breasts ever strive her beams to hide,
255 Shines, *really*, heedless of their earth-born sway,
In her own heaven of glory, far away;
So may my soul which seems, to eyes below,
Involved in life's thick mists of care and woe,
Far—far remote—from holy calm look down
260 On clouds of fleecy shine or stormy frown;
And while mankind its beams so shaded see,
Gaze steadfast on this life's inconstancy,
And find itself—like her—at home in heaven with Thee.

MAN thinks too often that his earth-born cares
    Bind chains on mind and can overcome its sway,
That faint and feeble proves the soul which wars
    Against its storm struck prison-house of clay;
5   But henceforth know that on its dreary way,
Whate'er of Ills with all its race it shares,
    Though pain and poverty becloud its day,
And want begins and sadness ends its years,
Soul still can brighten through its mortal gloom—
10   As THINE did, JOHNSON, England's trueborn son,
Who in they garret or a lordling's room
    Calmly let hunger creep or pride strut on,
    Intent on manly thoughts and honours won,
'Mid hours as darksome as thy dreaded Tomb.

O GOD! while I in pleasure's wiles
   Count hours and years as one,
And deem that, wrapt in pleasure's smiles,
   My joys can ne'er be done,

5   Give me the stern sustaining power
   To look into the past,
And see the darkly shadowed hour
   Which I must meet at last;

The hour when I must stretch this hand
10   To give a last adieu
To those sad friends that round me stand,
   Whom I no more must view.

For false though bright the hours that lead
   My present passage on,
15   And when I join the silent dead
   Their light will all be gone.

Then I must cease to seek the light
   Which fires the evening heaven,
Since to direct through death's dark night
20   Some other must be given.

T HE desolate earth, the wintry sky,
   The ceaseless rain-showers driving by—
The farewell of the year—
Though drear the sight, and sad the sound,
5   While bitter winds are wailing round,
Nor hopes depress, nor thoughts confound,
   Nor waken sigh or tear.

For, as it moans, December's wind
Brings many varied thoughts to mind
10   Upon its storm-drenched wing,
Of words, not said 'mid sunshine gay,
Of deeds, not done in summer's day,
Yet which, when joy has passed away,
   Will strength to sorrow bring.

15   For, when the leaves are glittering bright,
And green hills lie in noonday night,
   The present only lives;
But, when within my chimnies roar
The chidings of the stormy shower,
20   The feeble present loses power,
   The mighty past survives.

I cannot think—as roses blow,
And streams sound gently in their flow,
   And clouds shine bright above—
25   Of aught but childhood's happiness,
Of joys unshadowed by distress
Or voices tuned the ear to bless
   Or faces made to love.

But, when these winter evenings fall
30   Like dying nature's funeral pall,
   The Soul gains strength to say
That—not aghast at stormy skies—
That—not bowed down by miseries,—
Its thoughts have will and power to rise
35   Above the present day.

So, winds amid yon leafless ash,
And yon swollen streamlet's angry dash,
   And yon wet howling sky,
Recall the victories of mind
40   O'er bitter heavens and stormy wind
And all the wars of humankind—
   Man's mightiest victory!

The darkness of a dungeon's gloom,
So oft ere death the spirit's tomb,
45   Could not becloud those eyes
Which first revealed to mortal sight
A thousand unknown worlds of light,
And that *one* grave shines best by night
   Where Galileo lies.

50 But—into drearier dungeons thrown,
    With bodies bound, whose minds were gone—
        Tasso's immortal strain,
    Despite the tyrant's stern decree,
    Mezentius-like—rose fresh and free
55 And sang of Salem's liberty
        Forgetful of his chain;

    And thou, great rival of his song,
    Whose seraph-wings so swift and strong
        Left this world far behind,
60 Though poor, neglected, blind and old,
    The clouds round Paradise unrolled
    And in immortal accents told
        Misery must bow to mind.

    See, in a garret bare and low,
65 While mighty London roars below,
        One poor man seated lone;
    No favourite child of fortune he,
    But owned as hers by Poverty,
    His rugged brow, his stooping knee,
70   Speak woe and want alone.

    Now, who would guess that yonder form,
    Scarce worth being beaten by life's storm,
        Could e'er be known to fame?
    Yet England's love and England's tongue,
75 And England's heart, shall reverence long
    The wisdom deep, the courage strong,
        Of English *Johnson's* name.

    Like him—foredoomed through life to bear
    The anguish of the heart's despair
80   That pierces spirit through—
    Sweet Cowper, 'mid his weary years,
    Led through a rayless vale of tears,
    Poured gentle wisdom on our ears,
        And his was English too.

85 But Scotland's desolate hills can show
How mind may triumph over woe,
   For many a cottage there,
Where ceaseless toil from day to day
Scarce keeps grim want one hour away,
90 Could show if known how great the sway
   Of spirit o'er despair.

And he, whose natural music fills
Each wind that sweeps her heathy hills,
   Bore up with manliest brow
95 'Gainst griefs that ever filled his breast,
'Gainst toils that never gave him rest,
So, though grim fate Burns' life oppressed,
   His soul it could not bow.

ROBERT BURNS

HE little knows—whose life has smoothly passed
Unharmed by storm or strife, undimmed by care;
Who, clad in purple, laughs at every blast,
   Wrapped up contented in the joys that are—
5 He little knows the long and truceless war
Of one on poverty's rough waters cast,
   With eyes fixed forward on the glorious star
   That from Fame's temple beams, alas! how far—
Till backward buffeted o'er ocean's waste.

WHY hold young eyes the fullest fount of tears
   And why do youthful breasts the oftenest sigh
   When fancied friends forsake, or lovers fly,
Or fancied woes and dangers wake their fears:
5 Ah! He who asks has seen but spring tide years,
   Or Time's rough voice had long since told him why!
   Increase of days increases misery,
And misery brings selfishness, which sears
The heart's first feelings—'mid the battle's roar
10   In Death's dread grasp the soldier's eyes are blind
To comrades dying, and he whose hopes are o'er
   Turns coldest from the sufferings of mankind.
A bleeding spirit oft delights in gore—
   A tortured heart oft makes a Tyrant mind.

WHY dost thou sorrow for the happy dead?
  For if their life be lost, their toils are o'er
  And woe and want can trouble them no more,
Nor ever slept they in an earthly bed
So sound as now they sleep while, dreamless, laid
  In the dark chambers of the unknown shore
  Where Night and Silence seal each guarded door:
So, turn from such as these thy drooping head
And mourn the *dead alive* whose spirit flies—
  Whose life departs before his death has come—
Who finds no Heaven beyond Life's gloomy skies,
  Who sees no Hope to brighten up that gloom,
'Tis *He* who feels the worm that never dies—
  The *Real* death and darkness of the tomb.

THORP GREEN

I SIT, this evening, far away
  From all I used to know,
And nought reminds my soul to-day
  Of happy long ago.

Unwelcome cares, unthought-of fears,
  Around my room arise;
I seek for suns of former years,
  But clouds o'ercast my skies.

Yes—Memory, wherefore does thy voice
  Bring old times back to view,
As thou wouldst bid me not rejoice
  In thoughts and prospects new?

I'll thank thee, Memory, in the hour
  When troubled thoughts are mine—
For thou, like suns in April's shower,
  On shadowy scenes wilt shine.

I'll thank thee when approaching death
  Would quench life's feeble ember,
For thou wouldst even renew my breath
  With thy sweet word 'Remember'!

WHEN sink from sight the landmarks of our Home,
    And—all the bitterness of farewells o'er—
We yield our spirit unto Ocean's foam,
    And in the newborn life which lies before,
    On far Columbian or Australian shore
Strive to exchange time past for time to come,
    How melancholy then—if morn restore
(Less welcome than the night's forgetful gloom)
    Old England's blue hills to our sight again,
While we, our thoughts seemed weaning from her sky
    The *pang*—that wakes an almost silenced pain.
Thus, when the sick man lies resigned to die,
    A well-loved voice, a well-remembered strain,
Lets Time break harshly on Eternity.

I SEE a corpse upon the waters lie,
    With eyes turned, swelled and sightless, to the sky,
And arms outstretched to move, as wave on wave
Upbears it in its boundless billowy grave.
Not time, but ocean, thins its flowing hair;
Decay, not sorrow, lays its forehead bare;
Its members move, but not in thankless toil,
For seas are milder than this world's turmoil;
Corruption robs its lips and cheeks of red,
But wounded vanity grieves not the dead;
And, though these members hasten to decay,
No pang of suffering takes their strength away.
With untormented eye, and heart and brain,
Through calm and storm it floats across the main;
Though love and joy have perished long ago,
Its bosom suffers not one pang of woe;
Though weeds and worms its cherished beauty hide,
It feels not wounded vanity nor pride;
Though journeying towards some far-off shore,
It needs no care nor gold to float it o'er;
Though launched in voyage for eternity,
It need not think upon what is to be;
Though naked, helpless, and companionless
It feels not poverty, nor knows distress.

25 Ah, corpse! if thou could'st tell my aching mind
What scenes of sorrow thou hast left behind,
How sad the life which, breathing, thou hast led,
How free from strife thy sojourn with the dead;
I would assume thy place—would long to be
30 A world-wide wanderer o'er the waves with thee!
I have a misery, where thou hast none;
My heart beats, bursting, whilst thine lies like stone;
My veins throb wild, while thine are dead and dry;
And woes, not waters, dim my restless eye;
35 Thou longest not with one well loved to be,
And absence does not break a chain with thee;
No sudden agonies dart through thy breast;
Thou hast what all men covet—REAL REST.
I have an outward frame, unlike to thine,
40 Warm with young life—not cold in death's decline;
An eye that sees the sunny light of Heaven—
A heart by pleasure thrilled, by anguish riven—
But, in exchange for thy untroubled calm,
Thy gift of cold oblivion's healing balm,
45 I'd give my youth, my health, my life to come,
And share thy slumbers in thy ocean tomb.

EPISTLE FROM A FATHER TO A CHILD IN HER GRAVE

FROM Earth,—whose life-reviving April showers
Hide withered grass 'neath Springtide's herald
flowers,
And give, in each soft wind that drives her rain,
Promise of fields and forests rich again,—
5 I write to thee, the aspect of whose face
Can never change with altered time or place;
Whose eyes could look on India's fiercest wars
Less shrinking than the boldest son of Mars;
Whose lips, more firm than Stoic's long ago,
10 Would neither smile with joy nor blanch with woe;
Whose limbs could sufferings far more firmly bear
Than mightiest heroes in the storms of war;
Whose frame, nor wishes good, nor shrinks from ill,
Nor feels distraction's throb, nor pleasure's thrill.

15 I write to thee what thou wilt never read,
    For heed me thou *wilt not*, howe'er may bleed
    The heart that many think a worthless stone,
    But which oft aches for some belovèd one;
    Nor, if that life, mysterious, from on high,
20 Once more gave feeling to thy stony eye,
    Could'st thou thy father know, or feel that he
    Gave life and lineaments and thoughts to thee;
    For when thou died'st, thy day was in its dawn,
    And night still struggled with Life's opening morn;
25 The twilight star of childhood, thy young days
    Alone illumined, with its twinkling rays,
    So sweet, yet feeble, given from those dusk skies,
    Whose kindling, coming noontide prophesies,
    But tells us not that Summer's noon can shroud
30 Our sunshine with a veil of thundercloud.

    If, when thou freely gave the life, that ne'er
    To thee had given either hope or fear,
    But quietly had shone; nor asked if joy
    Thy future course should cheer, or grief annoy;

35 If then thoud'st seen, upon a summer sea,
    One, once in features, as in blood, like thee,
    On skies of azure blue and waters green,
    Melting to mist amid the summer sheen,
    In trouble gazing—ever hesitating
40 'Twixt miseries each hour new dread creating,
    And joys—whate'er they cost—still doubly dear,
    Those 'troubled pleasures soon chastised by fear;'
    If thou *had'st* seen him, thou would'st ne'er believe
    That thou had'st yet known what it was to live!

45 Thine eyes could only see thy mother's breast;
    Thy feelings only wished on that to rest;
    That was thy world;—thy food and sleep it gave,
    And slight the change 'twixt it and childhood's grave.
    Thou saw'st this world like one who, prone, reposes,
50 Upon a plain, and in a bed of roses,
    With nought in sight save marbled skies above,
    Nought heard but breezes whispering in the grove:
    I—thy life's source—was like a wanderer breasting

Keen mountain winds, and on a summit resting,
55 Whose rough rocks rose above the grassy mead,
With sleet and north winds howling overhead,
And Nature, like a map, beneath him spread;
Far winding river, tree, and tower, and town,
Shadow and sunlight, 'neath his gaze marked down
60 By that mysterious hand which graves the plan
Of that drear country called 'The Life of Man.'

If seen, men's eyes would loathing shrink from thee,
And turn, perhaps, with no disgust to me;
Yet thou had'st beauty, innocence, and smiles,
65 And now hast rest from this world's woes and wiles,
While I have restlessness and worrying care,
So sure, thy lot is brighter, happier far.

So let it be; and though thy ears may never
Hear these lines read beyond Death's darksome river,
70 Not vainly from the borders of despair
May rise a sound of joy that thou art freed from care!

WHEN all our cheerful hours seem gone for ever,
All lost that caused the body or the mind
To nourish love or friendship for our kind,
And Charon's boat, prepared, o'er Lethe's river
5 Our souls to waft, and all our thoughts to sever
From what was once life's Light; still there may be
Some well-loved bosom to whose pillow we
Could heartily our utter self deliver;
And if—toward her grave—Death's dreary road,
10 Our Darling's feet should tread, each step by her
Would draw our own steps to the same abode,
And make a festival of sepulture;
For what gave joy, and joy to us had owed,
Should Death affright us from, when he would her
restore?

SELECTED POEMS
OF
EMILY BRONTË

HIGH waving heather 'neath stormy blasts bending,
Midnight and moonlight and bright shining stars,
Darkness and glory rejoicingly blending,
Earth rising to heaven and heaven descending,
Man's spirit away from its drear dungeon sending,
Bursting the fetters and breaking the bars.

All down the mountain sides wild forests lending
One mighty voice to the life-giving wind,
Rivers their banks in the jubilee rending,
Fast through the valleys a reckless course wending,
Wider and deeper their waters extending,
Leaving a desolate desert behind.

Shining and lowering and swelling and dying,
Changing forever from midnight to noon;
Roaring like thunder, like soft music sighing,
Shadows on shadows advancing and flying,
Lightning-bright flashes the deep gloom defying,
Coming as swiftly and fading as soon.

LORD of Elbë, on Elbë hill
The mist is thick and the wind is chill
And the heart of thy friend from the dawn of day
Has sighed for sorrow that thou went away.

Lord of Elbë, how pleasant to me
The sound of thy blithesome step would be,
Rustling the heath that, only now
Waves as the night gusts over it blow.

Bright are the fires in thy lonely home.
I see them far off, and as deepens the gloom,
Gleaming like stars through the high forest-boughs
Gladder they glow in the park's repose.

O Alexander! when I return
Warm as those hearths my heart would burn,
Light as thine own, my foot would fall
If I might hear thy voice in the hall—

But thou art now on a desolate sea—
Parted from Gondal and parted from me—
All my repining is hopeless and vain,
Death never yields back his victims again.

SLEEP brings no joy to me,
Remembrance never dies;
My soul is given to misery
And lives in sighs.

Sleep brings no rest to me:
The shadows of the dead
My walking eyes may never see
Surround my bed.

Sleep brings no hope to me;
In soundest sleep they come
And with their doleful imagery
Deepen the gloom.

Sleep brings no strength to me,
No power renewed or brave;
I only sail a wilder sea,
A darker wave.

Sleep brings no friend to me
To soothe and aid to bear;
They all gaze, oh, how scornfully,
And I despair.

Sleep brings no wish to knit
My harassed heart beneath;
My only wish is to forget
In the sleep of death.

FALL, leaves, fall; die, flowers, away;
Lengthen night and shorten day;
Every leaf speaks bliss to me
Fluttering from the autumn tree.
I shall smile when wreaths of snow
Blossom where the rose should grow;
I shall sing when night's decay
Ushers in a drearier day.

THE night is darkening round me,
The wild winds coldly blow,
But a tyrant spell has bound me
And I cannot, cannot go.

The giant trees are bending
Their bare boughs weighed with snow
And the storm is fast descending
And yet I cannot go.

Clouds beyond cloud above me,
Wastes beyond wastes below,
But nothing drear can move me,
I will not, cannot go.

WHY do I hate that lone green dell?
Buried in moors and mountains wild
That is a spot I had loved too well
Had I but seen it when a child.

There are bones whitening there in the summer's heat
But it is not for that, and none can tell;
None but one can the secret repeat
Why I hate that lone green dell.

Noble foe, I pardon thee
10   All thy cold and scornful pride,
For thou wast a priceless friend to me
When my sad heart had none beside.

And leaning on thy generous arm
A breath of old times over me came;
15   The earth shone round with a long-lost charm;
Alas, I forgot I was not the same.

Before a day—an hour—passed by
My spirit knew itself once more;
I saw the gilded vapours fly
20   And leave me as I was before.

O WANDER not so far away!
  O love, forgive this selfish tear.
It may be sad for thee to stay
But how can I live lonely here?

5   The still May morn is warm and bright,
Young flowers look fresh and grass is green,
And in the haze of glorious light
Our long low hills are scarcely seen.

The woods—even now their small leaves hide
10   The blackbird and the stockdove well
And high in heaven so blue and wide
A thousand strains of music swell.

He looks on all with eyes that speak
So deep, so drear a woe to me!
15   There is a faint red on his cheek
Not like the bloom I used to see.

Call Death—yes, Death, he is thine own!
The grave must close those limbs around
And hush, for ever hush the tone
20   I loved above all earthly sound.

Well, pass away with the other flowers,
Too dark for them, too dark for thee
Are the hours to come, the joyless hours
That Time is treasuring up for me—

25   If thou hast sinned in this world of care
'Twas but the dust of thy drear abode—
Thy soul was pure when it entered here
And pure it will go again to God!

SONG TO A.A.

THIS shall be thy lullaby
    Rocking on the stormy sea,
Though it roar in thunder wild,
Sleep, stilly sleep, my dark-haired child.

5   When our shuddering boat was crossing
Eldern's lake so rudely tossing,
Then 'twas first my nursling smiled;
Sleep, softly sleep, my fair-browed child.

Waves above thy cradle break,
10   Foamy tears are on thy cheek,
Yet the Ocean's self grows mild
When it bears my slumbering child.

FOR him who struck thy foreign string
    I ween this heart hath ceased to care,
Then why dost thou such feelings bring
To my sad spirit, old guitar?

5   It is as if the warm sunlight
In some deep glen should lingering stay
When clouds of tempest and of night
Had wrapt the parent orb away—

It is as if the glassy brook
10 Should image still its willows fair
Though years ago, the woodman's stroke
Laid low in dust their gleaming hair:

Even so, guitar, thy magic tone
Hath moved the tear and woke the sigh,
15 Hath bid the ancient torrent flow
Although its very source is dry!

SONG BY JULIUS BRENZAIDA TO G.S.

GERALDINE, the moon is shining
With so soft, so bright a ray,
Seems it not that eve, declining
Ushered in a fairer day?

5   While the wind is whispering only,
Far—across the water borne,
Let us, in this silence lonely
Sit beneath the ancient thorn—

Wild the road, and rough and dreary;
10 Barren all the moorland round;
Rude the couch that rests us weary;
Mossy stone and heathy ground—

But when winter storms were meeting
In the moonless midnight dome,
15 Did we heed the tempest's beating
Howling round our spirits' home?

No, that tree, with branches riven,
Whitening in the whirl of snow,
As it tossed against the heaven,
20 Sheltered happy hearts below—

And at Autumn's mild returning
Shall our feet forget the way?
And in Cynthia's silver morning,
Geraldine, wilt thou delay?

O DREAM, where art thou now?
  Long years have passed away
Since last from off thine angel brow
I saw the light decay—

5   Alas, alas for me
Thou wert so bright and fair
I could not think thy memory
Would yield me nought but care!

The sun-beam and the storm,
10 The summer-eve divine,
The silent night of solemn calm,
The full moon's cloudless shine

Were once entwined with thee
But now, with weary pain—
15 Lost vision! 'tis enough for me—
Thou canst not shine again.

L OUD without the wind was roaring
  Through the waned autumnal sky,
Drenching wet, the cold rain pouring
  Spoke of stormy winters nigh.

5   All too like that dreary eve
Sighed within repining grief—
Sighed at first—but sighed not long,
Sweet—how softly sweet it came!
Wild words of an ancient song—
10 Undefined, without a name.

'It was spring, for the skylark was singing.'
Those words they awakened a spell—
They unlocked a deep fountain whose springing
Nor Absence nor Distance can quell.

15 In the gloom of a cloudy November
They uttered the music of May—
They kindled the perishing ember
Into fervour that could not decay.

Awaken on all my dear moorlands
The wind in its glory and pride!
O call me from valleys and highlands
To walk by the hill river's side!

It is swelled with the first snowy weather;
The rocks they are icy and hoar
And darker waves round the long heather
And the fern leaves are sunny no more.

There are no yellow-stars on the mountain,
The bluebells have long died away
From the brink of the moss-bedded fountain,
From the side of the wintery brae—

But lovelier than cornfields all waving
In emerald and scarlet and gold
Are the slopes where the north-wind is raving
And the glens where I wandered of old.

'It was morning, the bright sun was beaming.'
How sweetly that brought back to me
The time when nor labour nor dreaming
Broke the sleep of the happy and free.

But blithely we rose as the dusk heaven
Was melting to amber and blue,
And swift were the wings to our feet given
While we traversed the meadows of dew,

For the moors, for the moors where the short grass
Like velvet beneath us should lie!
For the moors, for the moors where each high pass
Rose sunny against the clear sky!

For the moors, where the linnet was trilling
Its song on the old granite stone—
Where the lark, the wild skylark was failling
Every breast with delight like its own.

What language can utter the feeling
That rose when, in exile afar,
On the brow of a lonely hill kneeling
I saw the brown heath growing there.

55 It was scattered and stunted, and told me
That soon even that would be gone;
It whispered, 'The grim walls enfold me;
I have bloomed in my last summer's sun.'

But not the loved music whose waking
60 Makes the soul of the Swiss die away
Has a spell more adored and heart-breaking
Than in its half-blighted bells lay—

The Spirit that bent 'neath its power
How it longed, how it burned to be free!
65 If I could have wept in that hour
Those tears had been heaven to me.

Well, well, the sad minutes are moving
Though loaded with trouble and pain—
And sometime, the loved and the loving
70 Shall meet on the mountains again.

A LITTLE while, a little while
The noisy crowd are barred away;
And I can sing and I can smile—
A little while I've holiday!

5 Where wilt thou go, my harassed heart?
Full many a land invites thee now;
And places near, and far apart
Have rest for thee, my weary brow.

There is a spot 'mid barren hills
10 Where winter howls and driving rain,
But if the dreary tempest chills
There is a light that warms again.

The house is old, the trees are bare
And moonless bends the misty dome
But what on earth is half so dear—
So longed for as the hearth of home?

The mute bird sitting on the stone,
The dank moss dripping from the wall,
The garden-walk with weeds o'ergrown,
I love them—how I love them all!

Shall I go there? or shall I seek
Another clime, another sky,
Where tongues familiar music speak
In accents dear to memory?

Yes, as I mused, the naked room,
The flickering firelight died away
And from the midst of cheerless gloom
I passed to bright, unclouded day—

A little and a lone green lane
That opened on a common wide;
A distant, dreamy, dim blue chain
Of mountains circling every side—

A heaven so clear, an earth so calm,
So sweet, so soft, so hushed an air
And, deepening still the dream-like charm,
Wild moor-sheep feeding everywhere—

That was the scene—I knew it well,
I knew the pathways far and near
That winding o'er each billowy swell
Marked out the tracks of wandering deer.

Could I have lingered but an hour
It well had paid a week of toil
But truth has banished fancy's power
I hear my dungeon bars recoil—

45   Even as I stood with raptured eye
Absorbed in bliss so deep and dear
My hour of rest had fleeted by
And given me back to weary care.

'HOW still, how happy!' Those are words
    That once would scarce agree together;
I loved the plashing of the surge—
The changing heaven, the breezy weather

5   More than smooth seas and cloudless skies
And solemn, soothing, softened airs
That in the forest woke no sighs
And from the green spray shook no tears.

    'How still, how happy!' Now I feel
10   Where silence dwells is sweeter far
Than laughing mirth's most joyous swell
However pure its raptures are.

    Come sit down on this sunny stone:
'Tis wintery light o'er flowerless moors—
15   But sit—for we are all alone
And clear expand heaven's breathless shores.

    I could think in the withered grass
Spring's budding wreaths we might discern;
The violet's eye might shyly flash
20   And young leaves shoot among the fern.

    It is but thought—full many a night
The snow shall clothe those hills afar
And storms shall add a drearier blight
And winds shall wage a wilder war

25   Before the lark may herald in
Fresh foliage twined with blossoms fair
And summer days again begin
Their glory-haloed crown to wear.

Yet my heart loves December's smile
As much as July's golden beam;
Then let us sit and watch the while
The blue ice curdling on the stream.

THE bluebell is the sweetest flower
    That waves in summer air;
Its blossoms have the mightiest power
To soothe my spirit's care.

There is a spell in purple heath
Too wildly, sadly dear;
The violet has a fragrant breath
But fragrance will not cheer.

The trees are bare, the sun is cold
And seldom, seldom seen—
The heavens have lost their zone of gold
The earth its robe of green;

And ice upon the glancing stream
Has cast its sombre shade
And distant hills and valleys seem
In frozen mist arrayed—

The bluebell cannot charm me now,
The heath has lost its bloom,
The violets in the glen below
They yield no sweet perfume.

But though I mourn the heather-bell
'Tis better far, away;
I know how fast my tears would swell
To see it smile to-day;

And that wood flower that hides so shy
Beneath the mossy stone
Its balmy scent and dewy eye:
'Tis not for them I moan.

It is the slight and stately stem,
30 The blossom's silvery blue,
The buds hid like a sapphire gem
In sheaths of emerald hue.

'Tis these that breathe upon my heart
A calm and softening spell
35 That if it makes the tear-drop start
Has power to soothe as well.

For these I weep, so long divided
Through winter's dreary day,
In longing weep—but most when guided
40 On withered bank to stray.

If chilly then the light should fall
Adown the dreary sky
And gild the dank and darkened wall
With transient brilliancy

45 How do I yearn, how do I pine
For the time of flowers to come
And turn me from that fading shine
To mourn the fields of home.

TO THE BLUEBELL

SACRED watcher, wave thy bells!
Fair hill flower and woodland child!
Dear to me in deep green dells—
Dearest on the mountains wild—

5 Bluebell, even as all divine
I have seen my darling shine—
Bluebell, even as wan and frail
I have seen my darling fail.
Thou hast found a voice for me
10 And soothing words are breathed by thee.

Thus they murmur, 'Summer's sun
Warms me till my life is done—
Would I rather choose to die
Under winter's ruthless sky?

15   Glad I bloom—and calm I fade;
Weeping twilight dews my bed;
Mourner, mourner, dry thy tears—
Sorrow comes with lengthened years!'

I AM the only being whose doom
  No tongue would ask, no eye would mourn;
I've never caused a thought of gloom,
A smile of joy, since I was born.

5   In secret pleasure, secret tears,
This changeful life has slipped away,
As friendless after eighteen years,
As lone as on my natal day.

There have been times I cannot hide,
10   There have been hours when this was drear,
When my sad soul forgot its pride
And longed for one to love me here.

But those were in the early glow
Of feelings not subdued by care;
15   And they have died so long ago
I hardly now believe they were.

First melted off the hope of youth
Then Fancy's rainbow fast withdrew
And then experience told me truth
20   In mortal bosoms never grew.

'Twas grief enough to think mankind
All hollow, servile, insincere;
But worse to trust to my own mind
And find the same corruption there.

MAY flowers are opening
And leaves unfolding free;
There are bees in every blossom
And birds on every tree.

5   The sun is gladly shining,
The stream sings merrily,
And I only am pining
And all is dark to me.

     O—cold, cold is my heart;
10   It will not, cannot rise;
It feels no sympathy
With those refulgent skies.

Dead, dead is my joy,
I long to be at rest;
15   I wish the damp earth covered
This desolate breast.

If I were quite alone
It might not be so drear;
When all hope was gone
20   At least I could not fear.

But the glad eyes around me
Must weep as mine have done
And I must see the same gloom
Eclipse their morning sun.

25   If heaven would rain on me
That future storm of care
So their fond hearts were free
I'd be content to bear.

Alas, as lightning withers
30   The young and aged tree,
Both they and I shall fall beneath
The fate we cannot flee.

LINES BY CLAUDIA

I DID not sleep, 'twas noon of day,
I saw the burning sunshine fall,
The long grass bending where I lay,
The blue sky brooding over all.

5　　I heard the mellow hum of bees
And singing birds and sighing trees,
And far away in woody dell
The music of the Sabbath bell.

I did not dream; remembrance still
10　　Clasped round my heart its fetters chill;
But I am sure the soul is free
To leave its clay a little while,
Or how in exile's misery
Could I have seen my country smile?

15　　In English fields my limbs were laid
With English turf beneath my head;
My spirit wandered o'er that shore
Where nought but it may wander more.

Yet if the soul can thus return
20　　I need not and I will not mourn;
And vainly did you drive me far
With leagues of ocean stretched between;
My mortal flesh you might debar
But not the eternal fire within.

25　　My Monarch died to rule forever
A heart that can forget him never,
And dear to me, aye, doubly dear,
Though shut within the silent tomb,
His name shall be for whom I bear
30　　This long-sustained and hopeless doom.

And brighter in the hour of woe
Than in the blaze of Victory's pride,
That glory shedding star shall glow
For which we fought and bled and died.

I KNOW not how it falls on me,
This summer evening hushed and lone;
Yet the faint wind comes soothingly
With something of an olden tone.

5 Forgive me if I've shunned so long
Your gentle greeting, earth and air,
But sorrow withers even the strong
And who can fight against despair?

AND now the housedog stretched once more
His limbs upon the glowing floor;
The children half resumed their play,
Though from the warm hearth scared away.
5 The goodwife left her spinning-wheel
And spread with smiles the evening meal;
The shepherd placed a seat and pressed
To their poor fare his unknown guest.
And he unclasped his mantle now
10 And raised the covering from his brow;
Said 'Voyagers by land and sea
Were seldom feasted daintily',
And checked his host by adding stern
He'd no refinement to unlearn.
15 A silence settled on the room,
The cheerful welcome sank to gloom;
But not those words, though cold and high
So froze their hospitable joy.
No—there was something in his face,
20 Some nameless thing they could not trace,
And something in his voice's tone
Which turned their blood as chill as stone.
The ringlets of his long black hair
Fell o'er a cheek most ghastly fair.

25　Youthful he seemed—but worn as they
　　Who spend too soon their youthful day.
　　When his glance drooped, 'twas hard to quell
　　Unbidden feelings' sudden swell,
　　And pity scarce her tears could hide,
30　So sweet that brow with all its pride;
　　But when upraised his eye would dart
　　An icy shudder through the heart.
　　Compassion changed to horror then,
　　And fear to meet that gaze again.
35　It was not hatred's tiger glare
　　Nor the wild anguish of despair;
　　It was not sullen misery
　　Which mocks at friendship's sympathy.
　　No—lightning all unearthly shone
40　Deep in those dark eyes' circling zone,
　　Such withering lightning as we deem
　　None but a spectre's look may beam;
　　And glad they were when he turned away
　　And wrapped him in his mantle grey,
45　Leant down his head upon his arm
　　And veiled from view their basilisk charm.

　　COME hither, child—who gifted thee
　　　With power to touch that string so well?
　　How daredst thou rouse up thoughts in me,
　　Thoughts that I would—but cannot quell?

5　Nay, chide not, lady; long ago
　　I heard those notes in Ula's hall,
　　And had I known they'd waken woe
　　I'd weep their music to recall.

　　But thus it was: one festal night
10　When I was hardly six years old
　　I stole away from crowds and light
　　And sought a chamber dark and cold.

I had no one to love me there,
I knew no comrade and no friend;
And so I went to sorrow where
Heaven, only heaven saw me bend.

Loud blew the wind; 'twas sad to stay
From all that splendour barred away.
I imaged in the lonely room
A thousand forms of fearful gloom;

And with my wet eyes raised on high
I prayed to God that I might die.
Suddenly in that silence drear
A sound of music reached my ear,

And then a note, I hear it yet,
So full of soul, so deeply sweet,
I thought that Gabriel's self had come
To take me to my father's home.

Three times it rose, that seraph strain,
Then died, nor breathed again;
But still the words and still the tone
Dwell round my heart when all alone.

SHED no tears o'er that tomb
For there are angels weeping;
Mourn not him whose doom
Heaven itself is mourning.

Look how in sable gloom
The clouds are earthward sweeping
And earth receives them home
Even darker clouds returning.

Is it when good men die
That sorrow wakes above?
Grieve saints when other spirits fly
To swell their choir of love?

Ah no, with louder sound
The golden harp-strings quiver
15 When good men gain the happy ground
Where they must dwell forever.

But he who slumbers there,
His bark will strive no more
Across the waters of despair
20 To reach that glorious shore.

The time of grace is past
And mercy scorned and tried
Forsakes to utter wrath at last
The soul so steeled by pride.

25 That wrath will never spare,
Will never pity know,
Will mock its victim's maddened prayer,
Will triumph in his woe.

MILD the mist upon the hill
Telling not of storms tomorrow;
No, the day has wept its fill,
Spent its store of silent sorrow.

5 O, I'm gone back to the days of youth,
I am a child once more,
And 'neath my father's sheltering roof
And near the old hall door

I watch this cloudy evening fall
10 After a day of rain;
Blue mists, sweet mists of summer pall
The horizon's mountain chain.

The damp stands on the long green grass
As thick as morning's tears,
15 And dreamy scents of fragrance pass
That breathe of other years.

'HOW long will you remain? The midnight hour
Has tolled its last note from the minster tower.
Come, come; the fire is dead, the lamp burns low;
Your eyelids droop, a weight is on your brow,
Your cold hands hardly hold the useless pen:
Come, morn will give recovered strength again.'
'No; let me linger, leave me, let me be
A little longer in this reverie.
I'm happy now, and would you tear away
My blissful dream that never comes with day?
A vision dear, though false, for well my mind
Knows what a bitter waking waits behind.'
'Can there be pleasure in this shadowy room
With windows yawning on intenser gloom
And such a dreary wind so bleakly sweeping
Round walls where only you are vigil keeping?
Besides, your face has not a sign of joy
And more than tearful sorrow fills your eye.
Look on those woods, look on that heaven lorn
And think how changed they'll be tomorrow morn:
The dome of heaven expanding bright and blue,
The leaves, the green grass sprinkled thick with dew
And sweet mists rising on the river's breast
And wild birds bursting from their songless nest
And your own children's merry voices chasing
The fancies grief not pleasure has been tracing.'
'Aye, speak of these—but can you tell me why
Day breathes such beauty over earth and sky
And waking sounds revive, restore again
Dull hearts that all night long have throbbed in pain?
Is it not that the sunshine and the wind
Lure from itself the mourner's woe-worn mind,
And all the joyous music breathing by
And all the splendour of that cloudless sky
Regive him shadowy gleams of infancy
And draw his tired gaze from futurity?'

'THE starry night shall tidings bring:
Go out upon the breezy moor,
Watch for a bird with sable wing
And beak and talons dropping gore.

5   Look not around, look not beneath,
       But mutely trace its airy way;
       Mark where it lights upon the heath
       Then, wanderer, kneel thee down and pray.

       What future may await thee there
10   I will not and I dare not tell,
       But Heaven is moved by fervent prayer
       And God is mercy—fare thee well!'

FAIR sinks the summer evening now
    In softened glory round my home;
       The sky upon its holy brow
       Wears not a cloud that speaks of gloom.

5   The old tower, shrined in golden light,
       Looks down on the descending sun—
       So gently evening blends with night
       You scarce can say that day is done—

       And this is just the joyous hour
10   When we were wont to burst away,
       To 'scape from labour's tyrant power
       And cheerfully go out to play.

       Then why is all so sad and lone?
       No merry footstep on the stair—
15   No laugh—no heart-awaking tone,
       But voiceless silence everywhere.

       I've wandered round our garden-ground
       And still it seemed at every turn
       That I should greet approaching feet
20   And words upon the breezes borne.

       In vain—they will not come to-day
       And morning's beam will rise as drear;
       Then tell me—are they gone for aye
       Our sun-blinks through the mists of care?

25   Ah no, reproving Hope doth say
Departed joys 'tis fond to mourn
When every storm that hides their ray
Prepares a more divine return.

THE wind, I hear it sighing
   With Autumn's saddest sound;
Withered leaves as thick are lying
As spring-flowers on the ground—

5   This dark night has won me
To wander far away—
Old feelings gather fast upon me
Like vultures round their prey.

Kind were they once, and cherished
10   But cold and cheerless now—
I would their lingering shades had perished
When their light left my brow.

'Tis like old age pretending
The softness of a child,
15   My altered hardened spirit bending
To meet their fancies wild.

Yet could I with past pleasures
Past woe's oblivion buy—
That by the death of my dearest treasures
20   My deadliest pains might die,

O then another daybreak
Might haply dawn above—
Another summer gild my cheek,
My soul, another love.

LOVE is like the wild rose-briar,
   Friendship, like the holly tree—
The holly is dark when the rose-briar blooms,
But which will bloom most constantly?

The wild rose-briar is sweet in spring,
Its summer blossoms scent the air;
Yet wait till winter comes again
And who will call the wild-briar fair?

Then scorn the silly rose-wreath now
And deck thee with the holly's sheen,
That when December blights thy brow
He still may leave thy garland green.

SYMPATHY

THERE should be no despair for you
   While nightly stars are burning;
While evening pours its silent dew
And sunshine gilds the morning.
There should be no despair—though tears
May flow down like a river:
Are not the best beloved of years
Around your heart for ever?

They weep, you weep, it must be so;
Winds sigh as you are sighing,
And Winter sheds his grief in snow
Where Autumn's leaves are lying:
Yet, these revive, and from their fate
Your fate cannot be parted:
Then, journey on, if not elate,
Still, *never* broken-hearted!

'WELL, some may hate and some may scorn
   And some may quite forget thy name,
But my sad heart must ever mourn
Thy ruined hopes, thy blighted fame.'

'Twas thus I thought an hour ago
Even weeping o'er that wretch's woe—
One word turned back my gushing tears
And lit my altered eye with sneers—

'Then bless the friendly dust', I said,
'That hides thy unlamented head.
Vain as thou wert, and weak as vain
The slave of falsehood, pride and pain—
My heart is nought akin to thine—
Thy soul is powerless over mine.'

But these were thoughts that vanished too,
Unwise, unholy and untrue—
Do I despise the timid deer
Because his limbs are fleet with fear?

Or would I mock the wolf's death-howl
Because his form is gaunt and foul?
Or hear with joy the leveret's cry
Because it cannot bravely die?

No—then above his memory
Let pity's heart as tender be:
Say, 'Earth lie lightly on that breast,
And Kind Heaven, grant that spirit rest!'

FAR, far away is mirth withdrawn;
'Tis three long hours before the morn
And I watch lonely, drearily—
So come, thou shade, commune with me.

Deserted one! thy corpse lies cold
And mingled with a foreign mould—
Year after year the grass grows green
Above the dust where thou hast been.

I will not name thy blighted name
Tarnished by unforgotten shame,
Though not because my bosom torn
Joins the mad world in all its scorn—

Thy phantom face is dark with woe,
Tears have left ghastly traces there;
Those ceaseless tears! I wish their flow
Could quench thy wild despair.

They deluge my heart like the rain
On cursed Gomorrah's howling plain—
Yet when I hear thy foes deride
20   I must cling closely to thy side.

Our mutual foes—they will not rest
From trampling on thy buried breast,
Glutting their hatred with the doom
They picture thine—beyond the tomb.

25   But God is not like human kind;
Man cannot read the Almighty mind;
Vengeance will never torture thee
Nor hunt thy soul eternally.

Then do not in this night of grief,
30   This time of overwhelming fear,
O do not think that God can leave,
Forget, forsake, refuse to hear!

What have I dreamt? He lies asleep
With whom my heart would vainly weep.
35   *He* rests—and *I* endure the woe
That left his spirit long ago.

IT is too late to call thee now—
I will not nurse that dream again,
For every joy that lit my brow
Would bring its after-storm of pain—

5   Besides, the mist is half withdrawn,
The barren mountain-side lies bare
And sunshine and awaking morn
Paint no more golden visions there.

Yet ever in my grateful breast
10   Thy darling shade shall cherished be,
For God alone doth know how blest
My early years have been in thee!

I'LL not weep that thou art going to leave me;
There's nothing lovely here,
And doubly will the dark world grieve me
While thy heart suffers there—

5   I'll not weep because the summer's glory
Must always end in gloom
And follow out the happiest story,
It closes with the tomb.

    And I am weary of the anguish
10   Increasing winters bear—
Weary to watch the spirit languish
Through years of dead despair.

    So if a tear when thou art dying
Should haply fall from me,
15   It is but that my soul is sighing
To go and rest with thee.

AT such a time, in such a spot
The world seems made of light;
Our blissful hearts remember not
How surely follows night.

5   I cannot, Alfred, dream of aught
That casts a shade of woe;
That heaven is reigning in my thought
Which wood and wave and earth have caught
From skies that overflow—

10   That heaven which my sweet lover's brow
Has won me to adore,
Which from his blue eyes beaming now
Reflects a still intenser glow
Than nature's heaven can pour.

15   I know our souls are all divine,
     I know that when we die
     What seems the vilest, even like thine
     A part of God himself shall shine
     In perfect purity.

20   But coldly breaks November's day;
     Its changes charmless all;
     Unmarked, unloved, they pass away;
     We do not wish one hour to stay
     Nor sigh at evening's fall.

25   And glorious is the gladsome rise
     Of June's rejoicing morn;
     And who, with unregretful eyes,
     Can watch the lustre leave its skies
     To twilight's shade forlorn?

30   Then art thou not my golden June
     All mist and tempest free?
     As shines earth's sun in summer noon
     So heaven's sun shines in thee.

     Let others seek its beams divine
35   In cell and cloister drear
     But I have found a fairer shrine,
     A happier worship here;

     By dismal rites they win their bliss,
     By penance, fasts and fears—
40   I have one rite—a gentle kiss;
     One penance—tender tears.

     O could it thus forever be
     That I might so adore,
     I'd ask for all eternity
45   To make a paradise for me,
     My love—and nothing more!

IF grief for grief can touch thee,
If answering woe for woe,
If any truth can melt thee
Come to me now!

5 I cannot be more lonely,
More drear I cannot be!
My worn heart throbs so wildly
'Twill break for thee—

And when the world despises—
10 When Heaven repels my prayer—
Will not mine angel comfort?
Mine idol hear?

Yes, by the tears I've poured,
By all my hours of pain
15 O I shall surely win thee,
Beloved, again!

'TIS moonlight, summer moonlight,
All soft and still and fair;
The solemn hour of midnight
Breathes sweet thoughts everywhere,

5 But most where trees are sending
Their breezy boughs on high,
Or stooping low are lending
A shelter from the sky.

And there in those wild bowers
10 A lovely form is laid;
Green grass and dew-steeped flowers
Wave gently round her head.

THE NIGHT WIND

IN summer's mellow midnight
A cloudless moon shone through
Our open parlour window
And rosetrees wet with dew—

5   I sat in silent musing—
The soft wind waved my hair;
It told me Heaven was glorious
And sleeping Earth was fair—

I needed not its breathing
10   To bring such thoughts to me,
But still it whispered lowly,
'How dark the woods will be!—

'The thick leaves in my murmur
Are rustling like a dream,
15   And all their myriad voices
Instinct with spirit seem.'

I said, 'Go, gentle singer,
Thy wooing voice is kind
But do not think its music
20   Has power to reach my mind—

'Play with the scented flower,
The young tree's supple bough—
And leave my human feelings
In their own course to flow.'

25   The Wanderer would not leave me;
Its kiss grew warmer still—
'O come', it sighed so sweetly,
'I'll win thee 'gainst thy will.

'Have we not been from childhood friends?
30   Have I not loved thee long?
As long as thou hast loved the night
Whose silence wakes my song.

'And when thy heart is resting
Beneath the churchyard stone
35   I shall have time for mourning
And thou for being alone.'

THERE let thy bleeding branch atone
  For every torturing tear;
Shall my young sins, my sins alone
Be everlasting here?

5   Who bade thee keep that cursed name
A pledge for memory?
As if oblivion ever came
To breathe its bliss on me;

As if through all the wildering maze
10   Of mad hours left behind
I once forgot the early days
That thou wouldst call to mind.

AND like myself lone, wholly lone,
  It sees the day's long sunshine glow,
And like myself it makes its moan
In unexhausted woe.

5   Give we the hills our equal prayer,
Earth's breezy hills and heaven's blue sea;
We ask for nothing further here
But our own hearts and liberty.

Ah! could my hand unlock its chain
10   How gladly would I watch it soar,
And ne'er regret and ne'er complain
To see its shining eyes no more.

But let me think that if to-day
It pines in cold captivity,
15   To-morrow both shall soar away
Eternally, entirely free.

THE OLD STOIC

RICHES I hold in light esteem
And Love I laugh to scorn
And Lust of Fame was but a dream
That vanished with the morn—

5 And if I pray—the only prayer
That moves my lips for me
Is—'Leave the heart that now I bear
And give me liberty.'

Yes, as my swift days near their goal
10 'Tis all that I implore—
In life and death, a chainless soul
With courage to endure!

SHALL Earth no more inspire thee,
Thou lonely dreamer now?
Since passion may not fire thee
Shall Nature cease to bow?

5 Thy mind is ever moving
In regions dark to thee;
Recall its useless roving—
Come back and dwell with me.

I know my mountain breezes
10 Enchant and soothe thee still—
I know my sunshine pleases
Despite thy wayward will.

When day with evening blending
Sinks from the summer sky,
15 I've seen thy spirit bending
In fond idolatry.

I've watched thee every hour—
I know my mighty sway—
I know my magic power
To drive thy griefs away.

Few hearts to mortals given
On earth so wildly pine,
Yet none would ask a Heaven
More like the Earth than thine.

Then let my winds caress thee—
Thy comrade let me be—
Since nought beside can bless thee,
Return and dwell with me.

AYE, there it is! It wakes to-night
Sweet thoughts that will not die
And feeling's fires flash all as bright
As in the years gone by!—

And I can tell by thine altered cheek
And by thy kindled gaze
And by the words thou scarce dost speak,
How wildly fancy plays.

Yes, I could swear that glorious wind
Has swept the world aside,
Has dashed its memory from thy mind
Like foam-bells from the tide—

And thou art now a spirit pouring
Thy presence into all—
The essence of the Tempest's roaring
And of the Tempest's fall—

A universal influence
From Thine own influence free—
A principle of life intense
Lost to mortality.

Thus truly when that breast is cold
Thy prisoned soul shall rise,
The dungeon mingle with the mould—
The captive with the skies.

I SEE around me tombstones grey
Stretching their shadows far away.
Beneath the turf my footsteps tread
Lie low and lone the silent dead;
Beneath the turf, beneath the mould—
Forever dark, forever cold,
And my eyes cannot hold the tears
That memory hoards from vanished years,
For Time and Death and Mortal pain
Give wounds that will not heal again.
Let me remember half the woe
I've seen and heard and felt below,
And Heaven itself, so pure and blest,
Could never give my spirit rest.
Sweet land of light! thy children fair
Know nought akin to our despair,
Nor have they felt, nor can they tell
What tenants haunt each mortal cell,
What gloomy guests we hold within—
Torments and madness, tears and sin!
Well—may they live in ecstasy
Their long eternity of joy;
At least we would not bring them down
With us to weep, with us to groan.
No—Earth would wish no other sphere
To taste her cup of sufferings drear;
She turns from Heaven a curseless eye
And only mourns that *we* must die!
Ah, mother, what shall comfort thee
In all this endless misery?
To cheer our eager eyes a while
We see thee smile, how fondly smile!
But who reads not through that tender glow
Thy deep, unutterable woe?
Indeed, no dazzling land above

Can cheat thee of thy children's love.
We all in life's departing shine
Our last dear longings blend with thine;
And struggle still, and strive to trace
40 With clouded gaze thy darling face.
We would not leave our native home
For *any* world beyond the Tomb.
No—rather on thy kindly breast
Let us be laid in lasting rest,
45 Or waken but to share with thee
A mutual immortality.

IN the same place, when Nature wore
The same celestial glow,
I'm sure I've seen these forms before
But many Springs ago;

5 And only *he* had locks of light
And *she* had raven hair;
While now, his curls are dark as night
And hers, as morning fair.

Besides, I've dreamt of tears whose traces
10 Will never more depart,
Of that agony that fast effaces
The verdure of the heart—

I dreamt, one sunny day like this
In this peerless month of May,
15 I saw her give the unanswered kiss
As his spirit passed away:

Those young eyes that so sweetly shine
Then looked their last adieu
And pale Death changed that cheek divine
20 To his unchanging hue;

And earth was cast above the breast
That beats so warm and free
Where her soft ringlets lightly rest
And move responsively.

25 Then She, upon the covered grave—
   The grass-grown grave did lie—
   A tomb not girt by Gondal's wave
   Nor arched by Gondal's sky.

   The sod was sparkling bright with dew
30 But brighter still with tears
   That welled from mortal grief, I knew,
   That never heals with years.

   And if he came not for her woe
   He would not now return;
35 He would not leave his sleep below
   When she had ceased to mourn.

   O Innocence, that cannot live
   With heart-wrung anguish long!
   Dear childhood's Innocence, forgive,
40 For I have done thee wrong!

   These bright rosebuds those hawthorns shroud
   Within their perfumed bower
   Have never closed beneath a cloud
   Nor bent before a shower—

45 Had darkness once obscured their sun
   Or kind dew turned to rain,
   No storm-cleared sky that ever shone
   Could win such bliss again.

   ## SELF-INTERROGATION

   'THE evening passes fast away,
        'Tis almost time to rest—
   What thoughts has left the vanished day,
   What feelings, in thy breast?'

5 'The vanished day? It leaves a sense
   Of labour hardly done;
   Of little gained with vast expense—
   A sense of grief alone!

'Time stands before the door of Death
Upbraiding bitterly;
And Conscience with exhaustless breath
Pours black reproach on me;

'And though I've said that Conscience lies,
And Time should Fate condemn;
Still, sad Repentance clouds my eyes,
And makes me yield to them!'

'Then art thou glad to seek repose?
Art glad to leave the sea,
And anchor all thy weary woes
In calm Eternity?

'Nothing regrets to see thee go—
Not one voice sobs "farewell",
And where thy heart has suffered so,
Canst thou desire to dwell?'

'Alas! The countless links are strong
That bind us to our clay;
The loving spirit lingers long
And would not pass away!

'And rest is sweet, when laurelled fame
Will crown the soldier's crest;
But a brave heart with a tarnished name
Would rather fight than rest.'

'Well thou hast fought for many a year,
Hast fought thy whole life through,
Hast humbled Falsehood, trampled Fear;
What is there left to do?'

''Tis true, this arm has hotly striven,
Has dared what few would dare;
Much have I done, and freely given,
But little learnt to bear!'

'Look on the grave, where thou must sleep,
Thy last and strongest foe—
It is endurance not to weep
If that repose seem woe.

45 'The long war closing in defeat,
Defeat serenely borne,
Thy midnight rest may still be sweet,
And break in glorious morn!'

HOW CLEAR SHE SHINES

HOW clear she shines! How quietly
I lie beneath her guardian light
While Heaven and Earth are whispering me,
'To-morrow wake, but dream to-night.'

5 Yes—Fancy, come, my Fairy love!
These throbbing temples, softly kiss;
And bend my lonely couch above
And bring me rest, and bring me bliss.

The world is going—Dark world, adieu!
10 Grim world, conceal thee till the day;
The heart thou canst not all subdue
Must still resist if thou delay—

Thy love I will not, will not share;
Thy hatred only wakes a smile;
15 Thy griefs may wound—thy wrongs may tear,
But, oh, thy lies shall ne'er beguile.

While gazing on the stars that glow
Above me in that stormless sea
I long to hope that all the woe
20 Creation knows, is held in thee!

And this shall be my dream to-night—
I'll think the heaven of glorious spheres
Is rolling on its course of light
In endless bliss, through endless years—

25   I'll think, there's not one world above,
Far as these straining eyes can see,
Where Wisdom ever laughed at Love,
Or Virtue crouched to Infamy;

Where, writhing 'neath the strokes of Fate,
30   The mangled wretch was forced to smile;
To match his patience 'gainst her hate,
His heart rebellious all the while.

Where Pleasure still will lead to wrong,
And helpless Reason warn in vain,
35   And Truth is weak, and Treachery strong,
And Joy the surest path to pain—

And Peace the lethargy of grief—
And Hope a phantom of the soul—
And Life a labour void and brief—
40   And Death the despot of the whole.

HOPE

HOPE was but a timid friend—
She sat without the grated den
Watching how my fate would tend
Even as selfish-hearted men—

5   She was cruel in her fear—
Through the bars, one dreary day,
I looked out to see her there
And she turned her face away!

Like a false guard, false watch keeping,
10   Still in strife she whispered, peace;
She would sing while I was weeping;
If I listened, she would cease—

False she was, and unrelenting;
When my last joys strewed the ground
15   Even Sorrow saw, repenting,
Those sad relics, scattered round—

Hope—whose whisper would have given
Balm to all my frenzied pain—
Stretched her wings and soared to heaven—
20   Went—and ne'er returned again!

MY COMFORTER

WELL hast thou spoken—and yet not taught
    A feeling strange or new—
Thou hast but roused a latent thought,
A cloud-closed beam of sunshine brought
5   To gleam in open view.

Deep down—concealed within my soul
    That light lies hid from men,
Yet glows unquenched—though shadows roll,
Its gentle ray cannot control—
10   About the sullen den.

Was I not vexed, in these gloomy ways
    To walk alone so long?
Around me, wretches uttering praise,
Or howling o'er their hopeless days—
15   And each with Frenzy's tongue—

A brotherhood of misery,
    With smiles as sad as sighs—
Whose madness daily maddened me,
Distorting into agony
20   The bliss before my eyes.

So stood I—in Heaven's glorious sun
    And in the glare of Hell
My spirit drank a mingled tone
Of seraph's song and demon's moan;
25   What my soul bore my soul alone
    Within itself may tell.

Like a soft air above a sea
Tossed by the tempest's stir—
A thaw-wind melting quietly
30 The snowdrift on some wintery lea;
No—what sweet thing resembles thee,
My thoughtful Comforter?

And yet a little longer speak,
Calm this resentful mood,
35 And while the savage heart grows meek,
For other token do not seek,
But let the tear upon my cheek
Evince my gratitude!

A DAY DREAM

ON a sunny brae alone I lay
One summer afternoon;
It was the marriage-time of May
With her young lover, June.

5 From her Mother's heart seemed loath to part
That queen of bridal charms;
But her Father smiled on the fairest child
He ever held in his arms.

The trees did wave their plumy crests,
10 The glad birds carolled clear;
And I, of all the wedding guests,
Was only sullen there.

There was not one but wished to shun
My aspect void of cheer;
15 The very grey rocks looking on
Asked, 'What do you do here?'

And I could utter no reply—
In sooth I did not know
Why I had brought a clouded eye
20 To greet the general glow.

So resting on a heathy bank
I took my heart to me
And we together sadly sank
Into a reverie.

25 We thought—'When winter comes again
Where will these bright things be?
All vanished like a vision vain—
An unreal mockery!

'The birds that now so blithely sing—
30 Through deserts frozen dry,
Poor spectres of the perished Spring
In famished troops will fly.

'And why should we be glad at all?
The leaf is hardly green
35 Before a token of the fall
Is on its surface seen.'

Now whether it were really so
I never could be sure—
But as in fit of peevish woe
40 I stretched me on the moor

A thousand thousand glancing fires
Seemed kindling in the air—
A thousand thousand silvery lyres
Resounded far and near.

45 Methought the very breath I breathed
Was full of sparks divine
And all my heather-couch was wreathed
By that celestial shine—

And while the wide Earth echoing rang
50 To their strange minstrelsy,
The little glittering spirits sang
Or seemed to sing to me,—

'O mortal, mortal, let them die—
Let Time and Tears destroy,
That we may overflow the sky
With universal joy.

'Let Grief distract the sufferer's breast
And Night obscure his way;
They hasten him to endless rest
And everlasting day.

'To Thee the world is like a tomb—
A desert's naked shore;
To us—in unimagined bloom
It brightens more and more.

'And could we lift the veil and give
One brief glimpse to thine eye
Thou wouldst rejoice for those that live
Because they live to die.'

The music ceased—the noonday Dream
Like dream of night withdrew,
But Fancy still will sometimes deem
Her fond creation true.

SONG

THE linnet in the rocky dells,
The moor-lark in the air,
The bee among the heather bells
That hide my lady fair,

The wild deer browse above her breast;
The wild birds raise their brood;
And they, her smiles of love caressed,
Have left her solitude!

I ween, that when the grave's dark wall
Did first her form retain,
They thought their hearts could ne'er recall
The light of joy again—

They thought the tide of grief would flow
Unchecked through future years,
15   But where is all their anguish now,
And where are all their tears?

Well, let them fight for Honour's breath,
Or Pleasure's shade pursue—
The Dweller in the land of Death
20   Is changed and careless too.

And if their eyes should watch and weep
Till sorrow's source were dry,
She would not in her tranquil sleep
Return a single sigh.

25   Blow, West wind, by the lonely mound,
And murmur, Summer streams,
There is no need of other sound
To soothe my Lady's dreams.

TO IMAGINATION

WHEN weary with the long day's care
And earthly change from pain to pain
And lost and ready to despair
Thy kind voice calls me back again—
5   O my true friend, I am not lone
While thou canst speak with such a tone!

So hopeless is the world without
The world within I doubly prize,
Thy world, where guile and hate and doubt
10   And cold suspicion never rise—
Where thou and I and Liberty
Have undisputed sovereignty.

What matters it that all around
Danger and guilt and darkness lie
15 If but within our bosom's bound
We hold a bright untroubled sky
Warm with ten thousand mingled rays
Of suns that know no winter days?

Reason indeed may oft complain
20 For Nature's sad reality
And tell the suffering heart how vain
Its cherished dreams must always be;
And Truth may rudely trample down
The flowers of fancy newly blown;

25 But thou art ever there to bring
The hovering vision back and breathe
New glories o'er the blighted Spring
And call a lovelier life from death,
And whisper with a voice divine
30 Of real worlds as bright as thine.

I trust not to thy phantom bliss
Yet still, in evening's quiet hour
With never-failing thankfulness
I welcome thee, benignant power,
35 Sure solacer of human cares
And sweeter hope when hope despairs.

PLEAD FOR ME

O, THY bright eyes must answer now,
When Reason, with a scornful brow,
Is mocking at my overthrow;
O, thy sweet tongue must plead for me
5 And tell why I have chosen thee!

Stern Reason is to judgement come
Arrayed in all her forms of gloom;
Wilt thou my advocate be dumb?
No, radiant angel, speak and say
Why I did cast the world away:

Why I have persevered to shun
The common paths that others run
And on a strange road journeyed on;
Heedless alike of wealth and power—
Of glory's wreath and Pleasure's flower.

These once indeed seemed Beings divine
And they perchance heard vows of mine
And saw my offerings on their shrine—
But, careless gifts are seldom prized
And mine were worthily despised.

So with a ready heart I swore
To seek their altar-stone no more,
And gave my spirit to adore
Thee, ever present, phantom thing,
My Slave, my Comrade, and my King!

A Slave because I rule thee still,
Incline thee to my changeful will
And make thy influence good or ill—
A Comrade—for by day and night
Thou art my intimate Delight—

My darling pain that wounds and sears
And wrings a blessing out from tears
By deadening me to earthly cares;
And yet a king—though prudence well
Have taught thy subject to rebel—

And am I wrong, to worship where
Faith cannot doubt, nor Hope despair,
Since my own soul can grant my prayer?
Speak, God of visions, plead for me,
And tell why I have chosen thee!

THE PHILOSOPHER

'ENOUGH of Thought, Philosopher;
    Too long hast thou been dreaming
Unlightened, in this chamber drear
While summer's sun is beaming—
Space-sweeping soul, what sad refrain
Concludes thy musings once again?

'O for the time when I shall sleep
Without identity—
And never care how rain may steep
Or snow may cover me!

'No promised Heaven, these wild Desires
Could all or half fulfil—
No threatened Hell—with quenchless fires,
Subdue this quenchless will!'

—So said I, and still say the same,
—Still to my Death will say—
Three Gods within this little frame
Are warring night and day—

Heaven could not hold them all, and yet
They all are held in me
And must be mine till I forget
My present entity—

O, for the time, when in my breast
Their struggles will be o'er—
O for the day when I shall rest
And never suffer more!

'I saw a Spirit standing, Man,
Where thou dost stand—an hour ago,
And round his feet, three rivers ran
Of equal depth and equal flow—

'A Golden Stream, and one like blood
And one like Sapphire, seemed to be,
But where they joined their triple flood
It tumbled in an inky sea—

35 'The Spirit bent his dazzling gaze
Down on that Ocean's gloomy night,
Then—kindling all with sudden blaze,
The glad deep sparkled wide and bright—
White as the sun; far, far more fair
40 Than its divided sources were!'

—And even for that Spirit, Seer,
I've watched and sought my lifetime long;
Sought him in Heaven, Hell, Earth and Air,
An endless search—and always wrong!

45 Had I but seen his glorious eye
Once light the clouds that 'wilder me,
I ne'er had raised this coward cry
To cease to think and cease to be—

I ne'er had called oblivion blest,
50 Nor stretching eager hands to Death
Implored to change for lifeless rest
This sentient soul, this living breath.

O let me die, that Power and Will
Their cruel strife may close,
55 And vanquished Good, victorious Ill
Be lost in one repose.

REMEMBRANCE

COLD in the earth and the deep snow piled above thee!
Far, far removed, cold in the dreary grave:
Have I forgot, my only Love, to love thee,
Severed at last by Time's all-severing wave?

5   Now, when alone, do my thoughts no longer hover
            Over the mountains on Angora's shore;
            Resting their wings where heath and fern-leaves cover
            That noble heart for ever, ever more?

            Cold in the earth, and fifteen wild Decembers
10   From those brown hills have melted into spring—
            Faithful indeed is the spirit that remembers
            After such years of change and suffering!

            Sweet Love of youth, forgive if I forget thee
            While the World's tide is bearing me along:
15   Other desires and other Hopes beset me,
            Hopes which obscure but cannot do thee wrong.

            No later light has lightened up my heaven;
            No second morn has ever shone for me;
            All my life's bliss from thy dear life was given—
20   All my life's bliss is in the grave with thee.

            But when the days of golden dreams had perished
            And even Despair was powerless to destroy,
            Then did I learn how existence could be cherished,
            Strengthened and fed without the aid of joy.

25   Then did I check the tears of useless passion,
            Weaned my young soul from yearning after thine;
            Sternly denied its burning wish to hasten
            Down to that tomb already more than mine!

            And even yet, I dare not let it languish,
30   Dare not indulge in Memory's rapturous pain;
            Once drinking deep of that divinest anguish,
            How could I seek the empty world again?

DEATH

DEATH, that struck when I was most confiding
In my certain faith of joy to be;
Strike again, Time's withered branch dividing
From the fresh root of Eternity!

5   Leaves, upon Time's branch, were growing brightly;
Full of sap and full of silver dew;
Birds, beneath its shelter, gathered nightly;
Daily, round its flowers, the wild bees flew.

Sorrow passed and plucked the golden blossom,
10   Guilt stripped off the foliage in its pride;
But, within its parent's kindly bosom,
Flowed forever Life's restoring tide.

Little mourned I for the parted gladness,
For the vacant nest and silent song;
15   Hope was there and laughed me out of sadness,
Whispering, 'Winter will not linger long.'

And behold, with tenfold increase blessing
Spring adorned the beauty-burdened spray;
Wind and rain and fervent heat caressing
20   Lavished glory on that second May.

High it rose; no winged grief could sweep it;
Sin was scared to distance with its shine:
Love and its own life had power to keep it
From all wrong, from every blight but thine!

25   Cruel Death, the young leaves droop and languish!
Evening's gentle air may still restore—
No, the morning sunshine mocks my anguish—
Time for me must never blossom more!

Strike it down—that other boughs may flourish
30   Where that perished sapling used to be;
Thus, at least, its mouldering corpse will nourish
That from which it sprung—Eternity.

STARS

AH! why because the dazzling sun
Restored our earth to joy
Have you departed, every one,
And left a desert sky?

5   All through the night, your glorious eyes
Were gazing down in mine,
And with a full heart's thankful sighs
I blessed that watch divine!

I was at peace—and drank your beams
10   As they were life to me
And revelled in my changeful dreams
Like petrel on the sea—

Thought followed thought—star followed star
Through boundless regions on,
15   While one sweet influence, near and far,
Thrilled through and proved us one.

Why did the morning dawn to break
So great, so pure a spell,
And scorch with fire the tranquil cheek
20   Where your cool radiance fell?

Blood-red he rose, and arrow-straight
His fierce beams struck my brow:
The soul of Nature sprang elate,
But mine sank sad and low!

25   My lids closed down—yet through their veil
I saw him blazing still;
And steep in gold the misty dale,
And flash upon the hill—

I turned me to the pillow then
30   To call back Night, and see
Your worlds of solemn light again
Throb with my heart and me!

It would not do—the pillow glowed
And glowed both roof and floor
35 And birds sang loudly in the wood
And fresh winds shook the door.

The curtains waved, the wakened flies
Were murmuring round my room,
Imprisoned there, till I should rise
40 And give them leave to roam.

O, Stars and Dreams and Gentle Night—
O, Night and Stars, return!
And hide me from the hostile light
That does not warm, but burn—

45 That drains the blood of suffering men—
Drinks tears, instead of dew—
Let me sleep through his blinding reign,
And only wake with you!

HEAVY hangs the raindrop
From the burdened spray;
Heavy broods the damp mist
On Uplands far away;

5 Heavy looms the dull sky,
Heavy rolls the sea—
And heavy beats the young heart
Beneath that lonely tree.

Never has a blue streak
10 Cleft the clouds since morn—
Never has his grim Fate
Smiled since he was born—

Frowning on the infant,
Shadowing childhood's joy,
15 Guardian angel knows not
That melancholy boy.

Day is passing swiftly
Its sad and sombre prime;
Youth is fast invading
20   Sterner manhood's time—

All the flowers are praying
For sun before they close
And he prays too, unknowing,
That sunless human rose!

25   Blossoms, that the west wind
Has never wooed to blow,
Scentless are your petals,
Your dew as cold as snow.

Soul, where kindred kindness
30   No early promise woke,
Barren is your beauty
As weed upon the rock—

Wither, Brothers, wither,
You were vainly given—
35   Earth reserves no blessing
For the unblessed of Heaven!

Child of Delight! with sunbright hair
And seablue, seadeep eyes;
Spirit of Bliss, what brings thee here
40   Beneath these sullen skies?

Thou shouldst live in eternal spring
Where endless day is never dim;
Why, seraph, has thy erring wing
Borne thee down to weep with him?

45   'Ah, not from heaven am I descended,
And I do not come to mingle tears;
But sweet is day, though with shadows blended;
And, though clouded, sweet are youthful years—

'I, the image of light and gladness,
50 Saw and pitied that mournful boy,
And I swore to take his gloomy sadness,
And give to him my beamy joy—

'Heavy and dark the night is closing;
Heavy and dark may its biding be;
55 Better for all from grief reposing,
And better for all who watch like me—

'Guardian angel he lacks no longer;
Evil fortune he need not fear:
Fate is strong, but love is stronger
60 And more unsleeping than angel's care.'

ANTICIPATION

HOW beautiful the Earth is still
To thee, how full of Happiness;
How little fraught with real ill
Or shadowy phantoms of distress;
5 How spring can bring thee glory yet
And summer win thee to forget
December's sullen time!
Why dost thou hold the treasure fast
Of youth's delight, when youth is past
10 And thou art near thy prime?

When those who were thy own compeers,
Equal in fortunes and in years,
Have seen their morning melt in tears
To clouded, smileless day;
15 Blest, had they died untried and young
Before their hearts went wandering wrong
Poor slaves, subdued by passions strong,
A weak and helpless prey!

'Because, I hoped while they enjoyed,
20 And by fulfilment, hope destroyed—
As children hope, with trustful breast,
I waited bliss and cherished rest.
A thoughtful Spirit taught me soon
That we must long till life be done;
25 That every phase of earthly joy
Will always fade and always cloy—

'This I foresaw, and would not chase
The fleeting treacheries,
But with firm foot and tranquil face
30 Held backward from the tempting race;
Gazed o'er the sands, the waves efface
To the enduring seas—

'There cast my anchor of desire
Deep in unknown eternity,
35 Nor ever let my Spirit tire
With looking for *What is to Be*.

'It is hope's spell that glorifies
Like youth to my maturer eyes
All Nature's million mysteries—
40 The fearful and the fair—

'Hope soothes me in the griefs I know,
She lulls my pain for others' woe
And makes me strong to undergo
What I am born to bear.

45 'Glad comforter, will I not brave
Unawed, the darkness of the grave—
Nay, smile to hear Death's billows rave,
Sustained, my guide, by thee?
The more unjust seems present fate
50 The more my Spirit swells elate
Strong in thy strength, to anticipate
Rewarding destiny!'

THE PRISONER

SILENT is the house—all are laid asleep;
One, alone, looks out o'er the snow-wreaths deep;
Watching every cloud, dreading every breeze
That whirls the wildering drifts and bends the groaning trees.

5   Cheerful is the hearth, soft the matted floor;
Not one shivering gust creeps through pane or door.
The little lamp burns straight; its rays shoot strong and far;
I trim it well to be the Wanderer's guiding star—

Frown, my haughty sire, chide, my angry dame;
10 Set yourselves to spy, threaten me with shame;
But neither sire nor dame, nor prying serf shall know
What angel nightly tracks that waste of winter snow.

In the dungeon crypts idly did I stray,
Reckless of the lives wasting there away;
15 'Draw the ponderous bars, open, Warder stern!'
He dare not say me nay—the hinges harshly turn.

'Our guests are darkly lodged', I whispered, gazing through
The vault whose grated eye showed heaven more grey than blue;
(This was when glad spring laughed in awaking pride.)
20 'Aye, darkly lodged enough!' returned my sullen guide.

Then, God forgive my youth, forgive my careless tongue!
I scoffed as the chill chains on the damp flagstones rung;
'Confined in triple walls, art thou so much to fear,
25 That we must bind thee down and clench thy fetters here?'

The captive raised her face; it was as soft and mild
As sculptured marble saint or slumbering, unweaned child;
It was so soft and mild, it was so sweet and fair
Pain could not trace a line nor grief a shadow there!

30 The captive raised her hand and pressed it to her brow:
    'I have been struck', she said, 'and I am suffering now;
    Yet these are little worth, your bolts and irons strong,
    And were they forged in steel they could not hold me long.'

    Hoarse laughed the jailor grim: 'Shall I be won to hear;
35 Dost think, fond, dreaming wretch, that *I* shall grant thy prayer?
    Or better still, wilt melt my master's heart with groans?
    Ah! sooner might the sun thaw down these granite stones.

    'My master's voice is low, his aspect bland and kind,
    But hard as hardest flint the soul that lurks behind;
40 And I am rough and rude, yet not more rough to see,
    Than is the hidden ghost that has its home in me.'

    About her lips there played a smile of almost scorn,
    'My friend', she gently said, 'you have not heard me mourn;
    When you my kindred's lives—*my* lost life can restore
45 Then may I weep and sue, but never, friend, before!

    'Still, let my tyrants know, I am not doomed to wear
    Year after year in gloom and desolate despair;
    A messenger of Hope comes every night to me
    And offers for short life, eternal liberty—

50 'He comes with western winds, with evening's wandering airs,
    With that clear dusk of heaven that brings the thickest stars;
    Winds take a pensive tone and stars a tender fire,
    And visions rise and fall that kill me with desire—

    'Desire for nothing known in my maturer years
55 When joy grew mad with awe at counting future tears;
    When, if my spirit's sky was full of flashes warm,
    I knew not whence they came, from sun or thunder-storm.

    'But first a hush of peace—a soundless calm descends;
    The struggle of distress and fierce impatience ends;
60 Mute music soothes my breast, unuttered harmony
    That I could never dream till earth is lost to me.

'Then dawns the Invisible, the Unseen its truth reveals;
My outward sense is gone, my inward essence feels:
Its wings are almost free—its home, its harbour found;
65   Measuring the gulf it stoops and dares the final bound.

'Oh, dreadful is the check—intense the agony—
When the ear begins to hear and the eye begins to see;
When the pulse begins to throb, the brain to think again,
The soul to feel the flesh and the flesh to feel the chain!

70   'Yet I would lose no sting, would wish no torture less;
The more that anguish racks, the earlier it will bless;
And robed in fires of Hell, or bright with heavenly shine,
If it but herald Death, the vision is divine!'

She ceased to speak, and we, unanswering, turned to go—
75   We had no further power to work the captive woe:
Her cheek, her gleaming eye, declared that man had given
A sentence, unapproved, and overruled by Heaven.

NO coward soul is mine,
  No trembler in the world's storm-troubled sphere;
I see Heaven's glories shine
And Faith shines equal arming me from Fear.

5   O God within my breast,
Almighty ever-present Deity
Life, that in me hast rest
As I, Undying Life, have power in Thee.

Vain are the thousand creeds
10   That move men's hearts, unutterably vain,
Worthless as withered weeds
Or idlest froth amid the boundless main

To waken doubt in one
Holding so fast by thy infinity,
15   So surely anchored on
The steadfast rock of Immortality.

With wide-embracing love
Thy Spirit animates eternal years,
Pervades and broods above,
20 Changes, sustains, dissolves, creates and rears.

Though Earth and moon were gone
And suns and universes ceased to be
And thou wert left alone
Every Existence would exist in thee.

25 There is not room for Death
Nor atom that his might could render void
Since thou are Being and Breath
And what thou art may never be destroyed.

SELECTED POEMS
OF
ANNE BRONTË

ALEXANDER AND ZENOBIA

FAIR was the evening and brightly the sun
   Was shining on desert and grove,
Sweet were the breezes and balmy the flowers
   And cloudless the heavens above.

5   It was Arabia's distant land
   And peaceful was the hour;
Two youthful figures lay reclined
   Deep in a shady bower.

    One was a boy of just fourteen
10   Bold beautiful and bright;
Soft raven curls hung clustering round
   A brow of marble white.

    The fair brow and ruddy cheek
   Spoke of less burning skies;
15   Words cannot paint the look that beamed
   In his dark lustrous eyes.

    The other was a slender girl,
   Blooming and young and fair.
The snowy neck was shaded with
20   The long bright sunny hair.

    And those deep eyes of watery blue,
   So sweetly sad they seemed.
And every feature in her face
   With pensive sorrow teemed.

25 The youth beheld her saddened air
     And smiling cheerfully
   He said, 'How pleasant is the land
     Of sunny Araby!

   'Zenobia, I never saw
30   A lovelier eve than this;
   I never felt my spirit raised
     With more unbroken bliss!

   'So deep the shades, so calm the hour,
     So soft the breezes sigh,
35 So sweetly Philomel begins
     Her heavenly melody.

   'So pleasant are the scents that rise
     From flowers of loveliest hue,
   And more than all—Zenobia,
40   I am alone with you!

   'Are we not happy here alone
     In such a healthy spot?'
   He looked to her with joyful smile
     But she returned it not.

45 'Why are you sorrowful?' he asked
     And heaved a bitter sigh,
   'O tell me why those drops of woe
     Are gathering in your eye.'

   'Gladly would I rejoice,' she said,
50   'But grief weighs down my heart.
   'Can I be happy when I know
     Tomorrow we must part?

   'Yes, Alexander, I must see
     This happy land no more.
55 At break of day I must return
     To distant Gondal's shore.

'At morning we must bid farewell,
  And at the close of day
You will be wandering alone
  And I shall be away.

60

'I shall be sorrowing for you
  On the wide weltering sea,
And you will perhaps have wandered here
  To sit and think of me.'

65

'And shall we part so *soon?*' he cried,
  '*Must* we be torn away?
Shall I be left to mourn alone?
  Will you no *longer* stay?

'And shall we never meet again,
  Hearts that have grown together?
70 Must they at once be rent away
  And kept apart for ever?'

'Yes, Alexander, we must part,
  But we may meet again,
75 For when I left my native land
  I wept in anguish then.

'Never shall I forget the day
  I left its rocky shore.
We thought that we had bid adieu
80 To meet on earth no more.

'When we had parted how I wept
  To see the mountains blue
Grow dimmer and more distant—till
  They faded from my view.

85 'And you too wept—we little thought
  After so long a time,
To meet again so suddenly
  In such a distant clime.

'We met on Grecia's classic plain,
    We part in Araby.
90
And let us hope to meet again
    Beneath our Gondal's sky.'

'Zenobia, do you remember
    A little lonely spring
95
Among Exina's woody hills
    Where blackbirds used to sing,

'And when they ceased as daylight faded
    From the dusky sky
The pensive nightingale began
100
    Her matchless melody?

'Sweet bluebells used to flourish there
    And tall trees waved on high,
And through their ever sounding leaves
    The soft wind used to sigh.

105
'At morning we have often played
    Beside that lonely well;
At evening we have lingered there
    Till dewy twilight fell.

'And when your fifteenth birthday comes,
110
    Remember me, my love,
And think of what I said to you
    In this sweet spicy grove.

'At evening wander to that spring
    And sit and wait for me;
115
And 'ere the sun has ceased to shine
    I will return to thee.

'Two years is a weary time
    But it will soon be fled.
And if you do not meet me—know
120
    I am not false but dead.'

*   *   *

Sweetly the summer day declines
  On forest, plain and hill
And in that spacious palace hall
  So lonely, wide and still.

125 Beside a window's open arch,
      In the calm evening air
    All lonely sits a stately girl,
      Graceful and young and fair.

    The snowy lid and lashes long
130   Conceal her downcast eye,
    She's reading and till now I have
      Passed unnoticed by.

    But see she cannot fix her thoughts,
      They are wandering away;
135 She looks towards a distant dell
      Where sunny waters play.

    And yet her spirit is not with
      The scene she looks upon;
    She muses with a mournful smile
140   On pleasures that are gone.

    She looks upon the book again
      That chained her thoughts before,
    And for a moment strives in vain
      To fix her mind once more.

145 Then gently drops it on her knee
      And looks into the sky,
    While trembling drops are shining in
      Her dark celestial eye.
    And thus alone and still she sits
150   Musing on years gone by.

    Till with a sad and sudden smile
      She rises up to go;
    And from the open window springs
      On to the grass below.

155 Why does she fly so swiftly now
       Adown the meadow green,
    And o'er the gently swelling hills
       And the vale that lies between?

       She passes under giant trees
160   That lift their arms on high
    And slowly wave their mighty boughs
       In the clear evening sky,

    And now she threads a path that winds
       Through deeply shaded groves
165 Where nought is heard but sighing gales
       And murmuring turtle doves.

    She hastens on through sunless gloom
       To a vista opening wide;
    A marble fountain sparkles there
170   With sweet flowers by its side.

    At intervals in the velvet grass
       A few old elm trees rise,
    While a warm flood of yellow light
       Streams from the western skies.

175 Is this her resting place? Ah, no,
       She hastens onward still,
    The startled deer before her fly
       As she ascends the hill.

    She does not rest till she has gained
180   A lonely purling spring,
    Where zephyrs wave the verdant trees
       And birds in concert sing.

    And there she stands and gazes round
       With bright and searching eye,
185 Then sadly sighing turns away
       And looks upon the sky.

She sits down on the flowery turf
  Her head drooped on her hand;
Her soft luxuriant golden curls
190 Are by the breezes fanned.

A sweet sad smile plays on her lips;
  Her heart is far away,
And thus she sits till twilight comes
  To take the place of day.

195 But when she looks towards the west
  And sees the sun is gone
And hears that every bird but one
  To its nightly rest is flown,

And sees that over nature's face
200 A sombre veil is cast
With mournful voice and tearful eye
  She says, 'The time is past!

'He will not come! I might have known
  It was a foolish hope;
205 But it was so sweet to cherish
  I could not yield it up.

'It may be foolish thus to weep
  But I cannot check my tears
To see in one short hour destroyed
210 The darling hope of years.

'He is not false, but he was young
  And time rolls fast away.
Has he forgotten the vow he made
  To meet me here today?

215 'No. If he lives he loves me still
  And still remembers me.
If he is dead—my joys are sunk
  In utter misery'

'We parted in the spicy groves
   Beneath Arabia's sky.
How could I hope to meet him now
   Where Gondal's breezes sigh?

'He was a shining meteor light
   That faded from the skies,
But I mistook him for a star
   That only set to rise.

'And with a firm yet trembling hand
   I've clung to this false hope;
I dared not surely trust in it
   Yet would not yield it up.

'And day and night I've thought of him
   And loved him constantly,
And prayed that Heaven would prosper him
   Wherever he might be.

'He will not come; he's wandering now
   On some far distant shore,
Or else he sleeps the sleep of death
   And cannot see me more!

'O, Alexander, is it thus?
   Did we but meet to part?
Long as I live thy name will be
   Engraven on my heart.

'I shall not cease to think of thee
   While life and thought remain,
For well I know that I can never
   See thy like again!'

She ceases now and dries her tears
   But still she lingers there
In silent thought till night is come
   And silver stars appear.

But lo! a tall and stately youth
  Ascends the grassy slope;
His bright dark eyes are glancing round,
  His heart beats high with hope.

255   He has journeyed on unweariedly
  From dawn of day till now,
The warm blood kindles in his cheek,
  The sweat is on his brow.

260   But he has gained the green hill top
  Where lies that lonely spring,
And lo! he pauses when he hears
  Its gentle murmuring.

He dares not enter through the trees
  That veil it from his eye;
265   He listens for some other sound
  In deep anxiety.

But vainly—all is calm and still;
  Are his bright day dreams o'er?
Has he thus hoped and longed in vain,
270   And must they meet no more?

One moment more of sad suspense
  And those dark trees are past;
The lonely well bursts on his sight
  And they are met at last!

A FRAGMENT
(Self-Congratulation)

'MAIDEN, thou wert thoughtless once
  Of beauty or of grace,
Simple and homely in attire
  Careless of form and face.
5   Then whence this change, and why so oft
  Dost smooth thy hazel hair?
And wherefore deck thy youthful form
  With such unwearied care?

'Tell us—and cease to tire our ears
　With yonder hackneyed strain—
Why wilt thou play those simple tunes
　So often o'er again?'
'Nay, gentle friends, I can but say
　That childhood's thoughts are gone.
Each year its own new feelings brings
　And years move swiftly on,

And for those little simple airs,
　I love to play them o'er—
So much I dare not promise now
　To play them never more.'
I answered and it was enough;
　They turned them to depart;
They could not read my secret thoughts
　Nor see my throbbing heart.

I've noticed many a youthful form
　Upon whose changeful face
The inmost workings of the soul
　The gazer's eye might trace.
The speaking eye, the changing lip,
　The ready blushing cheek,
The smiling or beclouded brow
　Their different feelings speak.

But, thank God! you might gaze on mine
　For hours and never know
The secret changes of my soul
　From joy to bitter woe.
Last night as we sat around the fire
　Conversing merrily,
We heard without approaching steps
　Of one well known to me.

There was no trembling in my voice,
　No blush upon my cheek,
No lustrous sparkle in my eyes
　Of hope or joy to speak.
But O my spirit burned within,
　My heart beat thick and fast.
He came not nigh—he went away
　And then my joy was past.

And yet my comrades marked it not,
50   My voice was still the same;
They saw me smile, and o'er my face—
     No signs of sadness came;
They little knew my hidden thoughts
     And they will never know
55 The anguish of my drooping heart,
     The bitter aching woe!

THE BLUEBELL

A FINE and subtle spirit dwells
  In every little flower,
Each one its own sweet feeling breathes
With more or less of power.

5 There is a silent eloquence
In every wild bluebell
That fills my softened heart with bliss
That words could never tell.

Yet I recall not long ago
10 A bright and sunny day,
'Twas when I led a toilsome life
So many leagues away;

That day along a sunny road
All carelessly I strayed,
15 Between two banks where smiling flowers
Their varied hues displayed.

Before me rose a lofty hill,
Behind me lay the sea,
My heart was not so heavy then
20 As it was wont to be.

Less harassed than at other times
I saw the scene was fair,
And spoke and laughed to those around,
As if I knew no care.

25   But when I looked upon the bank
My wandering glances fell
Upon a little trembling flower,
A single sweet bluebell.

Whence came that rising in my throat,
30   That dimness in my eye?
Why did those burning drops distil—
Those bitter feelings rise?

O, that lone flower recalled to me
My happy childhood's hours
35   When bluebells seemed like fairy gifts
A prize among the flowers,

Those sunny days of merriment
When heart and soul were free,
And when I dwelt with kindred hearts
40   That loved and cared for me.

I had not then 'mid heartless crowds
To spend a thankless life
In seeking after others' weal
With anxious toil and strife.

45   'Sad wanderer, weep those blissful times
That never may return!'
The lovely floweret seemed to say,
And thus it made me mourn.

LINES WRITTEN AT THORP GREEN (APPEAL)

O! I am very weary
    Though tears no longer flow;
My eyes are tired of weeping,
    My heart is sick of woe.

5   My life is very lonely,
    My days pass heavily;
I'm weary of repining,
    Wilt thou not come to me?

Oh didst thou know my longings
10   For thee from day to day,
My hopes so often blighted,
       Thou wouldst not thus delay.

OH, they have robbed me of the hope
  My spirit held so dear;
They will not let me hear that voice
       My soul delights to hear.

5   They will not let me see that face
       I so delight to see;
And they have taken all thy smiles,
       And all thy love from me.

Well, let them seize on all they can;—
10   One treasure still is mine,—
A heart that loves to think on thee,
       And feels the worth of thine.

FAREWELL to thee! but not farewell
  To all my fondest thoughts of thee:
Within my heart they still shall dwell;
       And they shall cheer and comfort me.

5   O, beautiful, and full of grace!
       If thou hadst never met mine eye,
I had not dreamed a living face
       Could fancied charms so far outvie.

If I may ne'er behold again
10   That form and face so dear to me,
Nor hear thy voice, still would I fain
       Preserve, for aye, their memory.

That voice, the magic of whose tone
       Can wake an echo in my breast,
15   Creating feelings that, alone,
       Can make my tranced spirit blest.

That laughing eye, whose sunny beam
    My memory would not cherish less;—
And oh, that smile! whose joyous gleam
    No mortal language can express.

Adieu, but let me cherish, still,
    The hope with which I cannot part.
Contempt may wound, and coldness chill,
    But still it lingers in my heart.

And who can tell but Heaven, at last,
    May answer all my thousand prayers,
And bid the future pay the past
    With joy for anguish, smiles for tears?

LINES WRITTEN AT THORP GREEN

THAT summer sun whose genial glow
    Now cheers my drooping spirit so
    Must cold and distant be,
And only light our northern clime
With feeble ray, before the time
    I long so much to see.

And this soft whispering breeze that now
So gently cools my fevered brow,
    This too, alas, must turn—
To a wild blast whose icy dart
Pierces and chills me to the heart,
    Before I cease to mourn.

And these bright flowers I love so well,
Verbena, rose and sweet bluebell,
    Must droop and die away.
Those thick green leaves with all their shade
And rustling music, they must fade
    And every one decay.

But if the sunny summer time
20 And woods and meadows in their prime
    Are sweet to them that roam—
Far sweeter is the winter bare
With long dark nights and landscape drear
    To them that are at home!

IN MEMORY OF A HAPPY DAY IN FEBRUARY

BLESSED be Thou for all the joy
    My soul has felt today!
O let its memory stay with me
    And never pass away!

5   I was alone, for those I loved
        Were far away from me,
    The sun shone on the withered grass,
        The wind blew fresh and free.

    Was it the smile of early spring
10   That made my bosom glow?
    'Twas sweet, but neither sun nor wind
        Could raise my spirit so.

    Was it some feeling of delight,
        All vague and undefined?
15 No, 'twas a rapture deep and strong,
        Expanding in my mind!

    Was it a sanguine view of life
        And all its transient bliss—
    A hope of bright prosperity?
20   O no, it was not this!

    It was a glimpse of truths divine
        Unto my spirit given
    Illumined by a ray of light
        That shone direct from Heaven!

25 I knew there was a God on high
  By whom all things were made.
I saw his wisdom and his power
  In all his works displayed.

30 But most throughout the moral world
  I saw his glory shine;
I saw his wisdom infinite,
  His mercy all divine.

Deep secrets of his providence
  In darkness long concealed
35 Were brought to my delighted eyes
  And graciously revealed.

And while I wondered and adored
  His wisdom so divine,
I did not tremble at his power,
40 I felt that God was mine.

I knew that my Redeemer lived,
  I did not fear to die;
I felt that I should rise again
  To immortality.

45 I longed to view that bliss divine
  Which eye hath never seen,
To see the glories of his face
  Without the veil between.

TO COWPER

SWEET are thy strains, Celestial Bard,
  And oft in childhood's years
I've read them o'er and o'er again
  With floods of silent tears.

5 The language of my inmost heart
  I traced in every line—
My sins, *my* sorrows, hopes and fears
  Were there, and only mine.

All for myself the sigh would swell,
      The tear of anguish start;
I little knew what wilder woe
      Had filled the poet's heart.

I did not know the nights of gloom,
      The days of misery,
The long long years of dark despair
      That crushed and tortured thee.

But they are gone, and now from earth
      Thy gentle soul is passed.
And in the bosom of its God
      Has found its Home at last.

It must be so if God is love
      And answers fervent prayer;
Then surely thou shalt dwell on high,
      And I may meet thee there.

Is He the source of every good,
      The spring of purity?
Then in thine hours of deepest woe
      Thy God was still with thee.

How else when every hope was fled
      Couldst thou so fondly cling
To holy things and holy men
      And how so sweetly sing—

Of things that God alone could teach?
      And whence that purity;
That hatred of all sinful ways,
      That gentle charity?

Are these the symptoms of a heart
      Of Heavenly grace bereft,
For ever banished from its God,
      To Satan's fury left?

Yet should thy darkest fears be true,
      If Heaven be so severe
That such a soul as thine is lost,
      O! how shall I appear?

TO—

I WILL not mourn thee, lovely one,
  Though thou art torn away.
'Tis said that if the morning sun
  Arise with dazzling ray

5   And shed a bright and burning beam
  Athwart the glittering main,
'Ere noon shall fade that laughing gleam
  Engulfed in clouds and rain.

And if thy life as transient proved,
10 It hath been full as bright,
For thou wert hopeful and beloved;
  Thy spirit knew no blight.

If few and short the joys of life
  That thou on earth couldst know,
15 Little thou knew'st of sin and strife
  Nor much of pain and woe.

If vain thy earthly hopes did prove,
  Thou canst not mourn their flight;
Thy brightest hopes were fixed above
20 And they shall know no blight.

And yet I cannot check my sighs,
  Thou wert so young and fair,
More bright than summer morning skies,
  But stern death would not spare;

25 He would not pass our darling by
  Nor grant one hour's delay,
But rudely closed his shining eye
  And frowned his smile away,

The angel smile that late so much
30 Could my fond heart rejoice;
And he has silenced by his touch
  The music of thy voice.

I'll weep no more thine early doom,
    But O! I still must mourn
35 The pleasures buried in thy tomb,
    For they will not return.

MY soul is awakened, my spirit is soaring,
  And carried aloft on the wings of the breeze;
For, above, and around me, the wild wind is roaring
Arousing to rapture the earth and the seas.

5 The long withered grass in the sunshine is glancing,
The bare trees are tossing their branches on high;
The dead leaves beneath them are merrily dancing,
The white clouds are scudding across the blue sky.

I wish I could see how the ocean is lashing
10 The foam of its billows to whirlwinds of spray,
I wish I could see how its proud waves are dashing
And hear the wild roar of their thunder today!

A WORD TO THE CALVINISTS
(A WORD TO THE ELECT)

YOU may rejoice to think yourselves secure,
  You may be grateful for the gift divine,
That grace unsought which made your black hearts pure
And fits your earthborn souls in Heaven to shine.

5 But is it sweet to look around and view
Thousands excluded from that happiness,
Which they deserve at least as much as you,
Their faults not greater nor their virtues less?

And wherefore should you love your God the more
10 Because to you alone his smiles are given,
Because He chose to pass the many o'er
And only bring the favoured few to Heaven?

And wherefore should your hearts more grateful prove
Because for *all* the Saviour did not die?
15   Is yours the God of justice and of love
And are your bosoms warm with charity?

Say does your heart expand to all mankind
And would you ever to your neighbour do,
—The weak, the strong, the enlightened and the blind—
20   As you would have your neighbour do to you?

And when you looking on your fellow men
Behold them doomed to endless misery,
How can you talk of joy and rapture then?
May God withold such cruel joy from me!

25   That none *deserve* eternal bliss I know:
Unmerited the grace in mercy given,
But none shall sink to everlasting woe
That have not well deserved the wrath of Heaven.

And O! there lives within my heart
30   A hope long nursed by me,
(And should its cheering ray depart
How dark my soul would be)

That as in Adam all have died
In Christ shall all men live
35   And ever round his throne abide
Eternal praise to give;

That even the wicked shall at last
Be fitted for the skies
And when their dreadful doom is past
40   To light and life arise.

I ask not how remote the day
Nor what the sinner's woe
Before their dross is purged away,
Enough for me to know

45   That when the cup of wrath is drained,
      The metal purified,
      They'll cling to what they once disdained
      And live by him that died.

THE CAPTIVE DOVE

POOR restless Dove, I pity thee,
      And when I hear thy plaintive moan
I'll mourn for thy captivity
And in thy woes forget mine own.

5   To see thee stand prepared to fly,
      And flap those useless wings of thine,
      And gaze into the distant sky
      Would melt a harder heart than mine.

      In vain! In vain! Thou canst not rise—
10   Thy prison roof confines thee there;
      Its slender wires delude thine eyes,
      And quench thy longing with despair.

      O! thou wert made to wander free
      In sunny mead and shady grove,
15   And far beyond the rolling sea
      In distant climes at will to rove.

      Yet hadst thou but one gentle mate
      Thy little drooping heart to cheer
      And share with thee thy captive state,
20   Thou couldst be happy even there.

      Yes, even there, if listening by
      One faithful dear companion stood,
      While gazing on her full bright eye
      Thou mightst forget thy native wood.

25   But thou, poor solitary dove,
      Must make unheard thy joyless moan;
      The heart that nature formed to love
      Must pine neglected and alone.

MUSIC ON CHRISTMAS MORNING

MUSIC I love—but never strain
Could kindle raptures so divine,
So grief assuage, so conquer pain,
And rouse this pensive heart of mine—
As that we hear on Christmas morn,
Upon the wintry breezes borne.

Though Darkness still her empire keep,
And hours must pass, ere morning break;
From troubled dreams, or slumbers deep,
That music *kindly* bids us wake;
It calls us, with an angel's voice,
To wake, and worship, and rejoice;

To greet with joy the glorious morn,
Which angels welcomed long ago,
When our redeeming Lord was born,
To bring the light of Heaven below;
The Powers of Darkness to dispel,
And rescue Earth from Death and Hell.

While listening to that sacred strain,
My raptured spirit soars on high;
I seem to hear those songs again
Resounding through the open sky,
That kindled such divine delight,
In those who watched their flocks by night.

With them I celebrate His birth—
Glory to God, in highest Heaven,
Good-will to men, and peace on earth,
To us a Saviour-king is given;
Our God is come to claim His own,
And Satan's power is overthrown!

A sinless God, for sinful men,
Descends to suffer and to bleed;
Hell *must* renounce its empire then;
The price is paid, the world is freed,

35   And Satan's self must now confess
      That Christ has earned a *Right* to bless;

      Now holy Peace may smile from heaven,
      And heavenly Truth from earth shall spring;
      The captive's galling bonds are riven,
40   For our Redeemer is our king;
      And He that gave his blood for men
      Will lead us home to God again.

                    HOME

      HOW brightly glistening in the sun
          The woodland ivy plays!
      While yonder beeches from their barks
          Reflect his silver rays.

5   That sun surveys a lovely scene
          From softly smiling skies;
      And wildly through unnumbered trees
          The wind of winter sighs:

      Now loud, it thunders o'er my head,
10   And now in distance dies.
      But give me back my barren hills
          Where colder breezes rise:

      Where scarce the scattered, stunted trees
          Can yield an answering swell,
15   But where a wilderness of heath
          Returns the sound as well.

      For yonder garden, fair and wide,
          With groves of evergreen,
      Long winding walks, and borders trim,
20   And velvet lawns between;

      Restore to me that little spot,
          With gray walls compassed round,
      Where knotted grass neglected lies,
          And weeds usurp the ground.

25 Though all around this mansion high
Invites the foot to roam,
And though its halls are fair within—
Oh, give me back my home!

MEMORY

BRIGHTLY the sun of summer shone
Green fields and waving woods upon
And soft winds wandered by.
Above, a sky of purest blue,
5 Around, bright flowers of loveliest hue
Allured the gazer's eye.

But what were all these charms to me
When one sweet breath of memory
Came gently wafting by?
10 I closed my eyes against the day
And called my willing soul away
From earth and air and sky;

That I might simply fancy there
One little flower—a primrose fair
15 Just opening into sight.
As in the days of infancy,
An opening primrose seemed to me
A source of strange delight.

Sweet memory, ever smile on me;
20 Nature's chief beauties spring from thee,
O, still thy tribute bring.
Still make the golden crocus shine
Among the flowers the most divine,
The glory of the spring.

25 Still in the wall-flower's fragrance dwell,
And hover round the slight bluebell,
My childhood's darling flower.
Smile on the little daisy still,
The buttercup's bright goblet fill
30 With all thy former power.

Forever hang thy dreamy spell
Round golden star and heatherbell,
  And do not pass away
From sparkling frost, or wreathed snow,
And whisper when the wild winds blow
  Or rippling waters play.

Is childhood then so all divine?
Or, memory, is the glory thine
  That haloes thus the past?
Not all divine; its pangs of grief
Although perchance their stay is brief,
  Are bitter while they last.

Nor is the glory all thine own,
For on our earliest joys alone
  That holy light is cast.
With such a ray no spell of thine
Can make our later pleasures shine,
  Though long ago they passed.

FLUCTUATIONS

WHAT though the sun had left my sky;
  To save me from despair
The blessed moon arose on high
  And shone serenely there.

I watched her with a tearful gaze
  Rise slowly o'er the hill;
While through the dim horizon's haze
  Her light gleamed faint and chill.

I thought such wan and lifeless beams
  Could ne'er my heart repay
For the bright sun's most transient gleams
  That cheered me through the day.

But as above that mist's control
  She rose and brighter shone
I felt her light upon my soul,
  But now—that light is gone!

Thick vapours snatched her from my sight
 And I was darkling left,
All in the cold and gloomy night
20 Of light and hope bereft.

Until methought a little star
 Shone forth with trembling ray
To cheer me with its light afar,
 But that too passed away.

25 Anon an earthly meteor blazed
 The gloomy darkness through.
I smiled yet trembled while I gazed,
 But that soon vanished too.

And darker, drearier fell the night
30 Upon my spirit then;
But what is that faint struggling light—
 Is it the moon again?

Kind Heaven, increase that silvery gleam
 And bid these clouds depart;
35 And let her kind and holy beam
 Restore my fainting heart.

THE ARBOUR

I'LL rest me in this sheltered bower,
 And look upon the clear blue sky
That smiles upon me through the trees,
Which stand so thickly clustering by;

5 And view their green and glossy leaves,
All glistening in the sunshine fair;
And list the rustling of their boughs,
So softly whispering through the air.

And while my ear drinks in the sound,
10 My winged soul shall fly away;
Reviewing long departed years
As one mild, beaming, autumn day;

And soaring on to future scenes,
Like hills and woods, and valleys green,
15   All basking in the summer's sun,
But distant still, and dimly seen.

Oh, list! 'tis summer's very breath
That gently shakes the rustling trees—
But look! the snow is on the ground—
20   How can I think of scenes like these?

'Tis but the *frost* that clears the air,
And gives the sky that lovely blue;
They're smiling in a *winter's* sun,
Those evergreens of sombre hue.

25   And winter's chill is on my heart—
How can I dream of future bliss?
How can my spirit soar away,
Confined by such a chain as this?

DREAMS

WHILE on my lonely couch I lie
I seldom feel myself alone,
For fancy fills my dreaming eye
With scenes and pleasures of its own.

5   Then I may cherish at my breast
An infant's form beloved and fair,
May smile, and soothe it into rest
With all a mother's fondest care.

How sweet to feel its helpless form
10   Depending thus on me alone;
And while I hold it safe and warm,
What bliss to think it is my own!

And glances then may meet my eyes
That daylight never showed to me,
15   What raptures in my bosom rise
Those earnest looks of love to see!

To feel my hand so kindly pressed,
To know myself beloved at last,
To think my heart has found a rest,
20   My life of solitude is past.

But then to wake and find it flown,
The dream of happiness destroyed,
To find myself unloved, alone,
What tongue can speak the dreary void?

25   A heart whence warm affections flow,
Creator, thou hast given to me,
And am I only thus to know
How sweet the joys of love would be?

VIEWS OF LIFE

WHEN sinks my heart in hopeless gloom,
   When life can shew no joy for me,
And I behold a yawning tomb
Where bowers and palaces should be,

5   In vain, you talk of morbid dreams,
In vain, you gaily smiling say
That what to me so dreary seems
The healthy mind deems bright and gay.

I too have smiled, and thought like you,
10   But madly smiled, and falsely deemed:
My present thoughts I know are true,
I'm waking now, 'twas then I dreamed.

I lately saw a sunset sky,
And stood enraptured to behold
15   Its varied hues of glorious dye:
First, fleecy clouds of shining gold;

These blushing took a rosy hue;
Beneath them shone a flood of green,
Nor less divine the glorious blue
20   That smiled above them and between:

I cannot name each lovely shade,
I cannot say how bright they shone;
But one by one I saw them fade,
And what remained when they were gone?

25   Dull clouds remained of sombre hue,
And when their borrowed charm was o'er,
The sky grew dull and charmless too
That smiled so softly bright before.

So gilded by the glow of youth
30   Our varied life looks fair and gay,
And so remains the naked truth
When that false light is past away.

Why blame ye, then, my keener sight
That clearly sees a world of woes
35   Through all the haze of golden light
That flattering Falsehood round it throws?

When the young mother smiles above
The first born darling of her heart
Her bosom glows with earnest love
40   While tears of speechless rapture start.

Fond dreamer! little does she know
The anxious toil, the suffering,
The blasted hopes, the burning woe,
The object of her joy will bring.

45   Her blinded eyes behold not now
What soon or late must be his doom,
The anguish that will cloud his brow,
The bed of death, the dreary tomb.

As little know the youthful pair
50   In mutual love supremely blest
What weariness and cold despair
Ere long will seize the aching breast.

And even should love and faith remain
(The greatest blessings life can show)
55 Amid adversity and pain
To shine throughout with cheering glow,

They do not see how cruel death
Comes on, their loving hearts to part;
One feels not now the gasping breath,
60 The rending of the earthbound heart,

The soul's and body's agony,
Ere she may sink to her repose;
The sad survivor cannot see
The grave above his darling close,

65 Nor how, despairing and alone,
He then must wear his life away
And linger feebly toiling on,
And fainting sink into decay.

O, youth may listen patiently,
70 While sad experience tells her tale;
But doubt sits smiling in his eye,
For ardent hope will still prevail.

He hears how feeble Pleasure dies,
By guilt destroyed, and pain and woe;
75 He turns to Hope—and she replies
'Believe it not—it is not so!'

'O! heed her not', experience says,
'For thus she whispered once to me;
She told me in my youthful days
80 How glorious manhood's prime would be.

'When in the time of early Spring
Too chill the winds that o'er me passed,
She said each coming day would bring
A fairer heaven, a gentler blast.

85   'And when the sun too seldom beamed,
They sky o'ercast too darkly frowned,
The frequent rain too constant streamed,
And mists too dreary gathered round,

      'She told me summer's glorious ray
90   Would chase those vapours all away,
       And scatter glories round,
With sweetest music fill the trees,
Load with rich scent the gentle breeze
       And strew with flowers the ground.

95   'But when beneath that scorching sky
I languished weary through the day
       While birds refused to sing,
Verdure decayed from field and tree,
And panting nature mourned with me
100   The freshness of the spring.

      "Wait but a little while", she said,
      "Till summer's burning days are fled,
       And Autumn shall restore
With golden riches of her own,
105   And summer's glories mellowed down
       The freshness you deplore."

      'And long I waited, but in vain;
That freshness never came again,
       Though summer passed away,
110   Though Autumn's mists hung cold and chill
And drooping nature languished still,
       And sank into decay;

      'Till wintry blasts foreboding blew
Through leafless trees—and then I knew
115   That hope was all a dream.
But thus, fond youth, she cheated me,
And she will prove as false to thee,
       Though sweet her words may seem.'

Stern prophet! cease thy bodings dire—
120 Thou canst not quench the ardent fire
 That warms the breast of youth.
O! let it cheer him while it may,
And gently, gently, die away
 Chilled by the damps of truth.

125 Tell him that earth is not our rest,
Its joys are empty, frail at best;
 And point beyond the sky;
But gleams of light may reach us here,
And hope the *roughest* path can cheer:
130 Then do not bid it fly.

Though hope may promise joys that still
Unkindly time will ne'er fulfil;
 Or if they come at all,
We never find them unalloyed—
135 Hurtful perchance, or soon destroyed,
 They vanish or they pall.

Yet hope itself a brightness throws
O'er all our labours and our woes,
 While dark foreboding care
140 A thousand ills will oft portend
That Providence may ne'er intend
 The trembling heart to bear.

Or if they come, it oft appears,
Our woes are lighter than our fears,
145 And far more strongly borne.
Then let us not enhance our doom,
But e'en in midnight's blackest gloom
 Expect the rising morn.

Because the road is rough and long,
150 Shall we despise the skylark's song,
 That cheers the wanderer's way?
Or trample down, with reckless feet
The smiling flowerets bright and sweet
 Because they soon decay?

155 Pass pleasant scenes unnoticed by,
Because the next is bleak and drear;
Or not enjoy a smiling sky
Because a tempest may be near?

No! while we journey on our way,
160 We'll notice every lovely thing,
And ever as they pass away,
To memory and hope we'll cling.

And though that awful river flows
Before us when the journey's past,
165 Perchance of all the pilgrim's woes
Most dreadful, shrink not—'tis the last!

Though icy cold, and dark, and deep;
Beyond it smiles that blessed shore
Where none shall suffer, none shall weep,
170 And bliss shall reign for evermore.

VANITAS VANITATIS ETC.

IN all we do, and hear, and see,
Is restless toil and vanity;
While yet the rolling earth abides,
Men come and go like Ocean tides;
5 And ere one generation dies,
Another in its place shall rise.
That sinking soon into the grave,
Others succeed, like wave on wave;
And as they rise, they pass away.
10 The sun arises every day,
And hastening onward to the west
He nightly sinks but not to rest;
Returning to the eastern skies,
Again to light us he must rise.
15 And still the restless wind comes forth
Now blowing keenly from the north,
Now from the south, the east, the west;
Forever changing, ne'er at rest.

The fountains, gushing from the hills,
Supply the ever-running rills;
The thirsty rivers drink their store,
And bear it rolling to the shore,
But still the ocean craves for more.
'Tis endless labour everywhere,
Sound cannot satisfy the ear,
Sight cannot fill the craving eye,
Nor riches happiness supply,
Pleasure but doubles future pain;
And joy brings sorrow in her train.
Laughter is mad, and reckless mirth,
What does she in this weary earth?
Should wealth or fame our life employ,
Death comes our labour to destroy,
To snatch th'untasted cup away,
For which we toiled so many a day.
What then remains for wretched man?
To use life's comforts while he can:
Enjoy the blessings God bestows,
Assist his friends, forgive his foes,
Trust God, and keep His statutes still
Upright and firm, through good and ill—
Thankful for all that God has given,
Fixing his firmest hopes on Heaven;
Knowing that earthly joys decay,
But hoping through the darkest day.

THE PENITENT (FRAGMENT)

I MOURN with thee and yet rejoice
That thou shouldst sorrow so;
With Angel choirs I join my voice
To bless the sinner's woe.

Though friends and kindred turn away
And laugh thy grief to scorn,
I hear the great Redeemer say
'Blessed are ye that mourn'.

Hold on thy course nor deem it strange
    That earthly cords are riven.
10   Man may lament the wondrous change
    But 'There is joy in Heaven'!

MONDAY NIGHT, MAY 11th 1846

WHY should such gloomy silence reign;
    And why is all the house so drear,
When neither danger, sickness, pain,
Nor death, nor want have entered here?

5   We are as many as we were
That other night, when all were gay,
And full of hope, and free from care;
Yet, is there something gone away.

The moon without as pure and calm
10   Is shining as that night she shone;
But now, to us she brings no balm,
For something from our hearts is gone.

Something whose absence leaves a void,
A cheerless want in every heart.
15   Each feels the bliss of all destroyed
And mourns the change—but each apart.

The fire is burning in the grate
As redly as it used to burn,
But still the hearth is desolate
20   Till Mirth and Love with *Peace* return.

'Twas *Peace* that flowed from heart to heart
With looks and smiles that spoke of Heaven,
And gave us language to impart
The blissful thoughts itself had given.

25   Sweet child of Heaven, and joy of earth!
O, when will Man thy value learn?
We rudely drove thee from our hearth,
And vainly sigh for thy return.

SEVERED and gone, so many years!
And art thou still so dear to me,
That throbbing heart and burning tears
Can witness how I clung to thee?

5 I know that in the narrow tomb
The form I loved was buried deep,
And left, in silence and in gloom,
To slumber out its dreamless sleep.

I know the corner, where it lies,
10 Is but a dreary place of rest:
The charnel moisture never dries
From the dark flagstones o'er its breast,

For there the sunbeams never shine,
Nor ever breathes the freshening air,
15 —But not for this do I repine;
For my beloved is not there.

O, no! I do not think of thee
As festering there in slow decay:—
'Tis this sole thought oppresses me,
20 That thou are gone so far away.

For ever gone; for I, by night,
Have prayed, within my silent room,
That Heaven would grant a burst of light
Its cheerless darkness to illume;

25 And give thee to my longing eyes,
A moment, as thou shinest now,
Fresh from thy mansion in the skies,
With all its glories on thy brow.

Wild was the wish, intense the gaze
30 I fixed upon the murky air,
Expecting, half, a kindling blaze
Would strike my raptured vision there,—

A shape these human nerves would thrill,
A majesty that might appal,
35   Did not thy earthly likeness, still,
Gleam softly, gladly, through it all.

False hope! vain prayer! it might not be
That thou shouldst visit earth again.
I called on Heaven—I called on thee,
40   And watched, and waited—all in vain.

Had I one shining tress of thine,
How it would bless these longing eyes!
Or if thy pictured form were mine,
What gold should rob me of the prize?

45   A few cold words on yonder stone,
A corpse as cold as they can be—
Vain words, and mouldering dust, alone—
Can this be all that's left of thee?

O, no! thy spirit lingers still
50   Where'er thy sunny smile was seen:
There's less of darkness, less of chill
On earth, than if thou hadst not been.

Thou breathest in my bosom yet,
And dwellest in my beating heart;
55   And, while I cannot quite forget,
Thou, darling, canst not quite depart.

Though, freed from sin, and grief, and pain
Thou drinkest now the bliss of Heaven,
Thou didst not visit earth in vain;
60   And from us, yet, thou art not riven.

Life seems more sweet that thou didst live,
And men more true that thou wert one:
Nothing is lost that thou didst give,
Nothing destroyed that thou hast done.

65 Earth hath received thine earthly part;
Thine heavenly flame has heavenward flown;
But both still linger in my heart,
Still live, and not in mine alone.

THE THREE GUIDES

SPIRIT of earth! thy hand is chill.
I've felt its icy clasp;
And shuddering I remember still
   That stony-hearted grasp.
5 Thine eye bids love and joy depart,
   O turn its gaze from me!
It presses down my sinking heart;—
   I will not walk with thee!

'Wisdom is mine', I've heard thee say,
10   'Beneath my searching eye,
All mist and darkness melt away,
   Phantoms and fables fly.
Before me, truth can stand alone,
   The naked, solid truth;
15 And man matured my worth will own,
   If I am shunned by youth.

'Firm is my tread, and sure, though slow:
   My footsteps never slide;
And he that follows me shall know
20   I am the surest guide.'
Thy boast is vain; but were it true
   That thou couldst safely steer
Life's rough and devious pathway through
   Such guidance I should fear.

25 How could I bear to walk for aye,
   With eyes to earthward prone,
O'er trampled weeds, and miry clay,
   And sand, and flinty stone.
Never the glorious view to greet
30   Of hill and dale and sky,
To see that Nature's charms are sweet
   Or feel that Heaven is nigh?

If, in my heart arose a spring—
   A gush of thought divine,
At once stagnation thou wouldst bring
   With that cold touch of thine!
If glancing up, I sought to snatch
   But one glimpse of the sky,
My baffled gaze would only catch
   Thy heartless, cold grey eye.

If, to the breezes wandering near,
   I listened eagerly,
And deemed an angel's tongue to hear
   That whispered hope to me,
That heavenly music would be drowned
   In thy harsh, droning voice,
Nor inward thought, nor sight, nor sound
   Might my sad soul rejoice.

Dull is thine ear; unheard by thee
   The still small voice of Heaven.
Thine eyes are dim, and cannot see
   The helps that God has given.
There is a bridge, o'er every flood,
   Which thou canst not perceive,
A path, through every tangled wood;
   But thou wilt not believe.

Striving to make thy way by force,
   Toil-spent and bramble torn,
Thou'lt fell the tree that stops thy course,
   And burst through briar and thorn;
And pausing by the river's side,
   Poor reasoner, thou wilt deem,
By casting pebbles in its tide
   To cross the swelling stream.

Right through the flinty rock thou'lt try
   Thy toilsome way to bore,
Regardless of the pathway nigh
   That would conduct thee o'er.
Not only art thou, then, unkind,

70   And freezing cold to me,
       But unbelieving, deaf, and blind—
         I will not walk with thee!

       Spirit of Pride! thy wings are strong;
         Thine eyes like lightning shine;
75   Ecstatic joys to thee belong
         And powers almost divine.
       But 'tis a false destructive blaze,
         Within those eyes I see,
       Turn hence their fascinating gaze—
80   I will not follow thee!

       'Coward and fool!' thou mayst reply;
         'Walk on the common sod;
       Go trace, with timid foot and eye,
         The steps by others trod.
85   'Tis best the beaten path to keep,
         The ancient faith to hold,
       To pasture with thy fellow sheep,
         And lie within the fold.

       'Cling to the earth, poor grovelling worm,
90   'Tis not for thee to soar
       Against the fury of the storm,
         Amid the thunder's roar.
       There's glory in that daring strife
         Unknown, undreamt by thee;
95   There's speechless rapture in the life
         Of those who follow me!'

       Yes; I have seen thy votaries oft,
         Upheld by thee their guide,
       In strength and courage mount aloft
100   The steepy mountain-side;
       I've seen them stand against the sky,
         And gazing from below
       Beheld thy lightning in their eye,
         Thy triumph on their brow.

105   Oh! I have felt what glory then—
         What transport must be theirs;
       So far above their fellow men,
         Above their toils and cares,
       Inhaling nature's purest breath,
110   Her riches round them spread,
       The wide expanse of earth beneath,
         Heaven's glories overhead!

       But—I have seen them downwards dashed,
         Down to a bloody grave;
115   And still thy ruthless eye has flashed,
         Thy strong hand did not save!
       I've seen some o'er the mountain's brow
         Sustained a while by thee,
       O'er rocks of ice and hills of snow
120   Bound fearless, wild, and free.

       Bold and exultant was their mien
         While thou didst cheer them on;
       But evening fell—and then, I ween,
         Their faithless guide was gone.
125   Alas! how fared thy favourites then—
         Lone, helpless, weary, cold—
       Did ever wanderer find again
         The path he left of old?

       Where is their glory, where the pride
130   That swelled their hearts before;
       Where now the courage that defied
         The mightiest tempest's roar?
       What shall they do when night grows black,
         When angry storms arise?
135   Who now will lead them to the track
         Thou taught'st them to despise?

       Spirit of Pride! it needs not this
         To make me shun thy wiles,
       Renounce thy triumph and thy bliss,
140   Thy honours and thy smiles.
       Bright as thou art, and bold, and strong,

That fierce glance wins not me,
And I abhor thy scoffing tongue—
  I will not walk with thee!

145 Spirit of Faith! be thou my guide,
    O, clasp my hand in thine,
And let me never quit thy side:
    Thy comforts are divine!
Earth calls thee 'blind misguided one',
150   But who can show like thee
Past things that have been seen and done,
    And things that are to be?

Secrets concealed from Nature's ken,
    Who like thee can declare;
155 Or who like thee to erring men
    God's holy will can bear?
Pride scorns thee for thy lowly mien;
    But who like thee can rise
Above this restless, clouded scene,—
160   Beyond the holy skies?

Meek is thine eye and soft thy voice
    But wondrous is thy might
To make the wretched soul rejoice,
    To give the simple light.
165 And still to all that seek thy way,
    Such magic power is given—
E'en while their footsteps press the clay
    Their souls ascend to heaven.

Danger surrounds them, pain and woe
170   Their portion here must be;
But only they that trust thee know
    What comfort dwells with thee,
Strength to sustain their drooping powers
    And vigour to defend.
175 Thou pole-star of my darkest hours,
    Affliction's firmest friend!

Day does not always mark our way;
  Night's terrors oft appal,
But lead me, and I cannot stray;
  Hold me: I shall not fall;
180 Sustain me, I shall never faint,
  How rough soe'er may be
My upward road,—nor moan nor plaint
  Shall mar my trust in thee.

185 Narrow the path by which we go;
  And oft it turns aside,
From pleasant meads where roses blow
  And murmuring waters glide;
Where flowery turf lies green and soft,
190   And gentle gales are sweet,
To where dark mountains frown aloft,
  Hard rocks distress the feet.

Deserts beyond lie bleak and bare,
  And keen winds round us blow;
195 But if thy hands conduct me there,
  The way is right, I know.
I have no wish to turn away:
  My spirit does not quail.
How can it while I hear thee say,
200   'Press forward—and prevail'?

Even above the tempest's swell,
  I hear thy voice of love.
Of hope and peace I hear thee tell,
  And that blest home above.
205 Through pain and death, I can rejoice,
  If but thy strength be mine.
Earth hath no music like thy voice;
  Life owns no joy like thine!

Spirit of Faith! I'll go with thee:
210   Thou, if I hold thee fast,
Wilt guide, defend, and strengthen me,
  And bring me home at last.
By thy help, all things I can do;
  In thy strength all things bear.
215 Teach me, for thou art just and true,
  Smile on me,—thou art fair!

SELF-COMMUNION

'THE mist is resting on the hill;
   The smoke is hanging in the air;
The very clouds are standing still;
A breathless calm broods everywhere.
Thou pilgrim through this vale of tears
Thou, too, a little moment cease
Thy anxious toil and fluttering fears,
And rest thee, for a while, in peace.'

'I would, but Time keeps working still
And moving on for good or ill:
   He will not rest nor stay,
In pain or ease, in smiles or tears,
   He still keeps adding to my years
   And stealing life away,
His footsteps in the ceaseless sound
   Of yonder clock, I seem to hear,
That through this stillness so profound
   Distinctly strikes the vacant ear,
   For ever striding on and on
He pauses not by night or day;
And all my life will soon be gone
As these past years have slipped away.
He took my childhood long ago,
And then my early youth; and lo,
   He steals away my prime!
I cannot see how fast it goes,
But well my inward spirit knows
   The wasting power of time.'

'Time steals thy moments, drinks thy breath,
Changes and wastes thy mortal frame;
But though he gives the clay to death,
He cannot touch the inward flame.
Nay, though he steals thy years away,
Their memory is left thee still,
And every month and every day
Leaves some effect of good or ill.

The wise will find in Memory's store
A help for that which lies before
        To guide their course aright;
40   Then, hush thy plaints and calm thy fears;
Look back on these departed years,
        And, say, what meets thy sight?'

'I see, far back, a helpless child,
Feeble and full of causeless fears,
45   Simple and easily beguiled
        To credit all it hears.
More timid than the wild wood-dove
Yet trusting to another's care,
And finding in protecting love
50   Its only refuge from despair,—
Its only balm for every woe,
The only bliss its soul can know:—
        Still hiding in its breast
A tender heart too prone to weep,
55   A love so earnest, strong and deep
        It could not be expressed.

Poor helpless thing! what can it do
Life's stormy cares and toils among;—
How tread this weary desert through
60   That awes the brave and tires the strong?
Where shall it centre so much trust
Where truth maintains so little sway,
Where seeming fruit is bitter dust,
And kisses oft to death betray?
65   How oft must sin and falsehood grieve
A heart so ready to believe
        And willing to admire!
With strength so feeble, fears so strong,
Amid this selfish bustling throng,
70   How will it faint and tire!

That tender love so warm and deep,
        How can it flourish here below?
What bitter floods of tears must steep
The strong soil where it would grow!

75 O earth! a rocky breast is thine—
A hard soil and a cruel clime,
Where tender plants must droop and pine,
Or alter with transforming time.
That soul, that clings to sympathy
80 As ivy clasps the forest tree,
How can it stand alone?
That heart so prone to overflow
E'en at the *thought* of other's woe,
How will it bear its own?

85 How, if a sparrow's death can wring
Such bitter tearfloods from the eye,
Will it behold the suffering
Of struggling, lost humanity?
The torturing pain, the pining grief,
90 The sin-degraded misery,
The anguish that defies relief?'

'Look back again—What dost thou see?'

'I see one kneeling on the sod,
With infant hands upraised to Heaven,
95 A young heart feeling after God,
Oft baffled, never backward driven.
Mistaken oft, and oft astray,
It strives to find the narrow way
But gropes and toils alone:
100 That inner life of strife and tears,
Of kindling hopes and lowering fears,
To none but God is known.
'Tis better thus: for *man* would scorn
Those childish prayers, those artless cries,
105 That darkling spirit tossed and torn,
But *God* will not despise!
We may regret such waste of tears,
Such darkly toiling misery,
Such wildering doubts and harrowing fears,
110 Where joy and thankfulness should be;
But wait, and Heaven will send relief.
Let patience have her perfect work:

Lo, strength and wisdom spring from grief
And joys behind afflictions lurk!

115　It asked for light, and it is heard;
God grants that struggling soul repose;
And, guided by his holy word,
It wiser than its teachers grows.
It gains the upward path at length,
120　And passes on from strength to strength,
　　Leaning on Heaven the while:
Night's shades departing one by one,
It sees at last the rising sun,
And feels his cheering smile.
125　In all its darkness and distress
For light it sought, to God it cried;
And through the pathless wilderness,
He was its comfort and its guide.'

'So was it, and so will it be;
130　Thy God will guide and strengthen thee;
　　His goodness cannot fail.
The sun that on thy morning rose
Will light thee to the evening's close,
　　Whatever storms assail.'

135　'*God* alters not; but Time on me
A wide and wondrous change has wrought;
And in these parted years I see
Cause for grave care and saddening thought,
I see that time, and toil, and truth
140　An inward hardness can impart,—
Can freeze the generous blood of youth,
And steel full fast the tender heart.'

'Bless God for that divine decree!—
That hardness comes with misery,
145　And suffering deadens pain;
That at the frequent sight of woe
E'en pity's tears forget to flow,
If reason still remain!
Reason, with conscience by her side

150
But gathers strength from toil and truth;
And she will prove a surer guide
Than those sweet instincts of our youth.
Thou that hast known such anguish sore
In weeping where thou couldst not bless,
155
Canst *thou* that softness so deplore—
That suffering, shrinking tenderness?
Thou that hast felt what cankering care
A loving heart is doomed to bear,
    Say, how canst *thou* regret
160
That fires unfed must fall away,
Long droughts can dry the softest clay,
    And cold will cold beget?'

'Nay, but 'tis hard to *feel* that chill
Come creeping o'er the shuddering heart,
165
Love may be full of pain, but still,
'Tis sad to see it so depart,—
To watch that fire, whose genial glow
Was formed to comfort and to cheer,
For want of fuel, fading so,
170
Sinking to embers dull and drear,—
To see the soft soil turned to stone
    For lack of kindly showers,—
To see those yearnings of the breast,
Pining to bless and to be blessed,
175
Drop withered, frozen one by one,
Till centred in itself alone,
    It wastes its blighted powers.

Oh, I have known a wondrous joy
In early friendship's pure delight,—
180
A genial bliss that could not cloy—
My sun by day, my moon by night.
Absence, indeed, was sore distress,
And thought of death was anguish keen,
And there was cruel bitterness
185
When jarring discords rose between;
And sometimes it was grief to know
My fondness was but half returned.
But this was nothing to the woe

With which another truth was learned:—
190 That I must check, or nurse apart
Full many an impulse of the heart
    And many a darling thought:
What my soul worshipped, sought, and prized,
Were slighted, questioned, or despised;—
195   This pained me more than aught.
And as my love the warmer glowed
The deeper would that anguish sink,
That this dark stream between us flowed,
Though both stood bending o'er its brink.
200 Until, at last, I learned to bear
A colder heart within my breast;
To share such thoughts as I could share,
    And calmly keep the rest.
I saw that they were sundered now,
205 The trees that at the root were one:
They yet might mingle leaf and bough,
But still the stems must stand alone.

O love is sweet of every kind!
'Tis sweet the helpless to befriend,
210 To watch the young unfolding mind,
To guide, to shelter, and defend;
To lavish tender toil and care,
And ask for nothing back again,
But that our smiles a blessing bear,
215 And all our toil be not in vain.
And sweeter far than words can tell
Their love whose ardent bosoms swell
    With thoughts they need not hide;
Where fortune frowns not on their joy,
220 And Prudence seeks not to destroy,
    Nor Reason to deride.
Whose love may freely gush and flow,
Unchecked, unchilled by doubt or fear,
For in their inmost hearts they know
225 It is not vainly nourished there.
They know that in a kindred breast
Their long desires have found a home
Where heart and soul may kindly rest

Weary and lorn no more to roam.
230   Their dreams of bliss were not in vain,
As they love they are loved again,
And they can bless as they are blessed.

O vainly might I seek to show
The joys from happy love that flow!
235   The warmest words are all too cold
The secret transports to unfold
Of simplest word or softest sigh,
Or from the glancing of an eye
      To say what rapture beams;
240   One look that bids our fears depart,
And well assures the trusting heart
It beats not in the world alone—
Such speechless raptures I have known,
      But only in my dreams.

245   My life has been a morning sky
Where Hope her rainbow glories cast
O'er kindling vapours far and nigh:
And, if the colours faded fast
Ere one bright hue had died away
250   Another o'er its ashes gleamed;
And if the lower clouds were grey,
The mists above more brightly beamed,
But not for long;—at length, behold,
Those tints less warm, less radiant grew,
255   Till but one streak of paly gold
Glimmered through clouds of saddening hue.
And I am calmly waiting, now,
To see that also pass away,
And leave, above the dark hill's brow
260   A rayless arch of sombre grey.'

'So must it fare with all thy race
Who seek in earthly things their joy:
So fading hopes lost hopes shall chase,
      Till Disappointment all destroy.
265   But they that fix their hopes on high
Shall, in the blue refulgent sky,

The sun's transcendent light,
Behold a purer, deeper glow
Than these uncertain gleams shall show,
    However fair or bright.
270
O weak of heart! why thus deplore
That Truth will Fancy's dreams destroy?
Did I not tell thee, years before,
Life was for labour, not for joy?
275
Cease, selfish spirit, to repine;
O'er thine own ills no longer grieve;
Lo, there are sufferings worse than thine,
Which thou mayst labour to relieve.
If Time indeed too swiftly flies,
280
Gird on thine armour, haste, arise,
    For thou hast much to do;—
To lighten woe, to trample sin,
And foes without and foes within
    To combat and subdue.
285
Earth hath too much of sin and pain;
The bitter cup—the binding chain
    Dost thou indeed lament?
Let not thy weary spirit sink;
But strive—not by one drop or link
290
    The evil to augment.
Strive rather thou, by peace and joy,
The bitter poison to destroy,
    The cruel chain to break,
O strive! and if thy strength be small,
295
Strive yet the more, and spend it all
    For Love and Wisdom's sake!'

'O I have striven both hard and long
But many are my foes and strong,
My gains are light—my progress slow;
300
For hard's the way I have to go,
And my worst enemies, I know
    Are those within my breast;
And it is hard to toil for aye,—
Through sultry noon and twilight grey
305
    To toil and never rest.'

'There is a rest beyond the grave'
A lasting rest from pain and sin,
Where dwell the faithful and the brave;
But they must strive who seek to win.'
'Show me that rest—I ask no more.
O drive these gloomy mists away;
And let me see that sunny shore,
However far away!
However wide this rolling sea,
However wild my passage be,
Howe'er my bark be tempest tossed,
May it but reach that haven fair,
May I but land and wander there,
With those that I have loved and lost;
With such a glorious hope in view,
I'll gladly toil and suffer too.
Rest *without* toil I would not ask;
I would not shun the hardest task:
Toil is my glory—Grief my gain,
If God's approval they obtain.
Could I but hear my Saviour say,—
"I know thy patience and thy love;
How thou has held the narrow way,
For my sake laboured night and day,
And watched, and striven with them that strove;
And still hast borne, and didst not faint",—
Oh, this would be reward indeed!'

'Press forward, then, without complaint;
Labour and love—and such shall be thy meed.'

BELIEVE not those who say
The upward path is smooth,
Lest thou shouldst stumble in the way
And faint before the truth.

It is the only road
Unto the realms of joy;
But he who seeks that blest abode
Must all his powers employ.

310
315
320
325
330
5

Bright hopes and pure delights
Upon his course may beam,
And there amid the sternest heights,
The sweetest flowerets gleam;—

On all her breezes borne
Earth yields no scents like those;
But he, that dares not grasp the thorn
Should never crave the rose.

Arm, arm thee for the fight!
Cast useless loads away:
Watch through the darkest hours of night;
Toil through the hottest day.

Crush pride into the dust,
Or thou must needs be slack;
And trample down rebellious lust,
Or it will hold thee back.

Seek not thy treasure here;
Waive pleasure and renown;
The World's dread scoff undaunted bear,
And face its deadliest frown.

To labour and to love,
To pardon and endure,
To lift thy heart to God above,
And keep thy conscience pure,—

Be this thy constant aim,
Thy hope and thy delight,—
What matters who should whisper blame,
Or who should scorn or slight?

What matters—if thy God approve,
And if within thy breast,
Thou feel the comfort of his love,
The earnest of his rest?

A DREADFUL darkness closes in
     On my bewildered mind;
O let me suffer and not sin,
     Be tortured yet resigned.

Through all this world of whelming mist
     Still let me look to Thee,
And give me courage to resist
     The Tempter till he flee.

Weary I am—O give me strength
     And leave me not to faint;
Say Thou wilt comfort me at length
     And pity my complaint.

I've begged to serve Thee heart and soul,
     To sacrifice to Thee
No niggard portion, but the whole
     Of my identity.

I hoped amid the brave and strong
     My portioned task might lie,
To toil amid the labouring throng
     With purpose pure and high.

But Thou hast fixed another part,
     And Thou hast fixed it well;
I said so with my breaking heart
     When first the anguish fell.

For Thou hast taken my delight
     And hope of life away,
And bid me watch the painful night
     And wait the weary day.

The hope and the delight were Thine;
     I bless Thee for their loan;
I gave Thee while I deemed them mine
     Too little thanks, I own.

Shall I with joy Thy blessings share
  And not endure their loss?
35 Or hope the martyr's crown to wear
  And cast away the cross?

These weary hours will not be lost,
  These days of passive misery,
These nights of darkness anguish tost
40   If I can fix my heart on Thee.

Weak and weary though I lie,
  Crushed with sorrow, worn with pain,
Still I may lift to Heaven mine eyes
  And strive and labour not in vain,

45 That inward strife against the sins
  That ever wait on suffering;
To watch and strike where first begins
  Each ill that would corruption bring,

50 That secret labour to sustain
  With humble patience every blow,
To gather fortitude from pain
  And hope and holiness from woe.

Thus let me serve Thee from my heart
  Whatever be my written fate,
55 Whether thus early to depart
  Or yet awhile to wait.

If Thou shouldst bring me back to life
  More humbled I should be;
More wise, more strengthened for the strife,
60   More apt to lean on Thee.

Should Death be standing at the gate
  Thus should I keep my vow;
But, Lord, whate'er my future fate
  So let me serve Thee now.

NOTES

CHARLOTTE BRONTË'S POEMS

p. 1 *Pleasure (A Short Poem or else not say I)* 'True pleasure breathes not city air'
Dated 8 February 1830.
This poem is a tribute to Charlotte's precocity as she was not yet fifteen when she wrote it. It is not particularly profound in thought or in language, but it is interesting to note the combination of the eighteenth-century praise of rural life (cf. Thomson's *Seasons*) and the romantic view of Nature as an inspiring force. We also see Charlotte's capacity to lose herself in dreaming, a capacity to which she constantly refers in both prose and poetry during the next ten years.

p. 2 *The Vision (A Short Poem)* 'The gentle showery Spring had passed away'
Dated 13 April 1830.
The influence of Wordsworth is here marked. Wordsworth was educated at the same Cambridge college as Mr Brontë, and the closeness to Haworth of the Lake District must have made him a special favourite of the Brontës, although Branwell's efforts in 1837 to interest Wordsworth in his poetry were unsuccessful. This poem was criticized by Branwell for being a repetition of earlier trifling efforts.

p. 4 *Matin* 'Long hath earth lain beneath the dark profound'
Dated 12 November 1830.
This poem is more pretentious and less successful. The second line, evoking an image of night as some stealthy night bird, is particularly unfortunate. The context of the poem is the love affair between the Marquis of Douro and Marian Hume, the daughter of his father's Scots physician, a recurring theme in Charlotte's prose and poetry during this period. Charlotte is never very successful with feminine rhymes, but it is possible to excuse some of her more exuberant words like 'umbrageous' as youthful excrescences, although the word recurs in *Villette*.

p. 6 *St John in the Island of Patmos* 'The holy exile lies all desolate'
Dated 30 August 1832.
For the text of this poem we are dependent upon a copy by Mr Nicholls. Mr Nicholls made copies of other poems for which we have the original, and he can be shown, unlike other editors, to have been a fairly faithful copyist. He may have tried to exercise a little editorial licence in crossing through the sixth stanza which might seem to refer to John the Baptist rather than John the Apostle, here clearly accepted as the author of the Book of Revelation. If Mr Nicholls's date for this poem is correct, it was written shortly after Charlotte's return from Roe Head. The year at Roe Head had interrupted the Angrian narrative, and, for some time after her return, Charlotte wrote comparatively little. This poem is on a religious rather than an Angrian theme, although the imagery used to describe the Apocalypse is a useful reminder that the world of Angria and the world of Charlotte's religious teaching were not all that far removed.

p. 8 'The cloud of recent death is past away'
Dated 27 November 1832.
The *Times Literary Supplement* (4 January 1907) entitled this poem *Lines on Bewick*. The painter Bewick died in 1828. These technically correct verses, written at a time when

Charlotte appeared to have not much interest in Angria, are principally interesting for students of *Jane Eyre*, where there is more than one reference to Bewick's paintings of birds. As this poem and the first chapter of *Jane Eyre* show, these pictures were not just of interest to ornithologists, but were a source of inspiration to all artists because of the dramatic landscape in which the birds were portrayed. When later Jane paints some strange pictures which Rochester studies, some might detect a strong resemblance between her portrait of the cormorant holding a bracelet in a scene of a storm at sea, and the twelfth and thirteenth stanzas of this poem.

p. 11 'O Hyle! thy waves are like Babylon's streams'
Undated, but around February 1833.
This poem was appended to *The African Queen's Lament*, a prose story in which the Duke of Wellington expresses his fear that the African tribes he has subdued may rise up in vengeance for their previous defeat. His anxieties are well founded, as Percy allies with the Africans under Quashia to make an attack on the Glass Town Federation. The Africans are compared to the Jews in captivity, the story of which Charlotte would know as a result of reading not only the Bible, but also Byron's *Hebrew Melodies*, more flagrantly plagiarized by Branwell. The comparison is odd, as is Charlotte's failure to spell Hyle consistently.

p. 11 'Justine, upon thy silent tomb the dews of evening weep'
Undated, but around February 1833.
Zamorna recalls his dead nurse, mother of his mistress, Mina Laury. Byronic guilt, the yearning for love, and a wish to return to childhood innocence, recurring themes in all the Brontës' works, are conspicuous in this poem, in which Charlotte handles the long line with more success than usual.

p. 13 *The Red Cross Knight* 'To the desert sands of Palestine'
Dated 2 October 1833.
This poem appears to take an oldfashioned view both of the Crusades and European colonialism in Africa, linked as Christian missions against the heathen. It should not, however, be taken too seriously, as John Gifford, named in the seventh stanza, is a Glass Town antiquarian, whose work is here being satirized by the Marquis of Douro. He is probably based on the real William Gifford, attacked by Byron in *English Bards and Scotch Reviewers*.

p. 15 *Lament* 'Lament for the Martyr who dies for his faith'
Dated 28 November 1834.
This poem has no particular merit, but has a certain interest because of the variety of interpretations placed upon it. Originally published in 1916 without the final twenty-one lines, it was used to show that the soldier dying in battle was as much a martyr as St Stephen and Socrates. It is difficult to know what Charlotte would have thought of her poem being used as First World War propaganda. Dr Alexander sees this poem as evidence for Charlotte's interest in religion, even in her juvenile writings, but, though the references to St Stephen and Socrates seem fairly clear, the newly published last section of the poem casts doubt on any Christian interpretation. Percy is clearly an Angrian character, probably Henry Percy, murdered by his father, the wicked Northangerland, as we learn in a poem of 15 June 1834. Maria Stuart is harder to identify. There are Stuarts in Angria, although they do not play a very important role. Henry's mother was called Maria, but she was hardly a traitress, and her surname was not Stuart. There is of course

one famous Maria Stuart, connected with martyrs, the wife of Charles I, and the mention of both Scotland and France might suggest that Charlotte's romantic and Royalist feelings were drawn to this particular martyr throughout the poem.

p. 17 *Memory* 'When the dead in their cold graves are lying'
Dated 13 February, 2 August and 2 October 1835.
Charlotte copied out this poem three times in 1835, the year in which she left for three years as a teacher at Roe Head. The two later versions are in the Berg Collection, New York and Beinecke Collection, Yale; owing to an error in the Abbreviations section of my edition of *The Poems of Charlotte Brontë*, this is not clear, and I make haste to remedy the omission. The context of the poem is not clear, but it is possible, as with the more famous 'We wove a web in childhood', to see this poem as representing an important watershed in Charlotte's attitude to her Angrian creations.

p. 18 'We wove a web in childhood'
Dated 19 December 1835.
This is perhaps Charlotte's most famous poem. It was written out during her first holidays at home, but the feelings expressed are those felt at Roe Head. Charlotte's homesickness is well reflected in lines 49–52, and her use of Angrian visions as an escape from the humble realities of life as a teacher is shown in a prose note to this poem, describing how she was awakened from dreaming about Zamorna by Miss Lister thrusting her little rough black head into her face. In her subsequent years at Roe Head until 1838 Charlotte wrote a great deal of poetry alluding to the gap between poetic fancy and mundane fact. Much of the poetry is incoherent, as vision follows vision, and the prose reflects a growing disturbance at the hold Charlotte's visions had over her.

p. 23 *Reason* 'Unloved I love, unwept I weep'
Undated, but around 1836.
This poem is difficult to interpret. It could be autobiographical, although no love affair of Charlotte has been discovered at this stage, and her dreary life as a teacher was not conducive to love affairs. She did incorporate the first stanza into her poem *Frances* (25), probably written after the visit to Belgium. At this early date these words are probably those of some Angrian heroine like Mina Laury, the story of whom Charlotte was to complete in 1838, although she had already in other stories alluded to the rather doomed love affair between the governess Mina and the aristocratic Zamorna. Some autobiography probably enters into both *Mina Laury* and this poem. The autobiographical dimension may explain why this poem bears some resemblance to Charlotte's novels, where she is able to fuse romance and reality, and why it is superior to many of the fantasies which she wrote at this time.

p. 24 'Again I find myself alone, and ever'
Undated, but around 1837.
The incoherence of this poem, written during the Roe Head period, may be due to the fact that it is part of another poem, but even so it is an interesting example of Charlotte's feelings at Roe Head where she shows growing guilt at her ability to lose herself in visions which probably had a strong sexual component. The language and the unworldliness of the poem are reminiscent of Shelley.

p. 25 'When thou sleepest, lulled in night'
Undated, but around 1837.
Another Roe Head poem takes a more cheerful attitude to Angrian dreams as an escape
from reality. In describing her visions soaring to heaven until she is dragged back in
baffled agony to earth, Charlotte is preaching a philosophy similar to that of Emily,
although her poetry lacks the force of poems like *The Prisoner* (112).

p. 27 *Stanzas* 'If thou be in a lonely place'
Dated 14 May 1837, but copied at Haworth in 1845 and revised again for publication in
1846.
There are not a great many differences between the three copies, although most of the
revisions are an improvement. The dangers of an exclusively Angrian or strongly
autobiographical interpretation are obvious if we consider the different dates at which the
poem was revised. The lover mourning for her lost love is a fairly conventional topic, and
is the subject of many of Charlotte's published poems. Mary Percy mourning for Zamorna
is the most obvious candidate to be the narrator of the original version.

p. 28 'Sit still—a breath, a word may shake'
Undated, but around 1837.
In 1846 Charlotte published a poem entitled *The Wife's Will* with a similar opening line
describing a vaguely similar situation, with two lovers united after a long and dangerous
separation. There ends all similarity between the two poems, as it is clear in the published
version that the narrator is married, and she rather primly insists upon the pure nature of
her love. Here the love is lawless, and even impious, as lines 6 and 57 make clear. Neither
poem is among Charlotte's best, but, unlike in some other poems which she revised for
publication, in this instance, her wish to comply with Victorian convention stifled the
poetry.

p. 30 'Obscure and little seen my way'
Undated, but around 1837.
This poem is capable of either an Angrian or an autobiographical interpretation. The
reference to the Great, conspicuous in the aristocratic circles of Angria, but not playing a
prominent part at Miss Wooler's school, suggests an Angrian fragment, but observant
criticism from the despised governess or teacher is common both in Charlotte's letters and
her novels.

p. 30 'Is this my tomb, this humble stone'
Dated 4 June 1837.
This poem has a certain elegaic melancholy and a good picture of the bleak Yorkshire
landscape. Charlotte's heroine, Mary Percy, had been killed off by Branwell in 1836, but
she had been revived by Charlotte, and there is no reason to believe that her burial was
particularly humble. So we do not know who the heroine of this poem is. It is indeed
uncertain for some time whether she is alive or dead, and the strange notion of her
returning to haunt her own grave seems more akin to the world of *Wuthering Heights* than
anything else in Charlotte's work.

p. 33 'Why should we ever mourn as those'
Undated, but around 1837.
This poem can be compared with Branwell's 'Cease mourner, cease thy sorrowing for the

dead', although it has not the same title, as errroneously reported in my edition of *The Poems of Charlotte Brontë*. Branwell's poem, a sonnet, is much more powerful with an original note of despair for the living dead, while conventional orthodoxy and insincere optimism makes Charlotte's poem sadly flat.

p. 34 *Presentiment* 'Sister, you've sat there all the day'
Dated 11 July 1837, but copied around 1843, and published in 1846.
There is nothing particularly autobiographical about the poem, although the contrast between the bleak atmosphere of winter, and the brief glimpse of summer reminds us of life at Haworth. On the other hand, Charlotte must have felt the force of this poem very keenly in 1848 and 1849.

p. 36 'What does she dream of, lingering all alone'
Undated, but around 1838.
Alone is a favourite word for Charlotte's heroines in poetry of this period. She also wrote poems beginning 'She was alone that evening—and alone' and 'Again I find myself alone, and ever'. It is probable that she identified herself with her lonely heroines, as she endured evenings of solitude at Roe Head. The identity of this particular heroine is obscure, although it has been conjectured that it is Mary Percy mourning her husband's desertion.

p. 36 ' "Oh, let me be alone," he said'
Undated, but around 1838.
This poem describes the thoughts of Lord Hartford, a former ally of Zamorna, who had fallen in love with Mina Laury, challenged Zamorna, his rival, to a duel, and been seriously wounded for his pains. We read about this in *Mina Laury*, completed in 1838. In Charlotte's next stories *Stancliffe's Hotel*, written in June 1838, and *Henry Hastings*, written in 1839, Lord Hartford has recovered.

p. 39 *The Town Besieged* 'With moaning sound a stream'
Dated June 1838, but copied with some changes around 1843.
Charlotte did write about war as well as love, although this poem is sung by an Angrian beauty, Jane Moore, in the middle of the prose story, *Stancliffe's Hotel*. The town being besieged is Evesham, the scene of the last major battle in the Angrian wars, when Zamorna returns to defeat his foes.

p. 39 'A Roland for your Oliver'
Dated February 1840.
The Revd William Weightman appears as a sunny gleam in the sombre Brontë story, and this poem's cheerful note comes as something of a shock. The Brontë sisters were all at home on Valentine's day 1840 and probably united in sending this effort. The verse is pedestrian, and the sentiments, though worthy, were doomed to be unfulfilled as Mr Weightman was to die in 1842. In 1841 Charlotte wrote rather sourly to Ellen Nussey, saying that she knew better than last year how to respond to Mr Weightman. It is a moot point how far, if at all, Anne Brontë was in love with Weightman. This poem, like the rest of Charlotte's correspondence, betokens nothing more than warm friendship.

p. 41 *Frances* 'She will not sleep, for fear of dreams'
Undated, but around 1843. Published in 1846.
The date is conjectured because the poem as well as reflecting the name of one of

Charlotte's Belgian heroines, Frances Henri, and the feelings of the other Belgian heroine, Lucy Snowe, might seem an accurate statement of Charlotte's feelings alone in Belgium with Monsieur Heger's affection suddenly grown cold. There are dangers in this interpretation, especially as lines 53–6 are almost identical with the first lines of a poem written at Roe Head, when Charlotte was equally bereft, filled with religious doubt, and a prey to escapist dreams. On the other hand just as Charlotte in the loneliness of 1852 worked over her experiences in 1843, when writing *Villette*, she may have done the same in writing this poem, which is one of her best, where the vigour of her despair and the shift between joy and anguish reminds us of the poetry of Emily.

p. 48 *Gilbert* 'Above the city hung the moon'
Undated, but around 1843. Published in 1846.
Charlotte's longest poem has received a certain amount of faint praise for its narrative interest, although the regular rhyme and metre hardly contribute to our understanding of Gilbert's changes of mood and fortune. As a kind of *Enoch Arden* in reverse, the poem might have appealed to Victorian sentiment. Students of Charlotte Brontë might be tempted, probably wrongly, to see autobiographical hints here, although Charlotte cannot really have thought or hoped she would return to haunt Monsieur Heger, whose conduct was never as selfish as that of Gilbert. A more promising source of enquiry might be to see parallels with the story of Jane Eyre. Rochester does not, it is true, treat Bertha Mason as Gilbert treats the drowned woman in this poem, but especially in the manuscript version there are echoes of Rochester's account of his West Indian experiences, and of the (perhaps) linked description by Jane of the pictures she is drawing.

p. 59 'He saw my heart's woe, discerned my soul's anguish'
Undated.
This poem may not refer to Monsieur Heger, but it is very tempting to suggest that it does. There seems a personal sincerity in the first half of the poem, perhaps lacking in the conventional religious note of the second part. We cannot date this poem. The four existing letters to Monsieur Heger are dated beween July 1844 and November 1845, but Charlotte may have decided to renounce him earlier or later than this period. The reference to a yearly appeal in the second stanza reminds us of the way in which Monsieur Heger clearly rationed Charlotte's letters to him, although six months rather than a year seems to have been the ration.

p. 60 'At first I did attention give'
Undated.
This poem was first printed in the edition of *Jane Eyre*, prepared by M. M. Smith (Oxford, 1973). I was not aware of this when I published this poem in *Brontë Facts and Problems* (London, 1983), where I discuss the problem fully. Mrs Smith's text is in places different from and better than mine, although the manuscript is very hard to read. I have taken a few of her readings, noted below. I remain convinced of an autobiographical interpretation for this poem, as Charlotte seems the obvious candidate for a respectful pupil being seized by a lawless love. It is then very interesting that the first lines of the poem are very similar to those of the decorous poem in *The Professor* where Frances Henri declares her love, and then the bulk of the poem, apart from the unhappy conclusion, are with an obvious change of sex used by Rochester to pronounce his love for Jane. We cannot unfortunately date this poem except to say that it preceded *Jane Eyre*.

In l. 7 *valued*, l. 31 *troubling*, l. 37 *wide as* and l. 68 *stains*, I have taken the readings of Mrs Smith.

p. 63 'My darling, thou wilt never know'
Dated 24 December 1848.
Emily Brontë died on 23 December 1848. This is in a way as moving as the prose account
of Emily's death recorded in *The Shakespeare Head Life and Letters* (London, 1932), Vol II,
pp. 294–5.

p. 63 'There's little joy in life for me'
Dated 21 June 1849.
Anne Brontë died on 28 May 1849, and Charlotte's poetic response to this tragedy,
though as heartfelt, was less immediate than her reaction to Emily's death. The death of
Anne was less sudden and more expected than that of Emily, but Charlotte's sense of
desolation must have been greater, and this poem is a sad tribute to the loneliness of the
last years of her life, during which she finished *Shirley* and wrote the whole of *Villette*.

BRANWELL BRONTË'S POEMS

p. 65 *The CXXXVIIth Psalm* 'By the still streams of Babylon'
Dated 1834, but transcribed 9 March 1837.
Cowper's poem with the same title, Byron's *Hebrew Melodies*, and *The Book of Common
Prayer*, are all sources for this poem which involves considerable plagiarism. According to
a note, these lines were originally composed by Alexander Percy, who was exiled, although
it is hard to see all that many similarities between his situation and that of the Israelites.

p. 66 *Morning* 'Morn comes and with it all the stir of morn'
Dated 6 December 1834, but transcribed on 11 March 1837.
This was originally a poem written by Henry Hastings at the battle of Gazemba.
    Although slightly overwritten, the poem has a certain sincerity, and by 1837, a poignant
relevance to the contrast between Branwell's ambitions and his achievements.

p. 67 *Lines* 'We leave our bodies in the Tomb'
Dated 1834, but transcribed 11 March 1837.
This poem was originally written as part of the life of Alexander Percy, but the religious
views expressed may reflect Branwell's own feelings. He does not see Heaven contrasted
with Hell, but imagines that the fate for the wicked is annihilation with the soul rotting in
the same way as the body. All the Brontës were worried about life after death, and at times
all of them adopted an unorthodox position.

p. 68 *Misery, Part I* 'How fast that courser fleeted by'
Undated in final version, but early 1836.
This poem is usually printed from an earlier version dated 18 December 1835, and this
date suggests that Branwell composed this long poem during the autumn of 1835. It is
possible that Charlotte may have copied out this version which was sent to *Blackwood's
Magazine*. We do not know who Albert and Maria are, and though the scenery of war and
lonely castles is appropriate to Angria, we cannot attribute the poem to any particular
Angrian incident. It may be that with Charlotte away at Roe Head in the later part of 1835,
Branwell tried to escape from Angria. It is probably fanciful to regard the name Maria here
and in the next poem as an autobiographical reminiscence of Branwell's eldest sister.

p. 77 *Misery, Part II* 'Wide I hear the wild winds sighing'
Undated in final version, but early 1836.
An early version of the poem is dated 2 March 1836. This text is taken from the version sent to *Blackwood's*. In spite of a promising romantic beginning, the poem adds little to its predecessor, and it is not difficult to see why *Blackwood's* rejected both poems. The religious doubts may be genuine, but the Byronic note of sinfulness is forced.

p. 86 'Still and bright, in twilight shining'
Dated 13 August 1836.
Wordsworth was sent an extract from this poem, or possibly the whole poem, in January 1837. The poem is full of reminders of Wordsworth's *Immortality Ode* as well as fairly direct copyings of Coleridge's *Kubla Khan* and hymns by Nahum Tate and Isaac Watts (lines 142–50, 196–201, 245–9). The message of the poem involving the deterioration of the innocent young Percy into the hardened sinner of Angrian tales can hardly have been to Wordsworth's taste even if he had been flattered by the plagiarism.

p. 95 'The light of thy ancestral hall'
Undated, but around 1837.
Branwell wrote three poems mentioning a dead Caroline, and sent them to his friend Leyland, who published them together. The other two poems are much longer. One of them, entitled variously *Sir Henry Tunstall* or *The Wanderer*, tells of a world-weary warrior returning from India to mourn his youthful Caroline. This poem has over 500 lines and Branwell revised it three times between 1838 and 1842. Some extracts were published in the *Halifax Guardian*, but modern taste would probably find it dreary. In a second poem, parts of which were written in 1837, Caroline is the sister of a lady called Harriet, who recalls her burial a little incoherently, and some have seen an autobiographical link with Branwell's sister here. The present poem, although a little stilted, is probably the best of the three. Attempts to show that the original of Caroline was a cousin of Branwell's friend William Dearden are fruitless, since though Dearden had a cousin called Caroline who died in 1828, Branwell did not meet Dearden until he went to Luddenden Foot in 1840.

p. 96 'Oh! on this first bright Mayday morn'
Dated May 1838.
This is a fragment of a poem sent to Leyland who supplies the date. The Romantic influence is again prominent with the contrast between youthful innocence and mature wickedness striking the same note as the poem which Branwell sent to Wordsworth. Once again it would seem that Percy is the speaker, although he may reflect Branwell's own feelings. By 1838 (as opposed to 1836) Branwell's feeling of failure may have had a little more justification, as he had by this time spent two years in unprofitable literary ventures.

p. 97 'Far off, and half revealed, 'mid shade and light'
Undated, but around 1840.
Branwell spent the first half of 1840 at Broughton tutoring the son of Mr Postlethwaite. The hill Black Comb is five miles from Brangaton, and it seems reasonable to assume that the poem was written during his time as a tutor. According to his own account Branwell was very drunk when he left for Broughton, and he left under discreditable circumstances, but it is at about this time when his life seemed to be taking a downward turn that Branwell's poetry becomes better. This is the first of a series of sonnets, some of which were published in the *Halifax Guardian*, and all of which deserve to be better known.

p. 97 'Oh Thou, whose beams were most withdrawn'
Dated 8 August 1841.
Branwell's despair at Luddenden Foot, and the religious feelings which accompany this despair, is both exaggerated and remarkable. He had still seven more years to live, and was to endure far more pain and despair. His other poems at Luddenden Foot, with their emphasis on heroic figures like Nelson and Johnson who overcame their difficulties, suggest that it was at this stage in his life that Branwell realized that he was not destined to achieve the greatness which fell to his sisters.

p. 98 *The Triumph of Mind over Body* 'Man thinks too often that the ills of life'
Undated, but around 1841.
Branwell wrote three versions of this poem, probably all three in the same year at Luddenden Foot, since all three mention the thirty-six year interval after the battle of Trafalgar in 1805. Nelson, who had the Italian title of Duke of Brontë, was an obvious hero for Branwell, who may have been especially attracted by the contrast between Nelson's insignificant appearance, and magnificent exploits. Branwell had an insignificant appearance and there was little opportunity for magnificence at Luddenden Foot. Taken by themselves, the concluding verses, which are not in one of the earlier versions, have a certain sincerity about them, although when linked to the story of Nelson, Branwell's reflections about himself may seem impertinent. The moon is a frequent source of inspiration in Branwell's poetry.

p. 105 'Man thinks too often that his earth-born cares'
Dated 3 September 1841.
This poem uses Johnson rather than Nelson as a source of inspiration. Branwell had presumably read Boswell, but it is possible to detect echoes of *The Vanity of Human Wishes* here, especially of the line 'Toil, envy, want, the patron and the goal', with which Branwell may have comforted himself in his garret at Luddenden Foot.

p. 106 'O God! while I in pleasure's wiles'
Dated 19 December 1841.
Drinking at the Lord Nelson public house appears to have been Branwell's major pleasure at Luddenden Foot, but this is quite an impressive poem to write after a sordid debauch with the haunting shorter second and fourth line of each stanza sometimes shocking the reader.

p. 106 'The desolate earth, the wintry sky'
Dated 25 December 1841.
Christmas was presumably spent by Branwell with his family at Haworth, but the mood of the poem is sombre. Charlotte, Emily and Anne were all due to leave home, and the climate of Haworth is at Christmas often not festive. Drink flowed less freely than at Luddenden Foot. Branwell adds Galileo, Tasso, Milton and Cowper to his pantheon of heroes. Johnson and Burns are celebrated in other poems.

p. 109 *Robert Burns* 'He little knows—whose life has smoothly passed'
Undated, but around 1842.
Burns's poetry and his drinking presumably made him a hero to Branwell; there is no record of Branwell being involved in any amorous escapades at this stage.

p. 109 'Why hold young eyes the fullest fount of tears'
Published in the *Halifax Guardian*, 7 May 1842.
In the preceding year Branwell had had a poem on the Afghan War published in the *Leeds Intelligencer*. In spite of its disillusioned note, the diction of this poem is impressive and its thought original. Leyland rightly praised it as he did the next poem printed.

p. 110 'Why dost thou sorrow for the happy dead'
Published in the *Halifax Guardian*, 14 May 1842, but an earlier version survives, perhaps written as early as 1837. The theological views expressed in this poem contrast both with religious orthodoxy and with the opinions expressed in the poem 'We leave our bodies in the Tomb' (33). Instead of a conventional heaven and hell, after death Branwell imagines the happy dead as suffering an annihilation of the senses, while hell on earth is reserved for those who have abandoned the life of the spirit.

p. 110 *Thorp Green* 'I sit, this evening, far away'
Dated 30 March 1843.
Branwell moved to the Robinsons as private tutor in January 1843. This is the only poem which we have in the next two years, although one would have thought that his duties would have allowed him some time for the writing of poetry. This poem strikes a more conventional and hopeful note than the gloomy sonnets of the previous year, but is less successful as poetry.

p. 111 'When sink from sight the landmarks of our Home'
Dated 6 May 1845.
This poem was written just before Branwell's disgrace at Thorp Green, but does not seem to have any autobiographical significance unless Branwell contemplated emigration as a way out of his difficulties, or more fancifully we imagine Branwell trying to break with Mrs Robinson and then finding her thrust before his sight again. Branwell wrote another sonnet which Leyland called *The Emigrant II*, as he called this poem *The Emigrant I*, but the later poem, describing a man in the tropics dreaming of his native shores, is much less impressive.

p. 111 'I see a corpse upon the waters lie'
Undated, but around 1846.
Leyland contrasts this poem with Charlotte's *Gilbert* (26), and compares it to Emily's *The Philosopher* (106). Written presumably after Branwell's disgrace at Thorp Green, the poem, though gloomy, has a certain melancholy dignity.

p. 112 *Epistle from a Father to a Child in her Grave* 'From Earth,—whose life-reviving April showers'
Dated 3 April 1846.
We do not know the circumstances which gave rise to this poem contrasting the innocence of youth with the troubles of maturity, but it shows enough technical skill for us to be able to dismiss the legend that by this date Branwell was a desperate and degenerate man, although the poet does seem in some sense to be anticipating his own death. The poem contains echoes of Branwell's earlier *Misery* poems as well as of *Wuthering Heights*.

p. 114 'When all our cheerful hours seem gone for ever'
Dated 28 April 1846.
This sonnet is a good place to leave Branwell. He still had two years to live, but his remaining poems are rambling affairs. In spite of the gloomy atmosphere and the melodramatic references, presumably to Mrs Robinson, this poem does show that Branwell was a real poet.

EMILY BRONTË'S POEMS

p. 115 'High waving heather 'neath stormy blasts bending'
Dated 13 December 1836.
The poem takes up one of Emily Brontë's favourite topics, the power and excitement of the wind. Often in her work it is 'life-giving'. This enthusiasm is probably traceable in part to the influence of Shelley, in part to an early acquaintance with the New Testament equation of wind with the Holy Spirit.
   In line 9, *jubilee* means 'celebration'. No notion of 'anniversary' is present here.

p. 115 'Lord of Elbë, on Elbë hill'
Dated 19 August 1837.
Gondal ascription A.G.A. to A.E.
Emily Brontë made several copies of the poem, and the text printed here is the latest. The date was copied out each time she recopied it, despite alterations introduced. In the first version Alexander (the A.E. may stand for 'Alexander of Elbë') is evidently not dead. Line 19 reads 'Longing to be in sweet Elbë again'. We may think it likely that his death was part of the rationalization process involved in the work done on 'Gondal Chronicles' by Anne and Emily Brontë during the period before 1845.
   Elbë as a Gondal name may be based on Napoleon's Elba. The Brontës showed interest in words ending in –ë. Emily Brontë uses the name Iernë as a persona.

p. 116 'Sleep brings no joy to me'
Dated November 1837.
Gondal ascription A.G.A.
In this poem, Emily Brontë's *alter ego*, A.G.A, considers the power of unhappy memory to banish sleep. It is hard to explain all the Gondal allusions. A.G.A. often appears as a tyrannical and treacherous lover, and we may assume that here the dreams are those of friends or lovers that have been betrayed or deserted.

p. 117 'Fall, leaves, fall; die, flowers, away'
Gondal ascription, apparently A.A.
It seems likely that the ascription is meant to be to the same Gondal princess who usually appears as A.G.A. It is not even clear from the manuscript whether a single or dual name is intended. The poem is perhaps an incantation said or sung by the princess on perceiving the dying year. It may owe something to Emily Brontë's reading of Shakespeare. At the moment the extent of any such reading is far from clear.

p. 117 'The night is darkening round me'
Dated November 1837.
There is no indication that this could have been a Gondal poem. We may suppose it originated in an observation of the poet, entranced with the natural world. However, there does not seem to have been heavy snowfall on that day. It seems likely that the intensity of the poem is to be ascribed to Emily Brontë's intensifying imagination.

p. 117 'Why do I hate that lone green dell?'
Dated 9 May 1838.
Gondal ascription A.G.A.
The poem is nominally written by Emily Brontë's strongest Gondal character, with whom she seems to identify. The allusions, however, are impossible to interpret clearly. It appears that the Gondal princess is speaking to an old enemy. The confused Gondal story seems to contain treacheries, revolts and reconciliations. Here, apparently, is one such.

Despite the Gondal tone, it is quite likely that the green dell of the poem was a real one, to be found on Haworth moor or nearby. The clear image of the whitening bones may have been based on an actual experience of discovering the remains of a dead moorland creature.

p. 118 'O wander not so far away!'
Dated 20 May 1838.
Gondal ascription A.G.A. to A.S.
We cannot now recover all the allusions of the poem, which is addressed in the name of 'A.G.A.' to a lover. It is worth noting that the poem is based in current reality ('The still May morn'). Interesting changes were made to the poem on recopying in 1844; for example, in line 10, the 'throstle' was replaced by 'stockdove'.

In line 17 *Call death* is Hatfield's emendation for manuscript 'Can'. Neither reading seems entirely adequate.

p. 119 *Song to A.A.* 'This shall be thy lullaby'
Dated May 1838.
Gondal ascription (in one manuscript only) Blanche.
It seems likely that Emily Brontë changed the Gondal context of the poem before recopying. The name 'Blanche' occurs only in the earlier manuscript, and in line 4 the adjective is changed from 'bright-haired' to 'dark-haired'.

The poem appears to be a lullaby sung by a woman cast out from her home, to her child, A.A. It is possible that the child is the girl later known as 'A.G.A.', but we have no sure proof of this.

p. 119 'For him who struck thy foreign string'
Dated 30 August 1838.
Gondal ascription A.G.A.
Charlotte made several alterations to this poem for her 1850 selection. The present text is that of the manuscript.

The guitar is addressed in Shelley's poem 'With a guitar to Jane' (1822). The popularity of Spanish guitars reached a peak during the Romantic movement. However, there is no evidence that the Brontës themselves ever owned one.

The 'woodman' of line 11 may reflect Brontë interest in the popular song of the time, in which a woodman is urged to spare a tree he is about to cut down.

p. 120 *Song by Julius Brenzaida to G.S.* 'Geraldine, the moon is shining'
Dated 17 October 1838.
The 'Geraldine S.' of the title cannot be positively identified with A.G.A., though there have been attempts to do this. Julius appears in a number of Gondal poems, and may be the same man who is later said to be king of Almedore. He is portrayed as a ruthless and treacherous character. He appears as the recipient of the funeral ode in the famous 'Cold in the Earth' (107).

p. 121 'O Dream, where art thou now?'
Dated 5 November 1838.
This is not a Gondal poem. The 'Dream' of the opening address is claimed to be a vision rather than a real person, and may possibly be identifiable with the poet Shelley. The poet associates this 'Dream' person with light and emotive facets of nature, which are experienced as animated by the spirit of a human or angelic being.

p. 121 'Loud without the wind was roaring'
Dated November 1838.
One manuscript suggests 11 November as the date, but the weather conditions on the day in question were inconsistent with the poem. It seems likely that spurious precision was added on recopying in 1844.
  The poem was written during Emily Brontë's short stay as a teacher at Law Hill School, Halifax. The words 'exile afar' are typical of her hyperbole, as Law Hill is not more than ten miles from Haworth. Lines 11 and 35 appear to be quotations from an actual 'ancient song', which I have not been able to identify accurately. They are similar to an Irish ballad known as 'The Mountains of Pomeroy', but this ballad in its present form postdates the Emily Brontë poem.

p. 123 'A little while, a little while'
Dated 4 December 1838.
This is a second Law Hill poem. In it Emily Brontë graphically describes her feelings during a short rest period from teaching. It is a fair autobiographical inference that teaching was most uncongenial to her.
  The reference to 'A little and a lone green lane' has often been taken to be to Haworth. Strictly, as careful reading will show, it is to a lane in Gondal. This opens up the whole question of the relation of Gondal geography to the geography of Haworth and the Yorkshire moors.

p. 125 '"How still, how happy!" Those are words'
Dated 7 December 1838.
This may be the last of the Law Hill poems, though there is a case to be made for including the next one. The subject of the poem is the tension of opposites. It exemplifies a strong characteristic of Emily Brontë, her tendency to think in terms of polarities, of which there are a number of excellent examples in *Wuthering Heights*. The characteristic is reflected in the frequency of poems with a dialogue element.

p. 126 'The bluebell is the sweetest flower'
Dated 18 December 1838.
It is impossible to tell whether Emily Brontë had returned home to Haworth when she wrote this poem. School terms generally did end about 15–18 December. However, the

last line seems to suggest that the poet was not in 'the fields of home' at the time of writing, and had still her journey before her. If she was still at Law Hill, the stream of the poem may be the Red Beck.

The manuscript bears traces of Charlotte Brontë's 1850 alterations, which are here excluded.

p. 127 *To the Bluebell* 'Sacred watcher, wave thy bells!'
Dated 9 May 1839.
Gondal ascription A.G.A.
By the time of writing this poem Emily Brontë had returned permanently from Law Hill and seems to have spent the first part of 1839 organizing and developing her poetry, apparently taking her poetic talent seriously for the first time.

The flowering period of the harebell (usually considered to be the Brontës' 'bluebell') is July–August. This makes it seem unlikely that the poet had a specimen before her as she wrote. On the other hand, as she associates the bluebell with the woods in this poem, it is just possible that she is referring to the true bluebell here.

p. 128 'I am the only being whose doom'
Dated 17 May 1839.
Though there is no formal Gondal ascription, the 'eighteen years' in line 8 shows that Emily Brontë is not overtly considering her own position at the time. Stanza five may be compared with Anne Brontë's 'Views of Life' (133), though it expresses thoughts and feelings of greater bitterness.

p. 129 'May flowers are opening'
Dated 25 May 1839.
The contrast between the feeling of the poet and those surrounding her, occurs elsewhere in Emily Brontë's work. The vein of pessimism found in the work of this spring may in part be due to a feeling of defeat resulting from the Law Hill experience, which is perhaps partly compensated for by the revision of poems during the first few months of the year. The repetitions in stanzas three and four are reminiscent of folk and parlour songs of the time.

p. 130 *Lines by Claudia* 'I did not sleep, 'twas noon of day'
Dated 28 May 1839.
The name 'Claudia' is otherwise totally unknown in Gondal. A strange mixture between real and imaginary appears in the poem. 'Claudia' has evidently died in England, as though Gondal characters travelled in the known as well as the imaginary world. We may associate this with the gradual tendency on the part of all the Brontës to move their work nearer to the actual world in which they lived.

In line 25, there is no way in which the 'Monarch' may be identified.

p. 131 'I know not how it falls on me'
Dated 8 June 1839.
This is generally taken to be a complete poem, but it comes from a fragment manuscript and was not recopied. In it the poet repeats her statement of confidence in nature, though in a muted tone. We have already noted the melancholy pessimism of the poems written during this period.

p. 131 'And now the housedog stretched once more'
Dated 12 July 1839.
The poem is not specifically Gondal, but clearly deals with a fictional encounter which might perhaps come from that story. The mysterious visitor, at first taken to be human, seems to have strayed from some fairyland or spirit world. There may be similarities between him and the sinister figure of Geraldine in Coleridge's 'Christabel'. We may recall that Emily Brontë is obsessed with the half-human, 'changeling'. Heathcliff himself exhibits many characteristics of such a creature, and perhaps developed from some such early idea of the author's.

p. 132 'Come hither, child—who gifted thee'
Dated 19 July 1839.
The manuscript is very much altered and the text at line 30 cannot be regarded as certain. That Emily Brontë was very absorbed in the poem is clear from these persistent alterations. Romer Wilson may be right to suggest a personal reference despite the Gondal name 'Ula'. It is certainly worth remarking that this apparently Gondal event takes place in a crowded 'hall' when the child is 'hardly six years old'—the age at which Emily Brontë was sent to Cowan Bridge school.

p. 133 'Shed no tears o'er that tomb'
Dated 26 July 1839.
The poem does not appear in a specifically Gondal MS and contains no Gondal names. The presumption must be that the person whose tomb is commemorated may be a real one. The argument of the poem is somewhat complex, but it seems that Emily Brontë is discussing the death, and life after death, of one whom angels mourn because of his wickedness on earth. It is not necessary to suppose that the conclusion represents any more than an imaginative exploration of the sinner's condition. The indications are that the poet did not take an orthodox view of hell.

p. 134 'Mild the mist upon the hill'
Dated 27 July 1839.
The Keighley meteorologist, Shackleton, records that almost an inch of rain fell on the day the poem was writen. This is another meditative poem of retrospection on the eve of Emily's twenty-fifth birthday.

p. 135 'How long will you remain? The midnight hour'
Dated 12 August 1839.
As in 'Come hither, child' (74), the MS bears evidence of much rewriting and pondering. The conversation in the poem may well reflect a real conversation, perhaps between Emily and Charlotte. The touches of fictionalization are slight, at least in the first part of the poem.
   The 'minster' tower (line 2) is a romanticized version of Haworth church tower. The identity of the 'blissful dream' (line 10) is harder to establish.

p. 135 'The starry night shall tidings bring'
Dated 13 August 1839.
This fragment seems likely to be part of a Gondal story the significance of which cannot now be recovered. F. B. Pinion in *A Brontë Companion* notes the 'Gothic relish for the horrible and ominous' of the fragment.

p. 136 'Fair sinks the summer evening now'
Dated 30 August 1839.
The feelings expressed in the poem appear to be those of the poet, both of whose sisters were away from home: Charlotte on holiday with Ellen Nussey, and Anne at Blake Hall.

p. 137 'The wind, I hear it sighing'
Dated 29 October 1839.
This poem occurs in Emily Brontë's non-Gondal MS. In it she laments her 'old feelings' which have ceased to cheer her. It has been natural for commentators to search for a real person who might have inspired such feelings, but so far no convincing case has been made.

p. 137 'Love is like the wild rose-briar'
Undated.
The poem occurs in Emily Brontë's non-Gondal MS. The poem cannot be later than 1844, but possibly dates from some time before this. The poem appears to be literary in tone, and there may be literary models which have so far not been identified.

p. 138 *Sympathy* 'There should be no despair for you'
Undated. Revised for publication in 1846.
The title was not originally written into the MS and appears to have been made up for the 1846 edition. There is no way in which the poem may be dated, though its location in the MS suggests that, like the previous poem, it may have been copied from a scrap written some time before 1844.

p. 138 'Well, some may hate and some may scorn'
Dated 14 November 1839.
This poem occurs in the non-Gondal MS. We may therefore reasonably presume that the person mourned is not a Gondal character. However, no obvious subject among Emily Brontë's limited circle of acquaintance presents himself. It seems likely that the dead man is a national political or literary figure. The name of Shelley has been suggested.

p. 139 'Far, far away is mirth withdrawn'
Dated March 1840.
It seems possible that the man commemorated in this poem is the same as that of the previous one. The man has a 'tarnished' name and lies in a foreign grave. His foes consider that he will be condemned to hell, but the poet believes that God is not vengeful. Some of the indicators here point quite strongly to Shelley being the person of whom Emily Brontë is thinking.

p. 140 'It is too late to call thee now'
Dated April 1840.
Another non-Gondal poem in the same series as the preceding one. If the subject is once again the poet Shelley, it is possible that Emily Brontë may have first encountered his work about 1832, at the age of about fourteen.

p. 141 'I'll not weep that thou art going to leave me'
Dated 4 May 1840.
It seems likely that this non-Gondal poem is inspired by the departure of Anne Brontë for

Thorp Green, though firm dates for this event are hard to establish. The final stanza moves away romantically from the actual scene, in a way which is very typical of Emily Brontë.

p. 141 'At such a time, in such a spot'
Dated 6 May 1840/28 July 1843.
The poem may have been begun in remembrance of the death of Maria Brontë on 6 May 1825. However, the bright weather of the opening soon turns to cold November, and the scene to Gondal. As in some other poems, Emily Brontë seems to be attacking religious practice in lines 34ff.

p. 143 'If grief for grief can touch thee'
Dated 18 May 1840.
The poem apparently reverts to the subject of previous poems of this year. The words used to describe the longed-for person, 'angel' and 'idol', do not help the case of those who seek an actual person as the subject of the poem. Overall, the tone seems to be much more one of longing for an ideal than reminiscence of a human and living lover.

p. 143 ''Tis moonlight, summer moonlight'
Dated 19 May 1840.
The poem occurs on an early fragment MS. It appears complete but was never recopied. Had it been incorporated into a longer poem, we might have been able to classify it as definitely a Gondal work. As it is, we may feel that the tone is fictional but no imaginary character may be in the poet's mind.

p. 144 *The Night Wind* 'In summer's mellow midnight'
Dated 11 September 1840.
The title was apparently added by the poet when revising for the 1846 edition. However, the poem was not in the end chosen for the selection, and first appeared in Charlotte Brontë's 1850 anthology. The Shelleyan influence would appear to predominate, though this refers to the thought rather than the form or language of the poem.

p. 145 'There let thy bleeding branch atone'
Undated; possibly written about 1839–40.
The forceful imagery of this poem has attracted critical attention, but a prosaic precis is impossible. The poem is incomplete, and it is hard to contextualize it. There is no evidence to suggest that it might have been intended as part of the Gondal cycle. The 'early days' of line 12 recalls the 'early years' of 'It is too late to call thee now'. It may be that the poem should be assigned to the cycle of poems possibly addressed to Shelley.

p. 145 'And like myself lone, wholly lone'
Dated 27 February 1841.
The poem occurs on a small fragment of paper and was never recopied. It has been thought to refer to the Brontë's pet hawk, Hero, and the bird of the poem certainly seems to be at home in moorland country: it 'soars' and has 'shining eyes'. This sounds quite like a description of a kestrel or similar bird. Emily Brontë strongly identifies with the bird, and uses it as a brief allegory of the human soul, set free to roam at death.

p. 146 *The Old Stoic* 'Riches I hold in light esteem'
Dated 1 March 1841.
The title first occurs in the 1846 edition and is not found in the manuscript. There is still considerable dispute as to how far this edition was superintended by Charlotte Brontë. The stoic attitude of the poem may have one root in Methodism, but is also frequently found in other parts of Emily Brontë's output. In particular, the notion of a 'chainless' soul appears to have been very close to the core of her thought.

p. 146 'Shall Earth no more inspire thee?'
Dated 16 May 1841.
This is one of the poems which Charlotte Brontë chose for her 1850 selection, to which she made no alteration. It expresses the closeness to Nature which appears in many of Emily Brontë's earlier poems, as well as pervasively in *Wuthering Heights*. Stanza 6 prefigures the famous scene in the novel in which Catherine is telling a dream in whch she found heaven uncongenial, and was flung back to the moorland. The reference to 'passion' in line 2 seems to imply that Nature is a refuge from an unsatisfying and intense emotion, possibly of love.

p. 147 'Aye, there it is! It wakes tonight'
Dated 6 July 1841.
The 'it' of line 1 seems likely to be the West wind, apparently her favourite, and the subject of Shelley's famous poem.
    The poem is presented as an observation by a third party, but it surely refers to the poet herself, whose 'altered cheek' reveals the fancy which allows her to feel merged in an immortal universe. The sentiment is Platonic, almost Buddhist.
    The capitals in line 15, and in subsequent lines, appear to be the manuscript reading, but we must remember that there are difficulties in attainting certainty over individual letters in Emily Brontë's minute script.

p. 148 'I see around me tombstones grey'
Dated 17 July 1841.
The poem continues the Shelleyan and Platonic feeling of the previous one. Throughout this group we encounter the notion of the soul as a prisoner in the body. Emily Brontë is in fact interested in prisoners in the literal as well as the metaphorical sense.
    In line 27, the reading 'curseless' was first noted by Derek Roper of Sheffield University.

p. 149 'In the same place, when Nature wore'
Dated 17 May 1842.
Gondal ascription H.A. and A.S.
It is impossible to discover the Gondal names to be attached to the two sets of initials. Miss Ratchford considers that the incident relates to the daughter of Lord Alfred of Aspin Castle and her adopted child. As I have already suggested, it may be a mistake to search for a coherent Gondal story in these poems.
    The manuscript is unclear at line 11. Emily Brontë's earlier suggestion was apparently 'the wild grief which'.

p. 150 *Self-Interrogation* 'The evening passes fast away'
Dated 23 October 1842–6 February 1843.
The poem was begun in Brussels and finished at Haworth. It is unfortunately impossible
to tell where the break came, as the poem is extant in copy-manuscript only.

The location in the copy-book rules out the possibility that this could be a Gondal
poem. We may therefore conclude that the poet is once again musing on her own destiny.
Both rhythm and subject matter strangely anticipate Houseman. Possibly both reflect
Horace, whom Branwell had translated and who could hardly fail to be known to Emily for
this reason.

p. 152 *How Clear She Shines* 'How clear she shines! How quietly'
Dated 13 April 1843. Revised for publication in 1846.
The poem includes a bitter attack on worldy attitudes as false and delusive. It goes on to
imagine a better world existing somewhere in the starry heaven. The source of this vein in
Emily Brontë's thought seems to be part-Christian, part-Romantic. In particular, one
suspects the influence of Shelley. The tone of the poem has been compared to that of
Johnson in *The Vanity of Human Wishes*.

p. 153 *Hope* 'Hope was but a timid friend'
Dated 18 December 1843. Revised for publication in 1846.
A further negative poem, which rather belies its title. In it, Hope is shown to be a frail
companion, to whom the prisoner looks in vain for succour. It is not clear what
biographical incident produced the gloom of this period in Emily Brontë's life. Possibly
there is no biographical reference, or else she may be writing with Branwell in mind. His
early promise at Thorp Green was perhaps beginning to fade. As so often, the poet sees
the world from the viewpoint of a caged animal.

p. 154 *My Comforter* 'Well hast thou spoken—and yet not taught'
Dated 10 February 1844. Revised for publication in 1846.
The poem is enigmatic. It appears to be referring once more to an earlier poet or writer,
whose words have comforted Emily Brontë. It seems unlikely to be concerned with a living
person, and the 'comforter' seems to have too much individual character to be thought of
as a disembodied spirit. In contrast to the comparison of the comforter to a 'thaw-wind' or
sea breeze, orthodox Christian belief, and in particular its conventional expression, is
regarded as 'a mingled tone/Of seraph's song and demon's moan'. It is important not to
scale down the forcefulness of this complaint.

p. 155 *A Day Dream* 'On a sunny brae alone I lay'
Dated 5 March 1845. Revised for publication in 1846.
The poem contains a dialogue between the poet and her 'heart'. During this colloquy, she
seems to have a vision of a celestial world, rather like the vision of 'How clear she shines'.
The vision follows a series of pessimistic thoughts concerning the brevity of time and the
transience of beautiful spring. The final stanza retreats rather mockingly from the intensity
of this vision. Here Emily Brontë uses the almost flippant word 'Fancy', and calls the
vision 'fond'. The influence of the Platonic Shelley seems to me evident in the visionary
stanzas of the poem.

p. 157 *Song* 'The linnet in the rocky dells'
Dated 1 May 1845.
Gondal ascription E.W.
The Gondal content of the poem is slight indeed. It proved possible to print the poem in 1846 without verbal modification. Contemporary reviewers soon picked it out for commendation, calling it 'sweet and pure', 'musical'; and noting its 'taste'.

The poem explores one of the favourite themes of all the Brontës, the power of time to wear down emotion, in this case the sharp emotions of bereavement. This softening down of fervid feeling is not uncriticized in stanza 4, where both 'Pleasure' and 'Honour' are selected to suggest scorn for the 'lady's' former followers.

p. 158 *To Imagination* 'When weary with the long day's care'
Dated 3 September 1844. Revised for publication in 1846.
Emily Brontë's ambivalent attitude to the power of imagination is illustrated in this poem. It is possible that the reference in lines 15–18 is to Gondal, but the 'hovering vision' of line 26 suggests that she may also be thinking of a more personal dream such as that we have encountered in 'If grief for grief can touch thee' (88).

p. 159 *Plead for Me* 'O, thy bright eyes must answer now'
Dated 14 October 1844. Revised for publication in 1846.
Once again this poem does not seem to refer to Gondal, but to the worship of a masculine 'vision' who can be both slave and king. In line 39 Emily Brontë goes so far as to call him 'God of visions'. The poem was quite considerably revised, as though the poet had a particular interest in it.

p. 161 *The Philosopher* 'Enough of Thought, Philosopher'
Dated 3 February 1845. Revised for publication in 1846.
The poem has been much commented on, but the comments still leave some matters obscure. It consists of a dialogue between a 'philosopher' and another. The philosopher turns out to be perhaps more a visionary. The vision of the 'Spirit' (lines 27ff) has a Platonic character, but is perhaps also related to the visions of *Revelations*. The speaker says he has watched a lifetime for this spirit but has never found him. The logical contradiction here is not fully resolved, and perhaps in a poem should not be. Interpretations of the three streams have been very various. It has been suggested that they may stand for the three Platonic divisions of the soul, the Father, Son and Holy Ghost, or the Gnostic body, soul and spirit. The triple division may possibly relate to Anne's 'The Three Guides' (138), though this was written much later. The manuscript title was *The Philosopher's Conclusion*.

p. 162 *Remembrance* 'Cold in the earth and the deep snow piled above thee!'
Dated 3 March 1845. Revised for publication in 1846.
Gondal ascription: R. Alcona to J. Brenzaida.
The Gondal context is hard to establish, as it is impossible to decide whether 'R. Alcona' (thought to be 'Rosina') is the same person as 'A.G.A.'. This is probably the best known of Brontë poems, and far outgrows its Gondal roots. Those who look for a real person, known to Emily Brontë in life, whom she may have loved, will seize on the apparent chronological clue in line 9. However, it may be worth pointing out that we may be dealing with an internal Gondal chronology, and this may not take us back to 1830, as it appears. There are several signs, both in Emily's poems and Anne's, that Gondal chronology is not to be equated with the chronology of Haworth.

p. 164 *Death* 'Death, that struck when I was most confiding'
Dated 10 April 1845. Revised for publication in 1846.
The poem is in the non-Gondal MS. The subject seems related to that of the previous poem, however. It is possible that Emily Brontë's mind returned at this time of the year to the death of her two elder sisters, twenty years ago.

p. 165 *Stars* 'Ah! why because the dazzling sun'
Dated 14 April 1845. Revised for publication in 1846.
Commentators have focusd on the sharp contrast between day and night, both here and elsewhere in Emily Brontë's work. It has also been called a 'Gnostic apostrophe to night' (Derek Stanford in M. Spark and D. Stanford *Emily Brontë*) and its similarity to the work of some German romantics, e.g. Novalis, has been noted.

p. 166 'Heavy hangs the raindrop'
Dated 28 May 1845.
Gondal ascription A.E. and R.C.
In Charlotte Brontë's 1850 edition, the title 'The Two Children' was given to this two-part poem. Little clue is to be gained from the Gondal initials, and the poem has been interpreted as a contrast between Emily and her sister Maria. Miss Ratchford considers the poem refers to the daughter of Lord Alfred and her adopted dark-haired son.

p. 168 *Anticipation* 'How beautiful the Earth is still'
Dated 2 June 1845. Revised for publication in 1846.
The poem underwent considerable change from the MS to the 1846 version, which is the basis of our text. It seems likely that its feeling reflects the situation at Haworth in mid-1845, when Branwell was dismissed from his post at Thorp Green and Anne also left her employment there. Lines 11ff appear to deal with these events and possibly also reflect the gloom of Charlotte during her inner struggle against her love for Monsieur Heger. The following stanza seems to suggest that Emily did not allow herself to fall in love with an earthly lover and this impression is strengthened by line 30, 'the tempting race'.

p. 170 *The Prisoner* 'Silent is the house—all are laid asleep'
Dated 9 October 1845. Revised for publication in 1846.
Gondal ascription: Julian M. and A. G. Rochelle.
The poem from which the 1846 version was taken originally consisted of 152 lines. It seems likely that its unity in the manuscript is false, and that Emily wrote the first three stanzas on a separate occasion from the others. Charlotte made a separate poem of them for the 1850 selection.
It has been decided to print a compromise version in the present anthology, including the first stanzas, but excluding other stanzas rejected by Charlotte and Emily when selecting for the 1846 edition. The final stanza printed here appears to have been composed on purpose for that edition, and serves the purpose of rounding off the story.
The kernel of the whole poem consists of 46–73, in which Emily Brontë appears to be giving an account of her own spiritual vision. The Gondal name 'Rochelle' is not met with elsewhere in the work of Emily and Anne Brontë.

p. 172 'No coward soul is mine'
Dated 2 January 1846.
Though not, as Charlotte seems to have thought, Emily's very last poem, this seems an apt

summary of her poetic and spiritual creed. The manuscript has little punctuation and many capitals.

The poem has been seen by C. Day Lewis as 'directly religious' and it has been claimed that it is not unorthodox. However, it seems quite closely allied to the poems about spirits and visions of which we have included many. All these need to be taken into account when forming an impression of Emily Brontë's religious positon, which is certainly complex and uncompromising.

ANNE BRONTË'S POEMS

p. 174 *Alexander and Zenobia* 'Fair was the evening and brightly the sun'
Dated 1 July 1837.
A Gondal poem telling of the separation and happy reunion of two young lovers. In Emily Brontë's diary paper of 26 June 1837, we have a thumbnail sketch of Anne writing this poem. It reflects the early joyful character and optimistic outlook of Anne Brontë.

p. 182 *A Fragment (Self-Congratulation)* 'Maiden, thou wert thoughtless once'
Dated 1 January 1840. Revised for publication in 1846.
The poem is here presented in its manuscript form, since there is reason to believe that the modifications introduced before publication were for concealment rather than literary improvement. A new pseudonym, 'Ellen', was used, but there seems little doubt that this is a poem about a first-hand experience of Anne Brontë. The original pseudonym, Olivia Vernon, is a name otherwise unknown in Gondal.

p. 184 *The Bluebell* 'A fine and subtle spirit dwells'
Dated 22 August 1840.
The poem seems to have been written at Scarborough where Anne was on holiday with her Thorp Green charges. There are no Gondal references in the poem, which represents a new stage in Anne's autobiographical work.

p. 185 *Lines Written at Thorp Green (Appeal)* 'O! I am very weary'
Dated 28 August 1840.
The manuscript title was abandoned in 1846 for the title *Appeal*. The poem is notable for its terse and economic style. It may be read as a poem directed to William Weightman, though there is of course no evidence that he may have read it.

p. 186 'Oh, they have robbed me of the hope'
Undated.
The poem appears in *Agnes Grey*. Style and content suggest a close association with the preceding poem, but there are some difficulties in a confident assertion of this. It seems hard to discover a subject for 'they' in line 1. It is possible that the poem was revised on the composition of *Agnes Grey*.

p. 186 'Farewell to thee! but not farewell'
Undated.
Like the previous poem, this appears in a novel, this time *Wildfell Hall*. In that context it is linked with music. We may see a number of Anne's poems as written to be sung. Several included in this anthology were intended as hymns.

p. 187 *Lines Written at Thorp Green* 'That summer sun whose genial glow'
Dated 19 August 1841.
Twelve days before the poem was written Charlotte Brontë wrote to her friend Ellen Nussey, 'She is more lonely—less gifted with the power of making friends even than I am'. The poem strongly echoes Charlotte's remark, though she was not always so well acquainted with her sister's character or feelings.

p. 188 *In Memory of a Happy Day in February* 'Blessed be Thou for all the joy'
Dated February–10 November 1842.
The poem was not completed until November, and poses an interesting problem. Was it originally intended as a religious poem? It may be worth noting the possibly coy 'those I loved' of line 5. By November, William Weightman was dead, but two years earlier he had sent a Valentine card to all the girls at the parsonage. If it is correct to see a special relationship developing between him and Anne, it is possible that this was recalled in 1842.

p. 189 *To Cowper* 'Sweet are thy strains, Celestial Bard'
Dated 10 November 1842. Extensively revised before publication in 1846.
At some point, not necessarily in preparation for the 1846 publication, Anne Brontë revised the poem metrically. The later version is printed here. Further slight alterations are notable between the final manuscript version and the printed text.
  It is worth noting the closeness of Anne's self-identification with the eighteenth-century poet. She may well have recently read a biography of Cowper, possibly during the few days she spent at home for the funeral of Aunt Branwell.

p. 191 *To* _____ 'I will not mourn thee, lovely one'
Dated December 1842.
This poem should probably be read as a valedication for William Weightman. The detailed arguments for this view cannot be rehearsed here. Anne would find many examples in her exemplars of Moore, Shelley, Keats and others, in which the name of the person to whom the poem is addressed is similarly suppressed.

p. 192 *Lines Composed in a Wood on a Windy Day* 'My soul is awakened, my spirit is soaring'
Dated 30 December 1842.
The title does not occur in the manuscript and has not been given in our text. It was added for the 1846 publication, though no further modifications were made. In a note, Anne ascribes it to 'the long plantation', a place apparently in Haworth, but not yet identified. The metre is common in the work of Thomas Moore, and thence perhaps derives from Irish folk song.

p. 192 *A Word to the Calvinists (A Word to the Elect)* 'You may rejoice to think yourselves secure'
Dated 28 May 1843. Revised for publication in 1846.
In the 1846 edition, the word 'Calvinists' was replaced by 'Elect'. The poem is a forceful attack on the implications of a Calvinistic insistence on the selective operation of divine grace, and goes on to present Anne Brontë's belief in 'Universalism', which is apparently the view also of Helen Burns in *Jane Eyre*.

p. 194 *The Captive Dove* 'Poor restless Dove, I pity thee'
Dated 31 October 1843. Very slightly revised for publication in 1846.
The manuscript states that the poem was 'mostly written in the spring of 1842' and
finished in October 1843. Anne's self-identification with the dove seems quite strong. It
occurs both in *Self-Communion* (139) (line 47) and in *Wildfell Hall*, where Helen draws a
picture of a girl watching two doves. Part of this may be due to the gospel injunction to be
'gentle as' doves, but Shelley too has a bird (this time a nightingale) identified with a girl in
Epipsychidion, a poem apparently known to both Emily and Anne Brontë.

p. 195 *Music on Christmas Morning* 'Music I love—but never strain'
Undated.
The poem appears in the 1846 edition, and there is no manuscript copy. It breathes the
optimistic and youthful spirit we have seen in *Alexander and Zenobia* (114). The Christmas
music thought of by Anne Brontë may have included the *Messiah* of Handel, well known to
the Brontës, but perhaps also traditional hymns such as 'Christians awake', which were
already finding their way into establishment services.

p. 196 *Home* 'How brightly glistening in the sun'
Undated, but perhaps about 1843–4.
As in the case of the previous poem, the manuscript of this poem is missing, and our text
depends on the 1846 edition. The poem is careful and accomplished, showing the kind of
work to which Anne Brontë was aspiring, and pointing to some heights left unscaled at her
death.

p. 197 *Memory* 'Brightly the sun of summer shone'
Dated 29 May 1844. Revised for publication in 1846.
The poem has appealed to a number of critics and appears to have a Wordsworthian
feeling at its core. Throughout her career, Anne Brontë was most sympathetic to
childhood and youth despite the appalling behaviour portrayed by her child characters in
Agnes Grey.
  We have retained the slightly more vivid manuscript readings in preference to the 1846
version.

p. 198 *Fluctuations* 'What though the sun had left my sky'
Dated 2 August 1844.
Certainly written at Scarborough, the poem is a strange one, apparently rehearsing in code
the history of Anne Brontë's friendships. Exact interpretation is hazardous. The meteor,
for example, *might* be William Weightman, and the moon of the last part either Emily
Brontë or Mary Robinson. Further biographical evidence would be valuable. Anne Brontë
made only one change in the poem for the 1846 volume, and we have retained the
manuscript version.

p. 199 *The Arbour* 'I'll rest me in this sheltered bower'
Undated, but probably written between 1843 and 1845.
The poem has no manuscript, but seems very likely to have been written at Thorp Green.
The prison metaphor, hinted at in the last stanza, is very typical of the poetry of both Emily
and Anne Brontë, who may in part have absorbed it from Wesley's hymns.

p. 200 *Dreams* 'While on my lonely couch I lie'
Dated Spring 1845.
It is likely, but not certain, that the poem was composed in late May or early June. By this time, Anne Brontë may well have been contemplating, or may even have started, *Agnes Grey*. The romantic attachment dreamed of in the poem may possibly have been the basis of part of the story of the novel.

p. 201 *Views of Life* 'When sinks my heart in hopeless gloom'
Dated June 1845. Revised for publication in 1846.
The poem was begun during the early part of 1844, then left until June 1845. Despite the sombre tone of large sections of the work, we need not be surprised at the hopeful final stanzas. It is typical of Anne Brontë's work that she travels, and allows her heroines to travel, through many trials, but ends on a hopeful note. This characteristic may be seen in the longer poems as well as the novels. We may often see the influence of *The Pilgrim's Progress* in her work. The present poem is also worth noting for its positive attitude towards youth. This may be compared with *Wildfell Hall*, Chapter 32, in which Helen and Millicent Hargrave discuss Esther's 'Romantic notions'.
   There are considerable similarities between this poem and some of Emily Brontë's, especially 'How beautiful the Earth is still' (111). In general, we have preferred the manuscript readings to those of 1846.

p. 206 *Vanitas Vanitatis etc.* 'In all we do, and hear, and see'
Dated 4 September 1845. Revised for publication in 1846.
Our text here includes a section (lines 19–23) not included in the manuscript. The poem has been compared to Johnson's 'The Vanity of Human Wishes', and indeed Johnson's general attitude to life might well appeal to Anne Brontë. However, we do note a typical Anne Brontë touch in the final 'But hoping through the darkest day'.

p. 207 *The Penitent (Fragment)* 'I mourn with thee and yet rejoice'
Dated 1845.
It has been suggested that the penitent in question is Branwell Brontë and this may well be so. Branwell seems to have alternated at this time between sorrow for his past and unrealizable ambitions for the future. The poem is likely to have been written soon after 'Vanitas Vanitatis'. It was printed unaltered in 1846.

p. 208 *Monday Night, May 11th 1846* 'Why should such gloomy silence reign'
Dated 11 May 1846.
The poem was first printed by Charlotte Brontë in her 1850 addition to her sisters' poems. It is very interesting in suggesting that the dissension which pervaded the parsonage in the early part of 1846 was not Branwell's fault alone. Anne appears to be contrasting this night in 1846 with a previous night 'when all were gay'. One has to go back a long time to find a night which might qualify, perhaps as far as 1835.

p. 209 'Severed and gone, so many years!'
Dated April 1847.
There can be little doubt that the poem is inspired by the Haworth curate William Weightman, whose influence on the whole house was cheering and on Anne permanent. She is undoubtedly romanticizing him. Though he had many good qualities, including a very hearty disposition, it may be going too far to find him 'true' (line 62). We note, too,

that in the final line Anne Brontë retreats from the impression that she claims the man in some personal way.

p. 211 *The Three Guides* 'Spirit of earth! thy hand is chill'
Dated 11 August 1847.
In many ways this is Anne's most notable poem, but it is also hard to interpret. We simply do not know with what to equate the 'three guides' of the title. One suggestion is that they are equivalent to the three Brontë sisters, but this would mean identifying Charlotte as the spirit of 'earth', which seems unlikely. We may also note the 'triple' flood of Emily's 'The Philosopher'. It certainly seems as though the spirit of 'pride' may be somehow associated with Emily and in particular with her character of Heathcliff, and his Gondal antecedents. As so often with Anne, the poem is moral polemic: almost all her writing is far from *ars gratia artis*.

p. 217 *Self-Communion* 'The mist is resting on the hill'
Dated November 1847–17 April 1848.
In this poem Anne shows the poetic talents which were beginning to unfold at the end of her life, and which were so different from those of her sisters and Branwell. There are still many problems with the poem's composition, but there are also passages in which form is closely adapted to meaning.

The poem consists of an inner dialogue in which are embedded autobiographical reflections. Carefully read, it appears to tell us a great deal about Anne's relations with her sister, Emily. This in turn may provide us with a way of interpreting other late poems and *Wildfell Hall*.

p. 225 'Believe not those who say'
Dated 24 April 1848.
A neat statement of Anne Brontë's philosophy, the poem has antecedents both in Puritan/Evangelical theology and in medieval Catholicism. In some ways it may be Anne's best and most even poem, with its deceptive simplicity and firm, plodding tread, accurately matching the content.

p. 227 'A dreadful darkness closes in'
Dated 7 January and 28 January 1849.
A most impressive work for the way in which it faces death, the poem holds in tension Anne Brontë's desire to live and devote herself to more moral/artistic creation, together with her willingness to trust the 'spirit of faith' which she had addressed fifteen months earlier. Though it was the last poem she wrote, we have her letter to Ellen Nussey of 5 April 1849, the tone of which is similar. With these, Anne Brontë establishes herself as a worthy companion in courage of Charlotte's Jane Eyre, and Emily in her poem 'No coward soul'.

INDEX OF TITLES AND
FIRST LINES